INSIDE THE MINDS OF SEXUAL PREDATORS

Katherine Ramsland and Patrick N. McGrain

PRAEGER
An Imprint of ABC-CLIO, LLC

A B C CLIO

Santa Barbara, California • Denver, Colorado • Oxford, England

Library of Congress Cataloging-in-Publication Data

Ramsland, Katherine M., 1953-
Inside the minds of sexual predators / Katherine Ramsland and Patrick N. McGrain.
p. cm.
Includes bibliographical references and index.
ISBN 978-0-313-37960-4 (hard copy : alk. paper) — ISBN 978-0-313-37961-1 (ebook)
1. Sex offenders—Case studies. 2. Sex offenders—Psychology. 3. Criminal psychology. I. McGrain, Patrick Norman. II. Title.
HV6556.R36 2010
364.15'3—dc22 2009034309

ISBN: 978-0-313-37960-4
EISBN: 978-0-313-37961-1

14 13 12 11 10 1 2 3 4 5

This book is also available on the World Wide Web as an eBook.
Visit www.abc-clio.com for details.

Praeger
An Imprint of ABC-CLIO, LLC

ABC-CLIO, LLC
130 Cremona Drive, P.O. Box 1911
Santa Barbara, California 93116-1911

This book is printed on acid-free paper ∞

Manufactured in the United States of America

Contents

	Acknowledgments	vii
1	Predators and Sexual Disorders	1
2	It's All about Me: Narcissism and Entitlement	11
3	Addiction and the Cycle of Sexual Violence	23
4	Child Molesters and Family Predators	35
5	Rapists	47
6	Lust Killers	61
7	Team Predators	75
8	Boys Gone Bad	87
9	Erotomania	97
10	Female Teacher Predators	109
11	Thou Shalt Not Prey: Offenders in the Clergy	123
12	Cyber-Predators	133
13	Catching Lies	145
14	Society's Response to the Sexual Predator	155

Notes 167

Selected Resources 183

Index 189

Acknowledgments

Books are never the solitary endeavors they seem. Behind every author is a cadre of people who opened doors, educated, and supported him or her. We wish to thank those who have assisted one or both of us with encouragement, information, and opportunities: Marilyn Bardsley, Dr. Robert Hare, former SSA Roy Hazelwood, Dr. Henry Lee, Coroner Zachary Lysek, former SSA Gregg McCrary, Detective Rich Peffall, Detective Joe Pochron, former SSA Robert Ressler, Dr. Robert Rieber, Ann Rule, Dr. Louis Schlesinger, and Dr. Cyril Wecht. We also appreciate the many professionals who did research in areas specific to this subject, as well as victims who offered insight into their experiences. In addition, both of us have worked out ideas while teaching classes devoted to this subject, and we wish to thank students at DeSales University who participated in the dialogue, and DeSales administrators who supported it. We'd also like to acknowledge members of our respective families who tolerated long hours and diverted attention, especially in the final stretch.

We're grateful to our editor, Michael Wilt, for helping to make the manuscript consistent in style and accessible for a broad audience.

And, finally, we thank our agent, John Silbersack at Trident Media Group, for his support.

1

Predators and Sexual Disorders

EXPLOITING TRUST

After Anthony Barron was convicted of eighty-nine sexual offenses against children, his wife of twenty-three years went on the record to say how shocked she was. "Everyone thought they could trust him," she said. "He could be so charming, but obviously there was more to it than that." With three children between them and several grandchildren, she could not understand why she had not seen any signs.

Successful predators are often so clever and secretive that even the people closest to them fail to recognize what they are doing. They devise a convincing façade, they have a long list of prepared excuses, and when suspicions arise they're skilled at reassuring others that nothing is wrong. They exploit trust and know how to twist what people want to believe into a false sense of security. Barron, fifty-four, had managed a bank and, in retirement, he was active in a parent-teacher organization. Around his neighborhood, he was a trusted babysitter. Children adored him, despite the fact that he was getting sexual gratification from at least eleven little girls.

Barron's oldest victim was twelve, the youngest only three, and a set of twins was four. His plan had been elaborate and his maintenance system cunning. First, he worked on the parents, earning their trust. Since he was himself a grandfather, many of Barron's neighbors allowed him to watch their children in his own home. Then, when he had the girls to himself, he charmed them with treats, games, and toys. Gradually, he would get them used to being filmed with a video camera, and then he progressed to touching them. He would assure them that they did not have to do anything that made them uncomfortable, but he gradually worked at getting them used to certain activities. Although self-centered and predatory, he knew he had to be patient if he wanted to exploit these children for his own sexual pleasure. When it was over, he bribed his victims to remain quiet with candy and more toys.

This behavior, right under the parents' noses, continued for nearly a decade until September 2006, when a five-year-old told her mother she had seen Barron's genitals. Alarmed, the woman sent the police to his home. As they entered, they saw all the toys, as well as fifty-two different computers, and a library full of home-made videotapes. When they confiscated and viewed the tapes, they knew they had a sexual predator of shocking proportions on their hands. But now he was caught. Parents of victims were notified and they were forced to watch these disturbing tapes to confirm their child's identity. It was a parent's worst nightmare: a man these parents had repeatedly trusted had exploited their trust to violate their child.

The charges ranged from multiple counts of indecent assault to several outright rapes. Barron admitted to eighty-seven of the charges and was tried on two more, being convicted on all eighty-nine counts. In a letter to the court, he offered several excuses: he blamed his divorce, his difficulty in being a single parent, and his reaction to the death of a close relative. He was sentenced to a minimum of nine years before he could apply for parole. Once released, his name will be on the sex offenders list for the rest of his life. The lead investigator and the senior prosecutor both told the press that it was the worst case of child abuse they had ever seen. In fact, the judge excused the jurors from jury duty for the next decade, as a reward for having to endure the disturbing images.[1]

Such deviance generally arises from sexual fantasies that develop over time. Essentially, a person becomes a predator through mental rehearsal that helps to prepare for opportunities and to empower him or her to act. Because sexuality is a complex human experience, it manifests in patterns unique to each person, deriving from the way the imagery merges with their sexual, social, and emotional development. Through a gradual process of enactment, these images provide a template for the future pattern of sexual offenses. They influence the choice of victim, the approach, the preferred sexual activities, the pre- and post-offense rituals, and the decision whether or not to complete the act with murder. Sometimes murder is merely a means for eliminating a witness, and sometimes it contributes to the erotic allure.

Not all who fantasize about sexual trespass become actual offenders; the fantasy might be sufficient to satisfy them. Similarly, not all who act on their fantasies become predators. Some act from a compulsion or in response to a sudden opportunity, such as frotteurism on a crowded bus; or they might simply commit acts of public indecency, such as masturbating in a movie theater. Often these offenders are ashamed and believe they will not repeat the behavior, but even if they do, their activities are considered "nuisance behaviors" rather than crimes that truly harm.[2]

Thus, there is a difference between paraphilic excitement that engenders crime and paraphilic excitement that is merely a victimless personal preference. There is also a difference between sexual offenders and sexual predators. Criminologist Eric Hickey puts it this way: a predator "denotes persons who are predatorial and seek out multiple victims, exploiting them sexually. These persons are prone to recidivism and not particularly amenable to treatment. Sex offenders, on the other hand, are more often persons who have one victim, often within their family, tend not to recidivate once punished, and are far more amenable to treatment."[3]

Most experts on sex crimes who offer typologies of sexual acts cover all types of offenses, but this book focuses on outright predators: males and females who plan their crimes against others, harm or kill their victims, repeat their offenses (even after punishment), and blame anyone but themselves when caught. Thus, we cover stalkers with sexual intent, serial rapists, serial lust killers, active pedophiles, cyber-offenders, and the relatively recent phenomenon of female teachers exploiting underage students. We present the distinct psychological dynamics involved in these types of crimes, partly by presenting detailed cases and partly with expert analysis, and offer a practical guide for recognition, assessment, and treatment.

FACTS AND FANTASIES

Deviant sexual desires have been organized into psychiatric categories known as paraphilias, which are recurrent, intense urges or behaviors that focus on objects, situations, or activities for sexual gratification. The fourth and current edition of the *Diagnostic and Statistical Manual of Mental Disorders*, hereafter the *DSM-IV-TR*, lists many of these conditions and offers criteria for each, but this nomenclature is not exhaustive. Other lists developed by sexologists and criminologists include even more. In fact, one expert lists fully 547 paraphilias.[4] They are psychosexual disorders, not sex crimes, and most are not even criminal acts, but they can fuel predatory criminal behavior, especially as they grow into addictions.

Paraphilias are primarily (but not exclusively) male disorders, many of which begin in childhood or adolescence and persist into adulthood. They generally derive from what any given society views as abnormal for sexual orientation—which, of course, can change from one society to another. The energy to sustain a paraphilia comes from repetitive fantasies or emotional needs.

Some examples are:

- Fetishism—sexual arousal from objects, such as shoes, underwear, candles, or ropes
- Acrophilia—sexual arousal from high places
- Arachnophilia—sexual arousal from spiders
- Agoraphilia—arousal from open spaces, or having sexual contact in public places
- Candaulism—forcing sexual partners to expose themselves in public, or to have sex with others
- Pictophilia—deriving principal gratification from erotic pictures
- Erotolalia—sexual gratification from describing, or listening to others describe, sexual acts
- Narratophilia—sexual gratification from listening to stories with sexual content
- Exhibitionism—the desire to expose one's genitals to others
- Auto-eroticism—a sexual fixation on oneself, often accompanied by self-strangulation that produces a loss of consciousness
- Frotteurism—touching or rubbing one's body surreptitiously against another person, usually a stranger in a crowded public place
- Telephone scatology/scatophilia—arousal from making obscene phone calls to strangers to hear their reaction
- Pedophilia/hebephilia—the focus of sexual attention involves children, either as pornography or as molestation of actual victims; hebephilia focuses specifically on prepubescent girls
- Masochism—gaining sexual pleasure from being hurt or humiliated, via verbal abuse, bondage, and even being beaten, whipped, or cut
- Necrophilia—gaining sexual arousal from handling or having intercourse with corpses
- Partialism—sexual arousal from some body part, such as the arch of a foot
- Mud eroticism—arousal from being covered in mud
- Pygmalionism/statuphilia—sexual desire for statues or dolls
- Coprophilia/coprolagnia—sexual excitement over the taste and smell of excrement
- Urophilia/undinism/urolagnia—sexual arousal from urine
- Klismaphilia—sexual arousal from receiving an enema

- Sadism—sexual pleasure from dominating, torturing, or abusing others via such activities as verbal abuse, whipping, burning, stabbing, raping, choking, and killing
- Gerontophilia—arousal from elderly persons of the opposite sex
- Infibulation—desire for self-torture
- Mysophilia—an erotic interest in filth
- Aquaerotism—gratification from sexual activity underwater
- Transvestitism—cross-dressing by heterosexual males, from wearing a piece of female clothing to dressing entirely as a female, and/or passing as one
- Triolism—a form of exhibitionism in which a person wants to perform a sexual act with several partners or in the presence of several people
- Mutilomania—arousal from the image or act of mutilating a living person or a corpse; sometimes fixated on a specific body part
- Piquerism—arousal from penetrating the body (one's own or another's) with a sharp object
- Vampirism—excitement over drinking blood
- Cannibalism—erotic pleasure from eating human flesh
- Scoptophilia (voyeurism)—deriving sexual pleasure from watching others from a clandestine position, such as peeking in windows where someone may be undressing or sleeping
- Vomerophilia—arousal from the act of vomiting
- Infantilism—erotic gratification in sexual role-playing when the individual pretends to be an infant
- Apotemnophilia—irresistible erotic desire to amputate a healthy body part
- Satyriasis—excessive sex drive in males (called nymphomania in females)
- Saliromania—gratification from destroying nude statues or paintings
- Pyrolagnia/pyrophilia—sexual gratification from witnessing, igniting, or extinguishing fires
- Fire-water complex—after lighting a fire, one exhibits oneself and then has a strong desire to urinate

Whenever such activities involve non-consenting partners (including animals) or where there is a resulting harm to others or destruction of property, a paraphilia becomes a crime. Clearly, given the sexual source of energy, paraphilias can trigger both addictive and predatory behavior, from physical trespass to murder, as one person forces another to do things that will satisfy his or her need. Many of the conditions listed above will show up in the behavior of perpetrators described in the following chapters.

FETISH AND MENTAL ILLNESS

It was Halloween in Manhattan when forty-one-year-old Peter Braunstein acted on his urgent fetish for shoes. He'd seen a pair on a young woman where he worked (but from where he had recently been fired) and decided to find out where she lived. Then he formed a plan. He went on eBay to purchase the items he would need to create a ruse to get into her Chelsea-area apartment. He watched her building on that night and when he was certain she was home, he entered, dressed as a fireman. Setting down a couple of Dixie cups filled with chemicals of his own concoction, Braunstein lit them and watched smoke fill the hallway. The plan was working.

Braunstein readied a police badge, also purchased online, and pounded on the woman's door, shouting, "Fire!" When she opened the door, he pushed his way in with a BB gun and a chloroform-soaked cloth. She had little time to be alarmed, and under the chloroform she collapsed, unconscious. Braunstein gagged her, undressed her, tied her arms together, and used duct tape to bind her to her bed. He donned a ski mask to hide his face, in case she revived, and over the next thirteen hours, he kept the young woman captive. She revived a few times and was aware of some of the things he was doing as he repeatedly groped her. He also videotaped her ordeal, forcing her to wear different pairs of her stiletto shoes. She had no idea what he planned or if she'd even survive. She could only endure it and wait to see what happened. In her bound position, there was no chance to fight back or escape. At one point, he gave her a sleeping pill and took one himself, lying beside her to take a nap. When he awoke early the next morning, he grabbed money, along with several items from her apartment, and left. She lay there, waiting and listening, but he did not return.

The victim struggled to free herself and ran for the phone to call the police. She then noticed an odd note on the mirror that said, "Bye—Hope things turn around for U soon." She was almost too scared to let responding officers through the door, but soon she related as much as she could recall of the bizarre assault. Although she was able to describe her assailant, she did not know who he was.

The next day, New York newspapers reported the incident, and a woman who read the accounts thought the man's behavior sounded suspiciously familiar. She even knew the victim, because they both worked at the same publishing company, so she called the police to name a possible suspect: former fashion writer Peter Braunstein. He, too, had worked at the publisher, so he could have seen the victim there. He was controlling and obsessive, the caller said, and when he did not get what he wanted, he resorted to harassment. He once had been her boyfriend and when she broke up with him, he had harassed her and her family for months.

The police got an arrest warrant, but Braunstein was on the run. When he was finally spotted and caught in Tennessee, he willingly returned to Manhattan for trial. During this proceeding, his state of mind during the crime was at issue, and several mental health experts examined him. Some said he had a history of anxiety and depression, and showed clear signs of schizophrenia—a "broken brain," his attorney said. However, others claimed that his methodical attack showed rational planning: Braunstein had purchased a number of items, had shielded his identity, and had learned how to make a potassium bomb. He had even written an article once about his long obsession with model Kate Moss, and some people who knew him said he had a sadistic streak.

Depression, obsession, and anxiety are not equivalent to a psychotic break. An obsessional disorder is recognized as a subcategory of obsessive compulsive disorder, yet based in obsessive thoughts rather than compulsive rituals. It can develop as a protective reaction to stress or the overwhelming feeling of chaos. Sufferers have intrusive or inappropriate thoughts and find relief in fantasies that reassure them that they're in control. When they attach to another person—for example, a woman wearing stiletto heels—they may believe they desperately need her and will then seek her out. It matters little to them what the target person wants; he or she will be perceived in whatever way the obsessed person needs. Drugs may diminish obsessions, but anxiety remains.[5]

During the months preceding the Halloween incident, Braunstein was in turmoil. He had lost his job, his girlfriend, and his elite standing in the fashion world. He had watched others surpass him whom he viewed as less intelligent and less worthy, and as an unemployed man facing midlife, he probably panicked over his future. Still, his need to be close to a woman who figured into his obsessions did not excuse his criminal behavior.

The legal issue was not whether he was anxious or delusional, because clearly he was; it was whether he was so delusional that he did not appreciate the wrongfulness of his conduct, or could not control it. The factors indicated that he was aware of the wrongfulness of the assault and that he had acted methodically. He had made eBay purchases with the idea of posing as a fireman or cop; he had built a smoke bomb and lit it inside an apartment building; he had terrorized and molested a woman. He had then fled the city, demonstrating that he understood what would happen if he was caught. Although people with schizophrenia can certainly plan, problematic for him was the fact that in four past clinical settings no psychologist or psychiatrist had diagnosed Braunstein with schizophrenia. This went against him. So did the fact that over the years he had maintained several exacting, high-pressure jobs and had achieved an advanced university degree. To those who listened to the case, Braunstein appeared to have been a high-functioning person. Using a mask during his crime only added proof that he knew that what he was doing was wrong.

The jury decided that Braunstein had the capacity to form criminal intent. On May 23, 2007, they convicted him of kidnapping, sex abuse, robbery and burglary, but acquitted him of second-degree arson.[6]

Braunstein's victim had clearly been terrified, and had probably believed that her captor intended to rape and kill her. However, Braunstein's shoe fetish had not been nearly as aggressive as it could have been. In Oregon, a similar paraphilia had inspired a man to murder, again and again. As a boy, Jerome Brudos developed an erotic fixation on women's shoes and underwear, which grew into complex fantasies as he grew up, got married, and adopted a fairly normal life. He kept his secret lust to himself. But when a pretty door-to-door salesgirl arrived at his home, he brought her into his workshop and killed her. Then he removed her foot to keep in the freezer so he could try on shoes and take photographs. As this foot decomposed, he went out looking for other victims, killing four women altogether before he was caught. In prison for life, his reading matter included catalogs for women's shoes.[7]

COMORBID CONDITIONS

The offender who probably holds the record for the most documented paraphilias is child molester and serial murderer Albert Fish. In 1928, he kidnapped twelve-year-old Grace Budd from her New York home after duping her parents about what a kindly old man he was. Six years later they received a letter from him in which he described in disgusting detail his fetish for cannibalism and his treatment of Grace: he had killed and cooked her into a vegetable stew, spending nearly a week savoring the tasty "meat." A detective traced the stationery to a flophouse, tracking down Fish. Under arrest, Fish admitted he had murdered Grace Budd; eventually he added dozens of cases of child molestation and three more child murders.

Before Fish's trial, Dr. Fredric Wertham, the senior psychiatrist at Bellevue Hospital, examined the deviant for more than twelve hours. He listened to Fish's excuses, as the old man, now in his sixties, blamed his faithless wife for his decision to let himself fully express his repressed sexual cravings. Fish told Wertham that he had always had the desire to inflict pain on others and to have others inflict pain on him, and he had become consumed with seeking ways to hurt himself. Over the course of their interview, Wertham counted eighteen different paraphilias, from cannibalism to coprophilia to infibulations—and this was before the diagnostic criteria in the *DSM* had even been conceived. He examined x-rays of Fish's pelvis, where the masochist had engaged in piquerism, shoving needles into his groin between the anus and scrotum. Many were still there, rusting. There was little doubt that Fish was sexually abnormal to the extreme.

Wertham learned that Fish's perverse predilections had begun when he was a child, apparently arising from severe spanking by a female teacher at a home for orphans. Fish had loved the attention, both to himself and the other children, and by his report, his emerging sexual desire fixated on the buttocks of children. To seduce them, he would go naked under his painter's overalls so that, whenever an opportunity was at hand, he could quickly undress. He generally chose victims from the poorest classes, because there was small chance of a serious investigation. Once he had a child under his control, he might castrate, torture, sodomize, or rape, mostly because he thrilled to their cries of pain.

But it was not just the torment of others that he enjoyed; Fish also liked whipping himself with spiked paddles. He wrote many obscene letters to strangers, hoping someone would respond with a similar inclination. One of his role models, Wertham learned, was Fritz Haarmann, the "Hanover Vampire" from Germany, who was convicted in 1924 of multiple counts of rape and murder. Haarmann's special trick had been to trap his victims underneath him and while sodomizing them, he would chew on their necks and taste their blood.

At the trial in 1935, Wertham testified for the defense, claiming that Fish had practiced "every known sexual abnormality." His deviant behavior appeared to be the result of an inherited history of psychiatric conditions, exacerbated by his obsession with religion. Fish had believed he could use murder to atone for his sins and, viewing himself as Abraham from the Old Testament, claimed that God had commanded it. Wertham was convinced that with all this psychological baggage, Fish could not possibly have controlled himself. He was dangerous, without a doubt, but in the midst of his sexual frenzies, he did not fully appreciate that what he was doing was wrong. He should therefore be institutionalized in a psychiatric facility, not locked up in a prison or executed. Fish's attorney agreed that he was a psychiatric phenomenon, stating that "no single case history report, either in legal or medical annals, contains a record of one individual who possessed all of these sexual abnormalities."[8]

Nevertheless, the jury convicted Fish of murder. As he awaited sentencing, he confessed to a murder in which he had cut a boy into pieces and roasted his buttocks with onions and carrots, consuming the tender meat over the course of four days. It was no surprise when Fish received the death sentence and on June 17, 1935, he went to the electric chair. Reportedly, despite being afraid, he thought the experience might be a supreme thrill—"The only one I haven't tried."[9]

In the following chapters, we explore more such cases, representing several different types of sexual predators. First, we examine the core dynamic of narcissism, and then we discuss the psychological and physiological components of the cycle of addiction. The most common predatory sex offenders are pedophiles, rapists, and lust murderers, so we tackle these subjects before taking on such specialized areas as juvenile offenders, cyberstalkers, and priests. We hope to shed light not only on how these perpetrators operate but also on how to spot them for self-protection. Whenever they themselves have offered insight about why they act as they do, we include it. In closing, we describe what victims have said and how society has devised ways to reduce or eliminate the threat of sexual predators. Since they are by nature cunning, secretive, and deceptive, we devote an entire chapter to behaviors that signal cover stories and other lies, along with the techniques that psychologists have devised for improving our ability to recognize a predator.

2

It's All about Me: Narcissism and Entitlement

COMPELLED TO KILL

Wendy Baribeault walked along a Connecticut highway one summer afternoon, on her way to the local convenience store. Several drivers noticed her and some even saw a dark-haired, bespectacled young man emerge from a compact blue car to proceed quickly toward her. When she failed to come home that afternoon, her mother called the police, but the seventeen-year-old seemed to have vanished. Local residents formed a search.

Two days later, Wendy's body was discovered behind a stone wall, and an autopsy showed that she had been raped and strangled. The police were concerned, because not only had her killer accosted her in broad daylight, with possible witnesses driving along, but she was one of several local females over the past two years who had been similarly assaulted.

It was 1984, two years before the first use of DNA analysis in a similar rape–murder in England, so there was little that investigators could do with the biological fluids. Chief investigator Michael Malchik sent officers to question residents, and they soon learned about the blue car. It was a recent foreign model, according to the description, which helped narrow down the possibilities. So did the fact that the white male driver wore glasses. The first person they went to see, whom they knew from DMV records owned a Toyota, was Michael Ross, a twenty-five-year-old Ivy League graduate who lived near the crime scene. He was a thin man, about five-foot-ten, sporting glasses that looked too large for his face. Since his car was not precisely like the one described and his demeanor was benign, Malchik nearly dismissed him as a suspect.

But Ross, an insurance salesman, asked about the killer's chances of being declared insane, which alerted Malchik to keep pressing for information. Soon Ross looked better and better for this crime—especially when his memory of his movements on the day Wendy disappeared seemed rehearsed. Malchik invited Ross to the station, where further probing finally got him to confess to raping and killing Wendy. When he'd seen her alone, he said, he'd acted quickly to drag her over the wall, to a private spot.

During the interrogation, Ross admitted to attacking nearly a dozen women and killing six, making him Connecticut's first known serial killer. However, his background challenged theories at the time about serial killers. He was neither a loner nor a loser; he was ambitious, personable, educated, and had a decent upbringing. Clearly, there was more to Michael Ross than a surface analysis revealed. He had been killing since 1981, and his violent fantasies and abuse of girls stretched back even farther. From his confessions it was apparent that he derived the greatest pleasure from the image of unclothed girls on their knees, terrified, and obedient to his every demand. Rape dominated his thoughts, but murder had also become part of the formula. One girl died too fast, he told his interrogators, so he had anally penetrated her, finding this experience interesting but unsatisfying. Sex was not his ultimate high; that came from domination. Ross needed to be the center of attention, and to be in charge.

These fantasies began before he was even a teenager, perhaps in reaction to his abusive mother's unpredictable mood swings. Unstable parents can traumatize children, and Ross' early efforts to feel safe involved imagining himself forcing girls to an underground cave, to hold them there until they fell in love with him. By the time he was fifteen, he had molested several girls, which got him arrested, but his fantasies continued to grow increasingly more violent.

As Ross was set to graduate from Cornell in 1981, he acted on an opportunity: he chased down a coed, grabbed her, and forced her into a secluded area. He ordered her to remove her clothing and get on her knees to give him oral sex. She complied and when he was finished, he fled. Ross convinced himself he would never do that again, but within three days, he had grabbed a second girl. This time he placed a rope around her neck to get her to perform, and he enjoyed this added sense of domination. By the following month, when the girl he accosted recognized him, he had committed murder. Although he had not intended this, he insisted later, the idea of killing a woman at the height of his orgasm soon obsessed him. Sexual gratification now demanded this form of total control.

One of Ross' victims was Robin Stravinsky, nineteen, who had disappeared while hitchhiking in November 1983. Her body was found and shortly linked to a double homicide in the same area: On Easter Sunday 1984, April Brunais and Lesley Shelley, both fourteen, were hitchhiking home after seeing a movie. Ross drove up and offered them a ride. They accepted and he took them to Rhode Island, where he raped one and strangled both, dumping the bodies in a culvert back in Connecticut. In 1982, Ross had also killed Debra Smith Taylor, twenty-three, and Tammy Williams, seventeen.

It was ten years before he offered more details. In an interview, he admitted to killing two young women in New York. One was sixteen-year-old Paula Perrera, who was out hitchhiking on March 1, 1982. He raped, sodomized, and strangled her. He did not name the other victim, but the police believed he was referring to twenty-five-year-old Dzung Ngoc Tu, a Cornell student. Her body had been thrown into a lake while she was still alive. This was probably the young woman who had recognized him, precipitating his first murder.

About his actions, Ross said it always felt as if he were outside his body, watching. His victims were a collage of faces that he quickly forgot, but whenever he targeted a woman, "she was as good as dead." One woman he had assaulted had managed to survive, but could only identify him after he had been arrested for murder. He thought she had been lucky. Ross dismissed all the talk that he was a serial killer, believing that compared to others, his victim toll was paltry. "Big deal," he said. Clearly, he had no feeling for the women he had harmed and terrorized. They meant nothing to him.

It was clear from his background that Ross had long experienced emotional problems. In college, he had taken Ritalin to suppress his hyperactivity. He drank heavily and became quite promiscuous. When he could not get enough sex, he masturbated until he rubbed himself raw. Even after he fell in love, his need for sex seemed to remain strong and demanding. He was also arrogant and boastful, although his parents' decision to separate at this time deeply affected him. He lost interest in school and changed his career trajectory, but failed to recover his momentum. He now thought of his fiancée as someone he needed to control. When she pulled away, he felt desperate, because his mother was preparing to leave as well. After each of two failed attempts to reconcile with his fiancée, he had gone out in a rage and raped and killed a woman.

Ross wrote an article in prison about how constant and compulsive his sexual urges always were. Despite the pleasure he received from raping a woman, he claimed he would feel disgusted afterward, growing depressed and suicidal. He said that the female hormone, Depo-Provera, given to him in prison, had reduced his urges and allowed him some relief, but then liver problems forced him to abandon this treatment. Directly afterward, the urges and fantasies returned full-force, supporting a psychiatrist's belief that his raging sex drive was the result of a hormone imbalance. Then Ross received another medication that he said helped to clear his mind, and for the first time, he was aware of what he had done. Still, he felt no remorse.

In July 1987, Ross went on trial for the murders of Deborah Taylor and Tammy Williams. He pled guilty and received a sentence of 120 years. Then he was found guilty in four other murders and received two life sentences and six death sentences. Psychiatrist Robert Miller was barred from testifying about Ross' diagnosis of compulsive sexual sadism, which Ross believed would have spared him the death penalty: it would show that he could not have controlled himself. He petitioned for a new trial, filing numerous appeals, and the Connecticut Supreme Court overturned his death sentences and ordered a new penalty hearing.

Dr. Stanley Kauchinski testified about how the hormonal imbalance had likely caused Ross' criminal behavior, and thus Ross could not resist his driving impulses. In addition, his mother had been emotionally unstable and abusive. There was also speculation among Ross' relatives that an uncle might have sexually abused him. However, no one could prove it. Ross had no memory of it and the alleged incident had not affected him in a way typical of victims of abuse. Instead, with an IQ in the superior range, he had excelled in school. It was not until his senior year at Cornell that he grew hostile and disinclined to follow his ambitions.

The jury, unimpressed, once more gave Ross four death sentences. He halted his appeals, ready to die, but then his attorney requested a competency hearing. Two more psychiatrists evaluated him and said that Ross suffered from a narcissistic personality disorder. As a result, he felt compelled to accept death, to avoid looking like a coward. His self-esteem was at issue.

In other words, as a narcissist, Ross could be charming, even pleasant and engaging, but an underlying sense of superiority and entitlement motivated his behavior. He considered himself to be special, untouchable. No one mattered but him. In fact, he had sometimes visited the decomposing bodies to offer a final insult by masturbating on them, thereby reassuring himself that he was in charge.

Given his need to be in control, it seems more likely that his decision to end his appeals came from his fear of becoming a nobody. It was not about cowardice or media attention, but about exercising his final leverage against ending up helpless in the prison system.

The judge listened to all the arguments and decided that Ross was competent to determine his fate, so in 2005, Ross was executed.[1]

THE CARE AND FEEDING OF THE BLOATED EGO

The narcissists' most prominent attitude is disdain. It arises from a smug sense of superiority that allows them to thoughtlessly exploit others for their own gain and to discard them as most people would a used tissue. In fact, no matter how badly narcissists treat someone, they believe their victims were "privileged" to have been in their orbit. This attitude is more than just overblown self esteem. It's a clinical disorder that distorts reality, because excessive narcissists are enveloped inside a cocoon of their own concerns that buffers them from what others may feel. In fact, they have trouble accurately assessing their own feelings (and may believe this is part of their superiority). One sexual torturer whom we will meet in Chapter 7, David Parker Ray, claimed that his greatest joy came from giving a woman pleasure—despite hearing one survivor scream at him in court and testify about nightmares that had plagued her for years after escaping his clutches.

Narcissists treat themselves well. They usually dress nicely and overspend on themselves. They cheat on others if they see an opportunity to puff themselves up with someone else. Each relationship is just an avenue for acquiring admiration, and if it flags or grows demanding, they move on to another. They're often certain they will have a major impact on the world, and they move with ease into leadership positions. With great skill, they seduce others into buying into their self-regard . . . at least initially. It's easy for a narcissist to start up a relationship; it's not as easy for them to keep one.

Sigmund Freud, who first used the term as a psychiatric concept, hypothesized that a certain amount of narcissism is innate, perhaps as a survival mechanism. The child naturally feels omnipotent and the parents affirm it, because the child represents ideals they have not reached. They thus over-value the child's qualities.[2] But this is not the type of narcissism that gives rise to the disorder, unless the child fails to process reality. (Some experts believe that narcissism is a fixation on the immaturity of childhood.) To distinguish the pathological version that victimizes people, some have labeled it "malignant narcissism," a self-love that maintains itself at others' expense. Such people tend to develop repetitive antisocial behavior, especially with paranoid and sadistic features. They look for people they can easily dominate; for those for whom making others feel pain is gratifying, it proves their superiority.

During the 1930s, psychoanalyst Karen Horney wrote that narcissism developed from the combination of a certain type of environment with a certain type of temperament. She believed parental over-indulgence was largely to blame (a theory commonly held today); the resulting ego was empty because it was based on the evaluation of others, not on genuine accomplishments.

In psychodynamic theories, the child develops an idealized notion about who he or she is, and narcissists retain this childish grandiosity. Heinz Kohut, a Viennese psychiatrist, coined the term, narcissistic personality disorder, to describe how the primitive ego retains a belief in self-perfection. A positive effect is resilience and ambition, but the negative side is an extreme self-centeredness that is blind to flaws.

Otto Kernberg also examined infantile narcissism and its need for affirmation, deciding that pathology develops from the refusal to accept reality. Narcissists cannot distinguish their idealized self from their actual self, because to see their flaws is intolerable to them. If someone tries to correct their view, it's not the view that changes, it's the relationship: the helpful friend becomes an enemy, or even ceases to exist as a significant person. In the extreme, this denial can be aggressive, even sadistic. Narcissists direct their rage at others, to make *them* feel helpless and out of control. This switch from victim to victimizer is eroticized, edgy, exciting.[3]

With male narcissists, sexual aggression can develop. Some lust killers like Michael Ross have said that to take a human life makes them feel as powerful as God. The driving force is the need for complete control, which for the narcissist confirms his strength and superiority.

The *DSM-IV-TR* includes narcissistic personality disorder (NPD) in Cluster B on Axis II, with three other disorders that can manifest in extreme forms of egocentric behavior. A personality disorder is a persistent pattern of maladaptive behavior that causes dysfunction in relationships or at work. Although not all people with NPD are criminals, NPD and its close cousin, psychopathy, are the two disorders most commonly found among predatory sex offenders and lust killers. They feel entitled to their victims and their self-involved arrogance puffs up their sense of personal importance. It fuels repetition.

The *DSM-IV-TR* lists a number of characteristics of NPD, most noticeably a pattern of grandiosity and excessive need for admiration.[4] People with NPD must be the center of attention and will sacrifice being liked for being admired. They may show a long-standing pattern of any five of the following behavioral manifestations:

- believe without merit that they're important
- obsess over power and success
- associate only with those considered "worthy"
- demand admiration

- believe they are entitled to immediate compliance with their wishes
- exploit others to advance their own ambitions
- exhibit little sense of what others feel or need
- believe others envy them
- exhibit arrogant behaviors or attitudes

Another diagnostic instrument, the Narcissistic Personality Inventory (NPI), is a forty-item forced-choice assessment based on *DSM-IV* criteria, but it aims toward measuring sub-clinical narcissism, i.e., people in the general population who have NPD. Subjects with high scores are more likely to exploit opportunities to cheat and manipulate, as well as to like looking at themselves in mirrors. Likewise, the Millon Clinical Multiaxial Inventory (MCMI), developed by Theodore Millon, includes a scale for measuring narcissism in the general population. In a twin study in 1993 that utilized 175 volunteer pairs of twins, of the eighteen personality dimensions measured, narcissism had the highest degree of heritability.[5]

Although it's not appropriate to diagnose anyone without an extensive assessment procedure and appropriate credentials, it's also not difficult to see in detailed stories about sexual predators that they do exhibit many of these traits. They are self-centered, insecure, incapable of learning from helpful comments, and they know how to provoke admiring recognition for anything they've done. Narcissistic criminals, when captured, will attempt to draw the limelight and turn themselves into the most superior criminal ever seen. Often, they will defend themselves during their trials because they think no one is sufficiently competent to do the job. Or they will choose whatever role in court will best put them on display. They're always certain they can rely on their charm to win the jury.

Former FBI profiler Robert R. Hazelwood has examined cases in which narcissistic criminals kept records of their crimes, using them to relive the moment of dominance. One man, James Mitchell DeBardeleben, was a sexual sadist/serial rapist who almost committed murder. Whenever he tortured victims, he made them follow a script. When he couldn't find a victim, he would tape himself reading the script in a high falsetto voice. He used himself as a prop for his sadistic fantasies. "The crime scene," Hazelwood wrote, "is a central feature of a sexual criminal's work product, his canvas, if you will. For many offenders, the work is so valuable that they devise elaborate and occasionally ingenious ways to preserve it for later delectation."[6] Despite the risk this can pose of incriminating evidence, these offenders are certain they will never be apprehended.

Narcissistic immunity or "Teflon narcissism," is a manifestation of criminal narcissism, and it arises from magical thinking, or the belief that one is untouchable. Often this develops in reaction to a world that feels too capricious, dangerous, or harsh. They're not accountable, they think, because nothing will really stick. They believe they're smarter than the police, and even if caught, they'll figure their way out of it: They're "protected" via their special status, so something will always save them. They have the "right" to immunity because they have a destiny; punishment is for ordinary people. Besides that, they think they're skilled at duping people. Being caught is only a temporary setback; they truly believe that others cannot see their manner of manipulation. (It's more often their charisma than their skill that works.)

The irony for narcissists is that although they believe they're set apart from others, they desperately need others to affirm their superiority. Unlike the myth that features the self-loving Greek figure Narcissus, gazing into a mirror is not sufficient. They must hear from others how great they are. Yet beneath their apparent self-confidence, their ego is in fact quite fragile, and they respond badly to being challenged or humiliated. They harbor grudges and fiercely defend their own view of themselves, blaming others whenever something goes wrong.

Despite their annoying over-estimation of themselves, narcissists are often popular, with an entourage of admirers, because they have worked hard to learn what it takes to become and remain the center of attention. They will have a terrific sense of humor, they can inspire others to believe that everything is under control, and they will act as if they have considerable influence, whether or not they actually do. They're also resilient, recovering quickly from stress, because they generally experience the invincible feeling of always being right. But they can also be defensive and needy. Most people will tire of them in a fairly short period, despite how fascinating they might be. Such relationships are a one-way street, with the narcissist reaping all the rewards. Clearly, they thrive best in ego-intensive careers, but they can only work on teams if they are the team leader.[7]

Narcissism overlaps considerably with the condition known as psychopathy, because extreme self-centeredness and a lack of empathy for others is at the heart of psychopathy. In fact, many people diagnosed with NPD might as easily be psychopaths. It can be difficult to make a distinction. It's probably safe to say that although not all narcissists are psychopaths, all predatory psychopaths have some form of malignant narcissism at the heart of their operations.

WITHOUT REMORSE

The poster boy for this type of psychopathy is Theodore Robert Bundy. He believed he was smarter than anyone investigating him; he thought that only he could ably defend himself in court; he felt nothing for his victims; and even when he was sentenced to death, he was confident he could beat the system. It's not known for certain if his claim to have murdered thirty young women is accurate, since he liked to play games by doling out information, but it is certainly true that he was an active killer between 1974 and 1978.

Several young women had disappeared in the Pacific Northwest during the mid-1970s, and investigators learned that they should look for a slender man named "Ted" who drove a tan or gold Volkswagen Beetle. Yet this was a popular car and the description was too vague to narrow down leads into a workable investigation. Not only that, Bundy had moved beyond their grasp when he headed to Utah and Colorado. He knew how to use mobility to his advantage. He often approached potential victims by acting as if he was disabled and needed assistance, or by posing as a cop. One day he picked up Carol Da Ronch by telling her she needed to accompany him to a police substation, but everything about him felt wrong to her, so she remained guarded. She did get into his car, but when he made his move, she was ready. She fought him and escaped. With her help, the Colorado police arrested Bundy, linking him from witness reports to a murder. Since he claimed to be a law student from Washington, they contacted investigators there. Bundy's tan Volkswagen raised red flags. However, Colorado already had him. As they processed him for trial, he pretended he needed to do some legal research for his defense, but when left alone in the law library he jumped out of a second-floor window and escaped.

In Tallahassee, Florida, on January 15, 1978, Bundy was snubbed by a date, which enraged him. As he drank that evening, he grew more upset. Like a true narcissist, this meant that someone had to pay for his frustration: he would transfer his humiliation to someone else and regain his sense of control. Late that night, Bundy entered the Chi Omega sorority house on the campus of Florida State University, where he raped and clubbed three girls in their beds. Lisa Levy and Martha Bowman died, but the third girl survived. There was also a witness in the hallway. Although Bundy eluded capture and even managed to grab a twelve-year-old girl in broad daylight a month later, a traffic violation did him in. Once in custody, Bundy was incensed that the officers did not realize his notoriety, so he informed them. As they called other jurisdictions, he manipulated the press, assuring reporters he would beat this rap. His arrogance and lack of remorse was palpable. He truly believed he was immune to the consequences of what he had done. He had slipped away before; he would do it again.

Bundy decided to represent himself in court. He knew journalists from all over the world would be covering it. Not only did he spot the opportunity to showcase his presumed superiority, but he believed he could fully control the proceedings. In courts, he preened, flirted with the girls who flocked to see him, and winked at people he knew. Author Ann Rule, who had known Bundy in Washington State, thought he was trying to give her the impression that he could hardly be bothered with the proceedings. At first she believed his claim of innocence, because he had so impressed her that she would trust her children with him. However, Bundy's arrogance was his downfall in court with everyone who watched. He took such delight in milking police officers on the stand for details about his crimes that he alienated the jury, and he once mistakenly referred to himself as the offender. A bite mark that he had left on a victim's buttocks was convincingly linked to his distinctive teeth, and the sorority witness confidently identified him as the midnight attacker. Despite Bundy's smirky demeanor and his certainty of acquittal, he was not quite as gifted as he believed. It did not take the jury long to convict him of three murders (including the twelve-year-old girl, whose body was found raped and strangled in the woods). Bundy was sentenced to death three times.

Even so, he was certain he could still beat the system. He appealed his cases on various grounds to the U.S. Supreme Court, and also tried to convince scientists that he was so unique that he ought to be kept alive and studied. He revealed more crimes, eventually confessing to thirty murders in six states, and hinted that he was not yet finished with what he could tell them. He discussed his compulsions as a predator to investigators who came to interview him, describing his need to totally possess his victim.

In addition, while a task force investigated the forty-plus murders attributed to the Green River Killer in Washington State during the 1980s, Bundy wrote from Florida's Death Row to offer them an "understanding" of the "Riverman's" mind. He knew the area intimately, he said, and he proposed to "figure out" how this new predator operated. A team came to question him, only because they believed that Bundy would describe his own modus operandi and perhaps close more cases. They accepted his "help," playing off Bundy's belief in his status as America's premier serial killer. As he described the Riverman's supposed modus operandi, Bundy revealed his indifference toward his victims. They were merely objects to him, to gratify his desires. He felt no remorse. To his mind, once he had them, they had belonged to him. He could not understand why their families were so grief-stricken over it. Like Michael Ross had said, Bundy felt nothing at all about the women he had killed, whose remains he had desecrated.

However, he did win a round for his sense of superiority when the FBI asked him to look over the forms they were developing for the database they called the Violent Criminal Apprehension Program. Bundy was happy to comply, letting them know, from the point of view of the world's most infamous offender, that they should correct some things. They thanked him, and he probably believed he had made his case that he was too valuable to execute.

Just before Bundy was to die in Florida, he tried again. This time, he lured an evangelical psychologist to take an interest in him by saying that pornography had played a significant role in his development into a killer. He gave the man a long interview, feigning sincerity in his search for "answers" for why he had become such a monster. However, only the most naïve people bought into this ploy. On February 24, 1989—probably to his surprise—Ted Bundy was finally executed.[8] He actually was *not* immune to the consequences of his actions.

During the 1980s, as Bundy sat in prison, psychopathy became diagnosable with a formal assessment instrument, which was developed by Dr. Robert Hare and other prison psychologists in Canada. The device was a twenty-two-item assessment, the Psychopathy Checklist (PCL). Now revised to twenty items, which are organized along four factors, the PCL-R is the preferred instrument throughout the world for assessing and predicting future violence. "Psychopathy is a personality disorder," Hare wrote in his classic book, *Without Conscience*, "defined by a distinctive cluster of behaviors and inferred personality traits, most of which society views as pejorative."[9]

The PCL-R is completed on the basis of a semi-structured interview with the subjects, along with information from their files. Each trait on the scale is rated from zero (the subject does not manifest it), to two (he or she definitely does). The highest possible score is forty, and a person is diagnosed as a psychopath if his or her score falls between thirty and forty.

In other publications, Hare has pointed out that among the most devastating features of psychopathy are a callous disregard for the rights of others and a propensity for predatory and violent behaviors. Without remorse, psychopaths charm and exploit others for their own gain. They lack empathy, and they manipulate, deceive, and con others, without regard for anyone's feelings. They're emotionally shallow, egocentric, and parasitic.

To add another dimension, Dr. Robert Rieber wrote in *Psychopaths in Everyday Life* that psychopathy may arise from a profound dissociation that affects how they process language and form goals. We all possess some degree of ability to ignore the moral or social requirements of a situation for our own self-interest, and psychopaths transform this ability into a skill. They can pathologically break from their conscience until they no longer have to exercise control over it. This makes them incapable of human concern, except to exploit. Adaptive psychopaths—those who can engage in a private fantasy—can fool others with a public persona until such time as they have a serious run-in with the law. That is, they can have long periods of normal behavior. However, risk and danger make them feel alive, and since they experience no deterring sense of morality or empathy, as an alternative to becoming psychotic, they simply dissociate from their harmful behavior and its consequences.[10]

With narcissism and a lack of remorse as a basis, we can better understand how the cycle of predatory exploitation and violence becomes addictive, and thus predictable: It's all about me. No one else matters. Although it can be difficult for normal people to grasp this motivation, to fully understand a sexual predator we must recognize how they motivate themselves.

3

Addiction and the Cycle of Sexual Violence

THE NEW FORENSICS

Tommie Lee Andrews began stalking and raping women in Florida in May 1986, and in less than a year he had victimized two dozen before he was caught. Only one woman could identify him, but to send him to prison for a longer sentence, the district attorney wanted to convict him of serial rape, so one more conviction was necessary. He decided to try the new DNA analysis, which had just succeeded in England in exonerating a suspect for two rape/murders under investigation there and in identifying the culprit for both. When the biological specimens from different cases in which Andrews was a suspect were tested, they identified him as the common source. This helped to convicted him of serial rape.[1]

Andrews' modus operandi was the same for most of his crimes: collecting a "trophy" from each scene, personalizing the rape, and making it something that he could look back on fondly. In the end, he received a sentence of 115 years. But the "who" is one issue; the "why" is another. What led Andrews, as well as other serial rapists, to repeatedly commit these heinous crimes? What drove him to stalk and rape, as well as collect personal items to relive his sexual conquest?

Few would argue that sexual predators think differently from most normal people, but it's not clear how their thinking gets off track. Although rape is not necessarily about sex, sometimes it is, and these sexual predators compulsively act on their craving. Yet it carries significant risk of incarceration, especially when they leave victims alive. Addiction of this nature is motivated from some overwhelming source, but it's not clear how it becomes so strong: Were the offenders born with a physiological malfunction that they could not control, or did their deviant behaviors arise from habits that formed after their initial decision to victimize? Whatever causes their "cycle of sexual violence," our first step is to examine the mechanism of sexual addiction.

CAN'T STOP THE CRAVING

Addiction can be defined as the inability to manage a desire for a specific behavior. With sexual addiction, the behavior is sex. Whether we call it sexual dependency, sexual compulsion, or hypersexuality, the idea is that individuals that suffer from sexual addiction cannot control their behaviors on their own, and crave sex under any circumstances. This is obviously not a problem when a person with the disorder can find a willing partner. However, in some instances, the target person's willingness is not what the addict wants. In fact, he may crave an unwilling partner, hoping that she will fight with him throughout the entire sexual experience. This is where the sexual addiction becomes a problem—when the addict might be a repeat pedophile, a deviant who commits criminal trespass, or even a rapist.

As an example of this cycle, we'll look at rape, which we'll deal with in a different manner in Chapter 5. Since rape is among the riskiest of major crimes, cases of serial rape afford a solid behavioral forum. The life of a serial rapist starts the same as any other individual, albeit usually with recognizable deficiencies.

Leonard Fraser, born in 1951, grew up in Ingham, North Queensland, Australia, the second youngest of four children. He dropped out of high school when he was fourteen, having difficulty with the workload and simple things like spelling his name. Then he began to get into trouble. At the age of fifteen, he was sentenced to serve a year in a boys' home for stealing. When he was released, he committed several other petty crimes, such as joyriding in a stolen car and driving without a license. At age twenty-one, he was arrested for burglary and prostitution, a hint that his sexual predilections may become a problem.

In the summer of 1974, Fraser attacked a woman from behind, twisting her arm behind her back to keep her under control. He pushed her down an embankment, away from public detection, and raped her. Worse, he believed she liked it, and he held her hand while walking back up the embankment as if he thought they now had some romantic bond. This rape indicated an elevation of criminal behavior, which is common among serial rapists.

Six days later, Fraser attempted to rape a second woman at a dry cleaner's shop. Utilizing the same modus operandi, he threw her arm behind her back. However, someone walked into the store interrupting him, so he fled. Three days later, he attempted to rape a third woman, this time twisting her arm behind her back and punching her several times in the face. In this case, however, the victim escaped by convincing Fraser that the sex would be better at *his* house. He believed so, too, so he started to walk with her back up the road. At that point, she was able to make a quick move and escape. Having outwitted her would-be rapist, she contacted the police, who found and arrested Fraser. He confessed to two rapes and two attempted rapes, saying that when he saw a woman alone, he felt driven to assault her.

Fraser was convicted and sentenced to twenty-two years in prison, but he was eligible for parole in just seven years. He was released in 1981, ready to pick up where he'd left off. Moving to Mackay in Queensland, Fraser committed several more rapes. In one instance, he duped a woman into believing he was interested in a car she had for sale. In a second case, he stalked a twenty-one-year-old girl for several days, eventually attacking her from behind, knocking her down in a secluded area, and raping her in the middle of the day. Since his victims all survived, they were able to contact the authorities and describe Fraser in detail, which allowed the police to find him quickly. Fraser was arrested and convicted once more, and sentenced to twelve years in prison. He seemed to have learned nothing from incarceration, as he continued to rape women as soon as he got out.

Fraser raped one woman who was terminally ill after she refused to come home with him. He subsequently moved into a flat with another woman and her eleven-year-old daughter, but that relationship ended when she accused him of having an inappropriate relationship with her daughter. When she found him having sex with her dog, she kicked him out. For Fraser, the need was sex; it did not matter who, what, or where, only that he needed it.

On April 22, 1999, Fraser graduated to murder. He kidnapped nine-year-old Keyra Steinhardt as she was walking home from school. A woman who lived in the neighborhood saw a man come behind Keyra and knock her over in the tall grass in the vacant lot. He fell on top of the girl, and the witness was unable to see what he was doing. She called the police, and they found Keyra's nude body in the trunk of Fraser's car. When the investigation was complete, it was clear that he had brutally raped and killed the girl by stabbing her repeatedly in the neck and upper body.

After Fraser's conviction and life sentence, investigators started to look at Fraser for other rapes and murders in the area, believing that he had killed more women before he killed Keyra. Between September 1998 and April

1999, four women and girls had gone missing, and the police now believed that Fraser was responsible. One was fourteen-year-old Natasha Ryan, who disappeared in the same area that Keyra was raped and murdered. The second victim was Julie Dawn Turner, who told friends that she was moving in with a man named "Lenny" and subsequently disappeared. Then Beverly Leggo, thirty-six, vanished in March 1999. An investigation turned up the fact that she had met Fraser two years before. In each case, circumstantial evidence, as well as testimony from friends and relatives, led to the conclusion that Fraser had been with each victim and was the last person seen with them before they disappeared.

Perhaps the most disturbing story is that of Sylvia Benedetti, who vanished April 17, 1999, just five days before the kidnapping, rape, and murder of Keyra Steinhardt. In room thirteen of the soon-to-be demolished Queensland Hotel, police were called to examine a blood-soaked area. The carpet was saturated, the walls and ceiling were covered with blood, and tiny bone fragments were sprayed all over the room. Police believed they had found the place where Fraser had committed his most heinous murder, but could not find the victim's body. The night before she disappeared, witnesses reported seeing Fraser with Benedetti at the Rockhampton city mall, and police now believed that he had killed her in the hotel room and disposed of the body elsewhere. After searching Fraser's car, they matched the blood in his trunk with that of Benedetti, and knew they had their killer.

Fraser eventually admitted to multiple murders. He said he had killed Natasha Ryan and put her in a shallow grave. In the case of Julie Turner, he confessed that he had raped and killed her after she rejected his advances. As for Beverly Leggo, he admitted to police that he had knocked her unconscious and then hanged her from a tree next to Nankin Creek, where he'd been swimming with her. When she was dead, he buried her in a ditch that he'd dug, covering his tracks. Finally, in describing the incident involving Sylvia Benedetti, he admitted that he beat her so hard that the bone fragments shattered and sprayed around the room; he also deliberately smeared her blood on the walls. When the judge sentenced Fraser to three additional life terms in prison, he concluded that Fraser's unusual sexual desire had ultimately motivated him to rape and kill.[2]

What kind of craving drove Fraser to commit these heinous crimes, raping and murdering so many innocent women? Based on his history, an obvious theory is sexual addiction. This can take many forms, often within the context of the paraphilias we described in Chapter 1, from rubbing against another person in an elevator to a desire to watch pornography and have sex several times a day. As is often the case, the addiction can lead to rape. In such cases, the behavior escalates, with the predator starting as something of an exhibitionist and eventually raping and possibly killing multiple victims. They become addicted to the rush; neurochemical events occur in the brain and body during sexual behavior, similar to the shot of adrenaline one might feel during an exhilarating activity, and they become addicted to the feeling. That is, the brain's chemicals create such euphoria during certain acts that the person develops a craving to repeat that experience.[3]

The addictive nature of rape for predators is not unlike the addictive nature of drugs or alcohol. In both cases, addicts are driven by the compulsion, often to the detriment of their family and other close relationships.[4] Rapists become consumed with their desire to rape as often as they can, and ignore the ramifications of their actions. That is, in the heat of the craving, they can focus on nothing else. In many instances, they will attempt to blame others for their behavior, just as drug addicts do, and this lack of responsibility helps to blind them to their problem. When they fail to see their problem, they will continue to feed their need.

ILL OR EVIL?

A common complaint from lay people is that rapists are afforded too much latitude, allowing mental health experts to deem them "diseased" or "broken," and equating their behavior to people who have an actual disability. However, the experts are in a better position to study sexual addiction. Dr. Helen Singer Kaplan, a clinical professor of psychiatry and the Founder and Director of the Human Sexuality Program at the Cornell Medical Center in New York, has argued that sexual motivation, or at least the control of one's sexual behaviors, is regulated by the central nervous system (CNS). She explains that an individual with a higher than average sex drive may simply be suffering from a malfunction of their CNS, the part of the body that adjusts and controls human sex drive. Furthermore, she argues that the mechanism that normalizes sexual desire takes into account the opportunity to rape and the hazards of such behavior, depending on the environment, but only if it's working properly.[5] In a sense, the rapists' systems go haywire, causing them to do whatever they can to achieve their sexual goals. While this theory might be correct, it's nevertheless difficult to feel pity for them when they choose to exercise their craving with such brutality.

Once a sexual predator rapes his first victim, there is a strong possibility that he will rape again. In fact, there are only a few serial rapists for a large number of serial rape victims.[6] The fact of the matter is that rapists enjoy the ritual aspect of the act as much as the act itself. For the serial rapist, the planning is almost as exciting as the actual rape. They look forward to it, and thinking about the details of how they will accomplish it stimulates them. The ritual of the serial rapist provides psychosexual arousal and gratification, above and beyond the rape itself.[7] In fact, the presence of a victim who witnesses it can be an essential component. Gathered from witnesses' reports, their sexual habits and predilections, both prior to and after the completion of the rape, become clues to their eventual detection.[8]

Psychiatrist Robert Simon says that antisocial activities that escalate indicate a need for the stimulation that derives from that activity.[9] Stephen Giannangelo, a psychologist who studies lust crimes, states that the excitement of an assault or rape can even induce a rapist to commit a murder. They may understand the crime's seriousness but will nevertheless experience a rush from discovering "what they truly need." If they get away with it, their confidence emboldens them to repeat it. This helps to fuel addiction.[10]

Giannangelo is among those researchers who have examined the mechanisms of addiction, in which the brain choreographs the body's information processing system, directing the neurotransmitters. Among those most implicated is dopamine, because it floods the system during novel or exciting situations, triggering the brain's reward system. Thus, we approach with anticipation those behaviors and situations that may feel good, and pending a continued pleasurable experience, dopamine provides an edgy high that spurs us to seek it again. It provides a biological investment in life's unpredictable twists. Dopamine helps us to focus and alerts us to new information. It fuels the thrill of being alive. Yet the brain adapts, and dopamine levels increase or decrease accordingly. When they diminish, the person seeks new avenues of stimulation and reward. In addition, research indicates that those people with fewer dopamine receptors in the brain are more prone to craving stimulation, which might be what makes them vulnerable to addiction or compulsive pleasure-seeking. For those who find their reward in rape or lust killing, it feels better in the brain and body to act out than to inhibit the impulse. The person grows bolder in pursuit of it.

Other bodily processes can also affect the dopamine surge as well. Comfort hormones such as oxytocin may diminish it, while elevated testosterone levels increase dopamine production. During risky situations, adrenaline kicks in as well. In addition, the longer reward is delayed, the more the brain produces these hormones, and frustration can have a facilitating effect.[11]

So to make this specific to the development of a predatory rapist, we propose an environmental/physiological feedback; the spiral of what we'll call erotic enthrallment.[12] An individual rapes someone and finds it stimulating. The brain responds with pleasure, rewarding an approach to the exciting object again, but the rapist eventually grows bored (the physiological thrill levels out) and he seeks more such stimulation. So the cycle repeats with some added stimulus (more challenge, more often, more intense, more violent), again reproducing the original erotic charge. In sum, the erotic enthrallment in causing harm to others for one's own gratification starts with environmental opportunities and associations, and becomes stronger via acts that stimulate the brain's reward mechanisms. The neural reward system processes these behaviors in a way that fends off boredom and ensures repetition.

METICULOUS AND DISTURBED

Most people introduced to Peter Norris Dupas saw a normal guy, average in stature, inconspicuous, and plain. However, his increasing predilection toward rape and murder made him one of the coldest and most calculating predators of all time. Born in July 1953 in Sydney, Australia, Dupas grew up in a normal family, with two loving parents and two older siblings. His parents were old enough to be his grandparents and they doted on him, treating him like an only child. However, at the age of fifteen, Dupas' criminal behavior began with a bang—or at least with a stab. On October 3, 1968, Dupas walked to the house next door, asked the babysitter if he could borrow a sharp kitchen knife to peel some vegetables, and proceeded to attack her with it, knocking her to the floor and stabbing at her several times. She was eventually able to stop him and call the police. Afterward, he was sent for psychiatric evaluation. The team concluded that he was unable to conform to his parents' high expectation of him and that his aggression was a symptom of his maturation. However loved, Dupas' relationship with his parents seemed to have sent him, in their opinion, down a path of brutality and violence. How this had occurred was not clarified.

Dupas' criminal behavior became more clearly sexual in 1972, when a man caught the nineteen-year-old predator staring at his wife through their bathroom window. About a year later, in November 1973, Dupas was questioned by police after they received a complaint that he was leering at a woman's twelve-year-old daughter. Coupled with the stabbing of the babysitter, these incidents of sexual deviance were a sign that Dupas was headed toward increased depravity. In an attempt to find vulnerable people, he applied to be a police officer, but he was rejected for being too short. However, he did not let this stop him from finding women to satisfy his sexual cravings.

From the first voyeuristic activity, it was clear that Dupas was a predator, not of opportunity but of planning. Two weeks after the complaint by the concerned parent, Dupas was arrested for the rape of a married woman, after carefully devising a plan to gain entry to her house. Knocking on the front door, he posed as a driver whose car had broken down. He claimed to need a screwdriver, and asked if she could assist him. She agreed, and once he was inside the house, he hid from her, and retrieved a knife from the kitchen. He threatened the woman and her eighteen-month-old baby with the knife, and proceeded to rape the mother, tying her up with a cord, rendering her defenseless. He was charged with rape, but released on bail, allowing him to continue his predatory acts while awaiting trial.

Dupas was subsequently sent to Mont Park Psychiatric Hospital, but it was an outpatient program from which he could come and go as he pleased. In fact, on three separate occasions, Dupas was seen entering a female toilet and shower block, eventually getting caught by a police stakeout. In July 1974, he was finally sentenced to nine years for sexual assault, serving the minimum of five.[13]

Two months after Dupas was released from prison, he was back to stalking and sexually assaulting women, but now his drive had accelerated. After devising his plan of attack, he molested and sexually assaulted four women over a ten-day period. His modus operandi changed slightly but still consisted of stalking and rape. Using a public restroom as his location of choice, he now attacked while wearing a ski mask and carrying a knife. In fact, he succeeded in raping one woman, but his next three victims managed to escape. Dupas was eventually caught and charged with assault, intent to rape, malicious wounding, assault with intent to rob, and indecent assault. He was sentenced to five years in prison, and it became increasingly obvious to many that he was past the point of treatment. Still, once he served his sentence, no one could stop him.

Released from prison in February 1985, Dupas waited only a month before raping his next victim. After seeing a twenty-one-year-old woman sunbathing on the beach, he walked up, held her to the ground at knifepoint, and raped her. This time the court was slightly less lenient, and he received a twelve-year sentence, with the possibility of parole after seven. He received medical treatment to try to reduce his sex drive. He served seven years and on release, he lived as a law-abiding citizen for a year and a half, but then his desire took over once more.

In January 1994, Dupas attacked a twenty-six-year-old woman who was vacationing with her fiancé at a house near Lake Eppalock in northern Victoria. As with his earlier rapes, he followed his victim into the public bathroom and, while wearing a ski mask and wielding a knife, attempted a rape. Again, he was unsuccessful, and soon the police apprehended him. This time, however, they found something more disturbing. When they searched Dupas, the police found a roll of PVC insulation tape, a pair of handcuffs, knives, and condoms, as well as a sheet of plastic and a shovel in his car. It was clear that his intent was to capture, rape, and torture, and eventually kill his victim—an acceleration of his already brutal pattern of sexual assault. After pleading guilty to the charge of false imprisonment, he received a sentence of three years and nine months, with a minimum of two years and nine months to be served. In September 1996, he was once again released from prison, and he moved into a house in Melbourne.

The following year, Dupas' history of planning, stalking, and rape culminated in a string of murders. On October 4, a prostitute named Margaret Maher went missing. When her body was eventually found, she had been stabbed several times and her breasts were mutilated: her left breast was cut off and shoved into her mouth. The crime was sexual, and given Dupas' prior incidents, he was an obvious suspect. In fact, a black wool glove was found near Maher's body, and DNA traces from it identified Peter Dupas as the source. However, this sadistic murder did not satisfy him, and Dupas was already searching for another victim.

Four weeks later, Mersina Halgavis was visiting her parents' grave. When she failed to meet her fiancé as planned, he went to the cemetery to find her. She was there in an empty grave, her shirt pulled up. She had been stabbed numerous times, mostly on the breasts. Investigators noticed that Dupas' grandparents had been buried here, less than 100 yards from where the body had been dumped, and this fact seemed too coincidental. An elderly man who was at the cemetery that day described a man who resembled Dupas leaving the cemetery. However, police were unable to positively connect Dupas to the murder.

Finally, on April 19, 1999, the body of Nicole Patterson was found, mangled and disfigured. She was naked from the waist down, with her skirt removed and her underwear around her ankles. Small pieces of tape were found attached to her body, indicating that she had been restrained with the same kind of yellow PVC tape that police found in Dupas' possession so many years ago. In addition, both of her breasts had been removed with a shape knife, indicating the sexual nature of the crime. Overall, she had been stabbed twenty-seven times.

The police suspected Dupas, and a search of his home revealed blood-stained clothing, PVC tape, a ski mask, and newspaper clippings of Nicole Patterson's murder.[14] On August 23, 2000, Peter Norris Dupas was convicted of her murder and finally put away for life, without the possibility of parole. Four years later, he received a second life term for the murder of Margaret Maher, and then a third life sentence for the murder of Mersina Halvagis.[15] The prison system's revolving door had finally stopped.

HOW FANTASY FUNCTIONS

While ritual plays an important role in the predator's behavior, so does fantasy. In fact, fantasy is often a strong motivator in serial rapists' behavior. Because they're taking such risks, they rely on secrecy. Typically, they have already developed a fantasy life as a child, which has grown more erotic as they move through puberty. As predators, they utilize their most stimulating private thoughts to rehearse for action. For most individuals, fantasy is enough to satisfy their desires. They do not feel the need to act them out, and are content to keep their wildest dreams to themselves. But for serial rapists, criminal paraphiliacs, and lust killers, fantasy is not sufficient.

Typically starting around the age of sixteen, sexually sadistic predators begin to fantasize about rape and sexually aggressive behavior. Before acting out their entire rape fantasy, they will often act out parts.[16] For instance, if their fantasy includes binding a victim's hands, they may go out and purchase rope. If their fantasy involves stalking a victim, they may follow a potential victim to her house, stopping short of approaching her. Eventually, serial rapists will follow through with their assault, raping their victims within the frame of their rape fantasies.

We mentioned the shoe fetish of Jerome Brudos in Chapter 1, and we return to him again for more details. He grew up as a solitary, browbeaten boy, who disappointed his mother. She made it clear she had wanted a girl. In solitude, he developed his erotic fantasies about women's shoes and underwear. His discovery of a pair of women's spike-heeled shoes at a local dump when he was five years old was the starting point. He took them home and tried them on in his bedroom, and when his mother caught him, she grabbed them, destroyed them, and let him know that such things were wicked. She was highly agitated and inexplicably upset, which signaled to the boy that there was something about those shoes that was deliciously forbidden. It's likely that making these shoes taboo gave them an aura that pervaded Brudos' developing sexuality. He also stole the shoes that his kindergarten teacher kept in her desk and received a reprimand.

As he grew up, Brudos often broke into neighborhood homes to steal these items, and continued to do this even after he was married and a father. Touching female underwear gave him some sense of comfort and the feeling of arousal, and he soon had quite a secret stash. As a seventeen-year-old in 1956, his fetish became edgier. Having dug a hole in a hillside to keep girls as sex slaves, he used a knife to accost a seventeen-year-old girl, demanding that she remove her clothing so he could photograph her nude body. He even beat her up, but after an elderly couple caught him he admitted what he'd done. Clearly, this sort of encounter was not going to satisfy him, not even after serving nine months for it on the psychiatric ward of Oregon State Hospital. In therapy there, doctors became aware that his sexual fantasies were centered around hatred for his demanding mother and revenge against women. They knew about his collection of women's clothing, but diagnosed him with an adolescent adjustment disorder. Apparently, they did not know, or did not think it was alarming, that his fantasies included placing girls into freezers so he could later arrange their stiff bodies in sexually explicit poses.

Brudos might have been content with his sexual fantasies, which sometimes involved assault, had not a young woman arrived at his door one day. Thus, his career as a murderer began. He had often imagined doing this and now he'd acted on it, killing four women before he was stopped.[17]

Jack Owen Spillman III was arrested in 1995 for the murder of a mother and daughter in Washington State. The fourteen-year-old had been stabbed and bludgeoned in the head, then raped, after which the killer had shoved a baseball bat into her vagina. He'd also placed skin from her genitals onto her face. The mother had been stabbed thirty-one times and her breasts were cut off and placed near the daughter. More appalling, her genital area had been excised and was stuffed into her mouth. Both victims were provocatively posed. Spillman was quickly caught for a local burglary and during his confession of this double homicide, he added a third. When this body was exhumed, it appeared that she had been buried in the same position as Spillman had posed the other girl. He had studied other killers and had fantasized about torturing girls and cutting out their hearts. He viewed himself as a werewolf, so in his fantasies he had stalked "prey." He then began following girls, reinforcing his identity as a beast-like predator. Finally, he killed one, digging up her body for necrophilic sex, and then went for two victims at once. He treated the bodies according to his most deviant fantasies.[18]

According to Louis Schlesinger, an expert on compulsive and criminal behavior, individuals who commit serial rape do so because they have a sex drive that they cannot satisfy.[19] These offenders start by simply fantasizing about rape, imagining all of the places they could commit the act and the types of women they would enjoy raping. Unfortunately, they eventually graduate to acting out their fantasies as best they can. The majority of sexual assaults by serial rapists are premeditated, based on the desire to find the "perfect" victim and avoid detection.[20]

Acting out fantasies before committing an actual rape is typical for sexual predators. In fact, using non-living things, such as dolls, pictures, videos, and clothing, is a common precursor to serial rape.[21] This is not to say that individuals who enjoy sex dolls, watching pornography, or wearing women's clothing are going to become sexual predators or lust killers. In fact, for many, the introduction of dolls and pornography is a fetish itself, but is as deviant as they will get. However, in the case of the developing serial rapist, this may be a stepping stone to criminal acts.

For serial rapists, fantasies become roadmaps to behavior, since they serve as a stage for rehearsal. As a predator grows older and acquires more experience, he "layers" the fantasy with more detail and more sophisticated ideas about what he wants to do. He works out the kinks in his head, and then imagines himself committing the act over and over, each time becoming more violent and more intricate, from the setting to the level of brutality.

Serial rapists will often choose a "type" of victim: blond or brunette, short or tall, young or old. This choice is something that they have played out in their mind dozens of times before committing their first rape. They envision the kind of woman whom they will be raping, and know what they would like their victim to look like. This is no different than an individual who prefers one "type" of person over another for a date or friendship, except that the predator uses these categories as characteristics to narrow his target possibilities. Vernon Geberth, an expert in the field of sex-related homicide and death investigation, has argued that fantasy is very important to the serial rapist for this reason; the rapist selects the "right type" of person to assault, and the victim is usually a stranger.[22]

As we see with any violent serial behavior, fantasies for serial rapists become more intense, vivid, and brutal as they continue to find and rape victims. Although they might start by fantasizing about a simple rape, their fantasies evolve; they begin to become more creative, as well as more aggressive. For more excitement, some introduce violent sexual behavior such as whipping, biting, choking, bondage, and various levels of torture. In fact, the escalation of violence appears to be necessary for achieving and sustaining arousal.[23]

Eric Hickey explains that serial rapists will often record their brutal behavior so that they may watch, listen, and relive the moment over and over again.[24] It is this lust for more degradation—this level of fantasy—that drives the serial rapist to increase the level of violence. Once he has accomplished one act, he raises his expectations, with the goal of trying something new, more intense, and more exciting. It becomes a vicious cycle; he craves control and violence, so he commits a more violent act, which makes him crave more control and violence. It is a cycle that will stop only when the rapist is apprehended.

The same can be said for all other predators who commit sexual crimes, including pedophiles and parents who commit incest. The cycle of violence is quite evident among these offenders, as we'll see in the next chapter.

4

Child Molesters and Family Predators

SCHOOL DAZE

On January 16, 2007, Lonnie Stiffler walked into Mingus Springs Charter School in Arizona, located an hour and a half from Phoenix. He was interested, he said, in enrolling his grandson, Casey, in the seventh grade. He told the secretary that, thus far, he had homeschooled the boy, but he now wished him to have more social experiences with boys his age. Stiffler filled out the paperwork and was pleased to learn that Casey could begin school the following day.

However, something about this encounter disturbed school administrators. After reviewing a birth certificate for Casey Edward Price and guardian papers that looked phony, the director suspected a possible case of child abduction. He contacted the authorities. His instincts were right, but this case ended up shocking not only the authorities, but even Casey's supposed grandfather.

Casey Price was actually Neil Havens Rodreick II, a twenty-nine-year-old convicted sex offender who was posing as a twelve-year-old to gain access to children in the charter school. By using a variety of techniques to disguise his age, including make-up to cover his stubble and the removal of his body hair, Rodreick had fooled not only the school administrators, but Lonnie Stiffler as well. Stiffler was a pedophile, and he had allowed his middle-aged partner, Robert James Snow, to bring Casey into their home. They were both under the impression that they had been having sex with a twelve-year-old boy. Having fallen for his disguise and fake background story, they were willing to continue the charade by enrolling Rodreick in school.

As a convicted sex offender, there is little question that Rodreick had created his persona with the intent of obtaining access to children who had just reached puberty. In fact, this was not the first time he had enrolled under this guise in an Arizona school. Starting in 2005, Rodreick had also attended charter schools in Surprise, Payson, and Prescott Valley, and he was able to fool teachers, students, and administrators alike.[1]

Although eventually caught, Rodreick had been able to perpetuate his pattern of sexual offending for years. Of real concern was why he went to such lengths to gain access to children. It is difficult for many people to imagine that a child could fulfill the needs of an adult, but that is the case with pedophiles. As strange as it is, pedophilic yearnings can be explained by examining their emotional development or lack thereof.

According to Sharon Araji and David Finkelhor, researchers who have completed numerous studies in the field of pedophilia and child sexual abuse, a pedophile's level of sexual arousal can be the direct result of formative experiences early in life.[2] Either through exposure to child pornography or through sexual abuse at the hands of a loved one, the early level of arousal the child experiences may eventually be incorporated into fantasy, disinhibiting control over his desires. Albert Fish, for example, who was described in Chapter 1, told a psychiatrist how his arousal over the buttocks of young boys began in a detention center, where he saw them being paddled by authority figures. Although some boys might develop an aversion to paddling from such experiences, or no particular attitude at all, Fish fixated on it as a source of sexual pleasure. Additionally, biological factors such as higher testosterone levels can contribute to this type of offender's desire and subsequent behavior.[3]

As would be expected with a crime of this nature, such offenders are overwhelmingly male. In fact, the chase of the child is often a significant factor in the thrill for these types of offenders. They will generally resort to stalking children, abducting them from places where children are known to gather, such as playgrounds and schools. In Rodreick's case, the creation of an elaborate plan allowed him to stalk his victims up close, giving him the ability to become friends with them, learn their behaviors, and build a level of trust that most offenders would not ordinarily be able to achieve. There was probably a certain amount of thrill in the act of duping others and seeing just how long he would get away with it. The success of a man nearing thirty in posing as barely adolescent may have surprised even him.

THE MOST PROLIFIC EVER

The ability to gain the trust of his victims was precisely how Dean Arthur Schwartzmiller was able to molest little boys at such an alarming rate.

Serving as a home improvement contractor, Schwartzmiller made a point of befriending parents to gain access to their children. In the early 1970s in Juneau, Alaska, Schwartzmiller started his thirty-year obsession, molesting and having sex with underage boys whenever the opportunity arose. Initially pleading ignorance about their age, he found himself drawn to these boys, eventually pleading guilty in one case to contributing to the delinquency of a minor, and then confessing to molesting a second boy. Schwartzmiller eventually left Alaska and moved to Mountain Home, Idaho, where he assumed the name Tim Lewis. While in Idaho, he followed his typical modus operandi: he coached football, befriended parents, and hired adolescent boys to work for him at his construction company.[4]

Focusing on boys who had little parental guidance in their lives, and were thus vulnerable to the attention of an adult male, Schwartzmiller befriended his victims with pot and beer. Targeting one boy at a time, he also arranged sleepovers. In some instances, he formed a relationship with a boy's mother, and one such victim from 1978 eventually testified against Schwartzmiller, claiming that he had been the man's sex slave for nearly a year.[5]

Schwartzmiller is considered one of the most prolific child molesters of all time, although the police cannot offer a total of his suspected number of offenses. When he was finally apprehended after several decades of sexual molestation and his property was searched, police found a large cache of child pornography, as well as Schwartzmiller's daily log of evil. Specifically, they found a 456-page journal that described his history of sexually abusing boys, as well as some 1,500 pages describing his victims and his sexual exploits in great detail. Headings such as "blond boys," "no, but yes boys," and "best of the best, thirteen and under" were all a part of his graphic memoir.[6] The handwritten notes, contained in seven spiral-bound notebooks, listed the names of 36,000 boys, as well as pages of coded symbols, which police believed described his various episodes of sexual depravity with children. Even James Missett, co-director of Stanford University's Center for Psychiatry and the Law and expert in the field of child molestation, was shocked by the meticulous nature with which the notebooks were kept. "What is different here are the numbers of youngsters, presuming the names refer to youngsters, and the extent to which they are cross-indexed and categorized. It's monstrous in its proportion. Thirty-six thousand is an awful lot." [7]

Schwartzmiller's forty-year period of child sexual abuse in eight states and three countries ended when he was sentenced to 152 years in prison for his deviant acts. He has been found guilty of twelve counts of child molestation and child pornography in connection with two California boys, as well countless other acts in both Idaho and Alaska.[8]

LITTLE BOY POT PIE

For pedophiles like Rodreick and Schwartzmiller, their passion for children, coupled with the excitement of the chase, can often lead to kidnapping, rape, and even murder. Such was the case with Nathaniel Bar-Jonah, a convicted child predator found guilty of repeatedly molesting, torturing, and murdering children. Born David Paul Brown, Bar-Jonah was a serial offender who went beyond the simple act of child molestation. Not only did he torture his victims, but he also cannibalized them.

Brown began his criminal career in 1974 at the age of seventeen, luring a boy into his car by posing as a police officer. He proceeded to beat and choke the eight-year-old, eventually letting him go. Although brutal, this was just the start to his heinous behavior. Three years later, Brown once again dressed as a police officer to lure his victim, this time kidnapping two boys, forcing them to undress before he began to strangle them. However, one boy escaped and reported the incident to the authorities. They responded immediately, stopping Brown and finding the other boy handcuffed but alive in the trunk of his car. For this, Brown received an eighteen-year prison sentence.[9]

In 1979, while housed in the Bridgewater State Hospital for Sexual Predators, Brown told his psychiatrist of his fantasies about kidnapping children, murdering them, and then cannibalizing their bodies. However, in 1991, the state deemed that he was not dangerous, and released him. After changing his name to Nathaniel Bar-Jonah, he attacked another boy, and the state decided that it would be most appropriate for him to leave Massachusetts and move to Montana, with the hope that living with his relatives would help to rehabilitate him. However, moving across the country simply gave Bar-Jonah the opportunity to continue his brutal behavior on unsuspecting prepubescents. Prison time had not deterred him; he was ready for more.

Once in Montana, Bar-Jonah remained anonymous for a while, until he was arrested in 1999 near an elementary school in Great Falls. A search of his home produced thousands of pictures of boys, as well as a diary that detailed his desire to eat his victims. Encrypted writings talked of "little boy stew," "little boy pot pie," and lunch served on the patio with roasted child.[10]

After a thorough investigation, it was determined that Bar-Jonah was responsible for the 1996 disappearance of Zachary Ramsay, who had vanished on the way to school one morning. Evidence suggested that he kidnapped, murdered, and cut up the boy's body for stews and hamburgers, which he served to unsuspecting neighbors at a cookout. A year later, in

2000, Bar-Jonah was charged with the kidnapping and sexual assault of three other boys who had lived in an apartment above him. Overall, Nathaniel Bar-Jonah's modus operandi was getting close to his victims before assaulting them. He was a predator who groomed his victims, spending months befriending them so that he could one day sexually abuse them.

OFFENDER PATTERNS

A comment we often hear is that some creepy person "looks like a child molester." However, it is nearly impossible to proactively determine who a sexual predator might be. Someone who looks "creepy" is no more an offender than a respectable person; conversely, just because someone looks respectable does not mean he's *not* a child molester. As an example, clean-cut John Joubert, who raped and murdered three young boys to satisfy a sexual craving, was in the military and volunteered with the local Boy Scouts. No one suspected him. Many researchers have attempted to create a typology of the average child molester, but none has helped to clarify this issue. Accurate prediction based on traits, appearance, or behavior still remains outside our reach.

Researchers have attempted to identify the characteristics of the offenders and the techniques they use to lure their child victims. In-depth interviews and questionnaires are among the methods used to learn what child molesters have to say about their behaviors. Getting inside their minds to try to determine causal factors is crucial for treatment, as well as to devise warnings to potential victims. In some cases, sexual preference has been gauged through the use of phallometry, wherein offenders are shown graphic pictures and pornographic sexual scenes, while a type of blood pressure cuff measures blood flow through the offender's penis. Unfortunately, even this research has not yielded anything definitive. Although the most obvious offenders who skulk around playgrounds or have difficulty hiding their desires are detectable, they're not that prevalent. Society must be concerned with those who skillfully hide their predilections in secret, practicing abuse for years.

Pedophiles can be placed into one of four categories. The first is the *mysoped*. These pedophiles are interested in molesting and sexually abusing their child victims because they want to physically harm them. They are often sadistic, and make a connection between sex and violence. They are male, generally a stranger to the victim, and will stalk a child before abducting him or her, often from a public place, such as a playground or school. For these individuals, harming the child is their highest priority.

A second type of pedophile is the *regressed child offender*. This individual generally has relations with adults, but offends against a child because of a precipitating event. Something happens in the offender's life, such as the collapse of a relationship or the loss of a job, and that makes him want to be with someone that he can physically control. He has feelings of inadequacy, and his inferiority complex manifests itself in alcohol use and child sexual abuse. The one positive thing about these offenders is that they have a low recidivism rate, because the precipitating event is generally not a perpetual event. In a sense, these are one-time offenders who will not feel the need to reoffend.

The *fixated child offender* has not emotionally matured, becoming stuck at an early stage of psychosexual development. There is no known precipitating cause and he comes across as a child who never grew up. He has little to no activity with people his own age, and is often uncomfortable around adults. He loves children, and does not want to hurt them. On the contrary, he "courts" them, buying them gifts and doing things to make them want to spend time with him.[11]

Finally, the *naïve pedophile* is the individual who, for all intents and purposes, has no sense of right and wrong. The offender is often mentally retarded, and does not understand the rules of normal society. In many cases, brain dysfunction influences their deviant behavior. This offender likes to cuddle with his victims, kissing and hugging rather than having sexual relations of any kind.[12]

Reuben Lang and Roy Frenzel, researchers at the Alberta Hospital in Alberta, Canada, interviewed fifty-two incest and fifty pedophilic offenders in an attempt to more clearly show what the average pedophile looks like. They found that the average age of child molesters is thirty-four. The typical modus operandi is to befriend the parents and offer to babysit the victims, as we saw in the case of the kindly grandfather in Chapter 1. They are attracted to situations in which children are easily attainable. In this vein, offenders tend to frequent malls, parks, arcades, and other places where children may hang out unattended. In many cases, their attraction may lead them to stalk single parents, for the purpose of creating an opportunity to be with their son or daughter.

Once the pedophile becomes a part of the child's life, the most common type of contact is "accidental" touching or cuddling. This allows the offender to be close to a child without him or her suspecting that anything out of the ordinary is occurring. In fact, an important part of their approach is to keep the child in the dark, so he or she will not report this activity to an adult.

Unfortunately, many pedophiles also use coercion, frightening the child into compliance with threats against the child or his family. They might also use bribes to ensure silence or gain consent. In either case, pedophiles will typically misrepresent normal moral standards to gradually seduce children into believing that nothing bad is happening to them. However, those pedophiles who target adolescents often exploit the emerging adolescent sex drive to lure the victims they desire.[13]

HOME SWEET HOME

William "Hank" Dufort was fixated on teenage boys. Between 1987 and 1989, he committed twenty-eight counts of sodomy, sexual abuse, and contributing to the sexual delinquency of a minor. All the while, he was serving as the director of the Children's Farm Home, a residential care facility in Corvallis, Oregon, for emotionally disturbed children. Exploiting his position, Dufort sexually abused six boys, ranging in age from twelve to seventeen. In fact, he admitted to sexually molesting and abusing dozens of boys during his tenure at the institution. Further, he admitted to being a longtime sex offender, and showed little remorse for his actions.[14]

Unlike Rodreick, Dufort did not care so much about the chase; instead, he thrived on the sexual act. Thus, he fits the classic definition of the *fixated child offender.* He has not completely matured, becoming fixated at an early stage of psychosexual development. Essentially, he is stuck in adolescence, and thinks and behaves like a child.

His desire for children is constant, with children becoming the sole target of his affections. His interest is persistent and compulsive, and he will do anything to get a child to spend time with him. For Dufort, his target was easily accessible, as his role of director of the boys' home gave him ample opportunity to spend time with the boys under his care. However, it is wrong to assume that he simply loved the boys. On the contrary, Dufort was emotionally immature, and his narcissism—he saw the boys as mirrors of him—drove him to continue his offending.[15]

As is the case with all fixated offenders, Dufort had a gender preference—male. In fact, it is rare that a fixated offender will pursue a female child. The fixated offender is easy to detect, as he has little to no activity with people his age; he is generally single, immature, and uncomfortable around adults. The fixated offender is the individual who will do whatever it takes to gain the trust and love of a child. Dufort was able to build a rapport with the children, projecting himself as a loving caretaker who would do anything to make them comfortable.

Understanding the predatory sex offender is paramount to public safety, but it is equally important to know the types of children whom pedophiles target. As expected, molesters will often choose victims who are vulnerable and needy, as well as victims already deemed socially troubled, because they know that such children seek a friend.[16] Children who are timid, shy, isolated, and dependent are the most likely targets. If a child does not have a sufficiently strong sense of self to resist an inappropriate adult and say no, he or she is more likely to become the victim of a predator who is actively looking for children of their type. Unfortunately, these children are submissive and inhibited, and are not likely to give the offender a hard time if he forces them into a sexual situation. They will also keep the secret, especially if bribed or threatened.[17]

It is difficult to detect a child molester until he has acted on his pedophilic desires. Unfortunately, believing that we can stop future victimization by determining who "looks like a child molester" will not protect children.

Just as disturbing as a stranger or acquaintance offender, and possibly more so, is the family pedophile—a parent or parental figure who targets a child. Concocting a plan to kidnap and sexually molest children is one thing, but victimizing your own children is an offense that few can understand.

CLOSE TO HOME

The vast majority of physical contact between an adult and child who are related does not constitute incest. Sexual child abuse is involved not with normal hugging and kissing, but when there is sexual involvement between a child and a relative, where law prohibits marriage. In many cases, the incestuous relationship is between the father and daughter, but it may also involve a mother and son, or extended family, such as stepparents, stepsiblings, and even grandfathers. In any case, the vast majority involves an aggressive male adult and a passive female as the victim.[18]

Incestuous relationships are not a modern-day phenomenon. In fact, they trace back to ancient civilizations. The word *incest* comes from the Latin term *incestum*, which means unchaste and low. Although many types of sexual deviance have been acceptable in certain cultures, incest is almost universally taboo.[19]

Elisabeth Fritzl had been the victim of her father's sexual abuse since she was eleven years old. At the age of sixteen, she had attempted to run away from home, but had failed and was planning to try it again. However, on August 28, 1984, Josef Fritzl asked sixteen-year-old Elisabeth to help him bring a door he had just purchased down to the basement. She thought it was an innocent request, but it was actually part of a plan for seduction and imprisonment: Fritzl, forty-eight, was looking for a sex slave. After luring Elisabeth downstairs, Fritzl drugged, handcuffed, and raped his daughter, locking her in the secluded basement. Unbeknownst to his wife, Rosemarie,

Fritzl kept his daughter in seclusion for the next two decades, visiting her every three days and raping her more than 3,000 times.[20]

During the next twenty-four years, neither Elisabeth's mother nor her six siblings knew where Elisabeth really was. In fact, when Rosemarie filed a missing persons report, Josef forced his daughter to write a letter to her mother, claiming that she was staying with a friend and no longer wanted to live with her family. In reality, Fritzl had his daughter locked in a dungeon.

Elisabeth gave birth to seven children; one died shortly after childbirth, three lived with Elisabeth in the basement dungeon, and Fritzl took in three of them. He told his wife that Elisabeth, who was in a cult, had abandoned them.[21] There seems to be no real explanation for how or why this heinous crime took place. However, Fritzl had been building up to it for some time, starting with the initial rape that brought Elisabeth under his power.

On April 19, 2008, Elisabeth's oldest daughter, Kerstin, fell unconscious, and Fritzl agreed to allow her to visit a doctor—the first time she had been outside the dungeon since her birth. Suffering from life-threatening kidney failure, Kerstin was admitted to the hospital, where doctors found a cryptic note attached to the patient's file, a note that Elisabeth hoped would grab the attention of whatever doctor took care of her daughter. Dr. Albert Reiter read the note and found the story troubling. He confronted Fritzl, and then contacted the police. Authorities went into the home, found the dungeon, and took Kerstin and Elisabeth into protective custody, where Elisabeth recounted the details of her long and traumatic captivity.

Although similar to other sexually predatory crimes, it is difficult to specifically characterize the incestuous offender. We cannot offer a profile of the typical incestuous predator, because incest cuts across every social, economic, and educational barrier. Further, the reasons for incestuous behavior can range from anger and frustration to revenge and sadism. However, research shows that most incestuous pedophiles are white, middle-class, married, educated men in their late thirties.[22]

The vast majority of incestuous fathers, including Fritzl, can be categorized as *sexually preoccupied*; they have a subconscious or obsessive sexual interest in their daughters. They become interested in the girl's lives, but also obsess about spending time with them sexually. In some instances, they will do whatever they can to spend more time with their daughters. In Fritzl's case, he wanted his daughter to be his slave.

Similarly, *adolescent regressive* men become sexually attracted to their daughters as they reach puberty. They have regressed sexually, and feel most comfortable around girls once they have reached puberty. Some fathers are emotionally dependent on their daughters, becoming depressed and lonely. Finally, some incestuous fathers become the *angry retaliator*, sexually abusing their daughters out of anger toward them or their mother who may have neglected or abandoned them.[23] One father took his anger to an extreme.

Ronald Gene Simmons, forty-seven, gunned down several people on the morning of December 28, 1987 in Russellville, Arkansas, before turning himself in. With a .22-caliber pistol, he shot a receptionist in the head at a law office, as well as four men at a convenience store. What appeared to police to have been a revenge shooting over a woman's rejection turned out to be much more sinister. Investigators learned that Simmons lived in a run-down house on isolated property outside town, so they went to notify his family of his arrest. When no one answered the door, the place seemed so strangely quiet that they suspected Simmons might have shot some people here as well. They entered the home through a window.

Inside the home decorated for Christmas were a number of bodies: Simmons' son, daughter, and their spouses had been shot. His granddaughter, age six, had been smothered to death. The officers immediately sought more resources for searching the thirteen-acre property.

The next day, investigators came across disturbed earth under barbed wire and sheet metal. When they dug down, they found two more bodies. They kept digging until they had found the remains of seven people, just barely covered by dirt. In the makeshift grave were Simmons' wife, two sons, three daughters, and a three-year-old granddaughter. Another team found two more corpses in the trunks of junked cars: Simmons' infant grandsons.

All of the adults had been shot and the children asphyxiated. A coroner determined that they had been killed a few days earlier, just before Christmas. Altogether, including the two people who had died in town, Simmons was charged with sixteen counts of first-degree murder and four counts of attempted murder. Then his true motive was revealed.

During a psychiatric exam, Simmons admitted that he had been physically abusing his wife and daughters. No mail came for them, no calls, and no friends were allowed. The reason lay in his flight from the law in New Mexico, where he was wanted on charges of incest. He had impregnated his fifteen-year-old daughter, Sheila, and this child was now among the dead. Simmons claimed he had loved her, and that they had been "soul mates," but then she had gotten involved with a young man. To his shock, she got married, which Simmons counted as an outright betrayal. Thus, he had planned the Christmas gathering as his moment of revenge: he killed his entire family.

Simmons was declared competent to stand trial and was convicted of the two murders in town. After he was found guilty of killing his family, he was sentenced to death. He told the jury they had done the right thing and refused to appeal, so on June 25, 1990, Simmons was given a lethal injection.[24]

A tragic tale of ongoing incest in a family tribe came out of California in 2003. On March 12, police officers responded to a phone call from two women in Fresno who sought access to their children. The father, Marcus Wesson, fifty-seven, was blocking them from his home. Although they had granted him custody, they were afraid for their children's welfare. The sound of gunshots filled the air as police arrived and ordered Wesson to come out, but only two women emerged. These four women, collectively, were Wesson's girlfriends or wives, and the mothers of the children inside. Eventually Wesson surrendered, presenting himself as a beefy 300-pound man with filthy dreadlocks down to his hips, covered in what appeared to be blood. The police arrested him and went in.

To their horror, they saw twelve coffins stacked against a wall. They pressed on to the next room, where they found a pile of bodies. One was an adult woman, another was a seventeen-year-old girl, and the rest were children, including two infants. There were nine in all, shot to death, and the woman had shot herself. The children had been fathered with six different women, including Wesson's own daughters. Wesson reportedly told the officers that he had killed his children to prevent them from being taken from him. They charged him with numerous counts for sexual crimes, alleging long-term sexual abuse going back to 1988 and forcible rape of underage females living with him.

At the end of his trial, the jury decided that even if his eldest daughter had shot some of the children, Wesson had to have shot others, making his brainwashed daughter participate. He was convicted of nine counts of first-degree murder and fourteen sex crimes, including the rape and molestation of his underage daughters and nieces. He received the death penalty.[25]

Incestuous fathers often feel entitled to their children, in the sense that their children are sexual property. These fathers are true to their role of patriarchy, believing that the father rules the roost and will do whatever he wants to whomever he chooses. He believes that his role in the family gives him the right, including victimizing his children on a consistent basis.

In many cases, incest is a symptom of a family with multiple problems, not just a single skeleton in the closet. Indicators of a family in a sexual crisis include the family's social isolation from the rest of society; a domineering father with a high level of control within the family; a highly distressed relationship between the parents; and parents who have reported substantial sexual discord between them.[26] In any case, it is difficult to imagine an adult craving sex with a child, particularly when that child is his flesh and blood. Yet such things occur, and the cases that emerge when the instigator is caught help us to understand how they develop.

5

Rapists

SEXUAL TRESPASS

For over a decade on the South Side of Lafayette, Louisiana, a man had entered the homes of a dozen different women to rape them. Despite numerous tips and the descriptions from each victim, police were unable to build solid leads. They knew that the predator was a stocky, white male who wore a knit hat, knit gloves, and a mask. He held a flashlight up high to blind the victims when he spoke, and used a gun to threaten them. After raping the women, he made them urinate or take a shower. He also told them that if they reported the incident he would know. Then he suggested they lock their doors and windows. One woman looked outside after he left and saw a brown Ford pickup truck drive away. But there were many such trucks in the area, and the sighting wasn't necessarily the perpetrator, so this tip led nowhere.

Investigators suspected, from the way in which this intruder held the flashlight and his threat that he'd "know," that he was familiar with law enforcement, but no one they knew matched the physical description. In 1998, the Lafayette police invited Dr. Kim Rossmo to apply his computerized program of geographical profiling. Rossmo went to each scene and pointed out that most of the houses had no curtains. Thus, the offender had a perfect opportunity to watch and wait for the right moment. He could also see whether a woman lived alone. With the program, Rossmo predicted where the rapist probably lived: a half-mile square area, within two miles from each scene. However, this procedure, too, failed to drum up solid leads.

Then a tip identified a police officer named Ernest Randy Comeaux, but he did not live anywhere near the target zone. Deeper digging revealed that during the period of the rape activity, Comeaux had indeed resided in this area. He also had a relative with a brown truck like the one the victim had described, and he was engaged to a rape crisis center volunteer. Comeaux was a good bet, so detectives surreptitiously acquired a sample of his DNA, which conclusively linked him to the rapes. He was arrested early in 1999, convicted of several rapes, and given life terms for each.[1]

Of all crimes, the thought of being raped instills a greater level of fear than most other types of victimization. Although societal focus has shifted from stranger to acquaintance and marital rape, the majority of women are still most concerned about being raped by a stranger. In this book, we're focusing specifically on predatory rape, which generally involves repetitive behavior, not on rape that arises within relationships. We're also aware that although some women who molest or assault children have been convicted of rape, we're looking at the phenomenon of rape by males. Female assault comes up in later chapters.

Predatory rape can be difficult to classify, because the offenders and victims include a variety of ages, races, and occupations. However, rape by a stranger, which lacks the complex factors of prior relationships, can be categorized according to one of three motivators: anger, desire for power, and sadism.[2]

Stranger rape is often the result of pent-up anger, frustration and hostility; the victim is typically a symbolic target. In a sense, the rape occurs because of an external event, something traumatic that the rapist has recently gone through. The loss of his job, an argument with his wife, or any other stressful incident can be the impetus for an anger rape. The offender seeks an outlet, and for such people, rape is the most gratifying way to acquire it. Sex becomes a weapon, allowing him to express his frustration.

The second motivation for rape is a need or *desire for power.* In this case, the predator rapes because he has feelings of inadequacy or insecurity, and the act of rape allows him to feel powerful or to gain control over another person. It is often the case that the rapist leads a life in which he feels he has little control. He may feel oppressed at work, has a job or relationship that makes him subservient, or even have feelings of inadequacy from his lower socioeconomic status.[3]

The most dangerous and predatory of all rapes is the *sadistic* rape. This offender eroticizes aggression, and is turned on and excited by the rape and torture of another person. He utilizes the most force and brutality possible, causing his victim severe pain, often for extended periods of time. In many cases, the kidnapped rape victim is tortured and/or held in bondage, and, if not killed, scarred for life.

WHO THEY ARE

Experts believe that the mentality, or belief system, of a rapist is wholly different from that of non-criminal society. The goal, then, is to determine what traits give rise to this type of thinking and triggers acting out. Although no single variable predicts future or serial rape, rapists appear to possess four distinct traits or characteristics that are noticeably absent from non-criminal males.[4]

The first characteristic is a set of *misogynist beliefs*. Rapists tend to agree with stereotyped views of sexual and gender roles and adversarial sexual beliefs. For instance, they may believe that women are inferior to men and should play the socially prescribed role of a subservient housewife. They may believe that women exist to please men sexually, not to have careers. Additionally, they may accept rape myths as fact, such as "if she didn't want it, she wouldn't have dressed like that," or "no means yes." These attitudes first show up during early adolescence, between the ages of twelve and fourteen, and remain fixed. Misogynistic beliefs reveal a general hatred for women, carried out in angry or sadistic sexual behavior.

The second characteristic is an *aggressive style*, often manifested as the use of force or violence to solve problems. This rapist will not stop when his victim begs and pleads, and in fact might be aroused by pleas for mercy. Such rapists are often seen as being hypermasculine, adopting a tough-guy attitude and proving their masculinity whenever possible, particularly when challenged by a woman. The attitude will show up in the type of cars they drive, pets they own, and even the guns they purchase.

Third, rapists often have a recognizable *personality functioning*, meaning that they tend to have consistent personality-test profiles. In other words, they fit the "classic" portrayal of a rapist. The personality variables include low levels of interpersonal responsibility and poor social skills. These men are uncomfortable in social settings and unreliable in either a personal or work setting.

Finally, rapists have specific *sexual styles*, and are often dissatisfied with their level of sexual activity. They show a pattern of intensely seeking sexual outlets, and are incapable of ever really being sexually satisfied. Sex serves many purposes, including the need for power, the ability to vent stress or anger, and the need to satisfy sexual desires.[5]

Understanding the behavior of a rapist can be helpful when attempting to identify suspects in a sexual assault case. However, understanding how a rapist *became* a sexual predator can be helpful in preventing the crime before it occurs. Changing behaviors and attitudes can decrease the number of rapes and sexual assaults that occur annually, and understanding the drive behind a predator's behavior is an important step.

ROOT CAUSES

On November 5, 1964, while police were seeking the man responsible for killing eleven women in their homes in the Boston area, Albert DeSalvo was arrested for entering women's apartments and raping them. He had been called the "Green Man," because he wore green work clothes; on one occasion, he raped four women in a single day. He generally forced his way in and ordered his victim at knifepoint to take off her clothes. He caressed them, and if they wanted it, he had sex with them. He insisted later, after he was identified, that he never had an unwilling victim. He often apologized before he left.

In late October, the Green Man subjected a young married woman to a long period of sexual abuse. She called the police and helped an artist to make a sketch. One officer thought he looked familiar, recalling the exploits of another sexual deviant known as the "Measuring Man."

A couple of years before, a series of sex offenses had occurred in the Cambridge area. A dark-haired man in his late twenties would knock at the door of an apartment, and if a young woman answered, he would tell her he was from a modeling agency that had received a recommendation for her. He was there to get her measurements. Apparently a number of women were flattered enough to let him measure them, but when he disappeared and no one contacted them, they realized they had been duped. Some of these women contacted the police. On March 17, 1961, Cambridge police caught him and learned that his name was Albert DeSalvo. A blue-collar worker with numerous burglary arrests, he lived nearby with his wife and two small children. He told an officer that he needed sex six times a day, but no one suggested that he get psychiatric help. Instead, he received a reduced sentence of eighteen months, releasing him just two months before the Boston Strangler killed his first victim.

Brought back in for questioning in the Green Man rapes, DeSalvo hinted there was much more, and he soon confessed to being the Boston Strangler. His attorney, F. Lee Bailey, worked out a deal that sent him to prison for the rapes, so he was never prosecuted for the notorious murders. Nevertheless, the police believed they had the Strangler behind bars. DeSalvo would eventually recant his controversial confession, although many people today still view him as the Boston Strangler. Regardless, he was a prolific rapist.

Different theorists approach the cause of rape from different angles, so we'll summarize three basic approaches: the biological/evolutionary approach, the psychological approach, and the sociological approach.

The Biological/Evolutionary Approach

According to this perspective, rape is an evolved behavior that men cannot control. Females generally make the choices when it comes to partners, so males have to prove that they are worthy of being chosen. When they appear inferior, which would include being physically unattractive, lacking a high-paying job, or lacking the connections to compete and become successful, they have few sexual options. Forced copulation becomes the only viable alternative for reproduction.

Randy Thornhill, a biologist at the University of New Mexico, and Craig T. Palmer, an anthropologist at the University of Colorado, have devised one version of this theory. They believe that women choose men based on "superior" genetic make-up and resources. However, they also believe that the selection process may not be about resources, but sexual desire. They argue that females are interested in finding a partner with whom they can spend their lives, while males want to have sex with as many different partners as possible. This biological difference is what leads females to be selective, while males will rape to satisfy their biological need for sex without investment. Plainly, males rape because they are "sexually engineered" to do so.[6]

In his study of serial rapists, Dennis Stevens describes thirty-two-year-old Darin, a man who enjoys committing rape. Darin, who is five-foot-nine and 130 pounds, began to enjoy sexual experiences at an early age. Before first grade, Darin experimented with masturbation, which offered him a feeling of relief and serenity. As he manipulated himself, he imagined being intimate with girls, but he had no urge to develop a relationship. When he was in sixth grade, he babysat for a little girl while her mother ran errands. He imagined what it would be like to ejaculate in the child's mouth. Eventually, he assaulted her until her vagina bled. Darin felt sorry for causing her pain, but not for his drive to molest her. He eventually ejaculated on her, pretending to spank her while he masturbated.[7]

As Darin got older, he broke into houses, with the notion that he could outwit the owner and possibly have sex with his wife. For him, the idea of forced intercourse became an obsession; whenever he masturbated at night, he imagined ramming his penis deep inside his victim, ejaculating and "getting her fluids on him." As he continued to rape more women, he found that only aggression would get him aroused, so he increased the intensity. Finally, he decided to rape the little girl's mother, despite the fact that she knew him and could identify him. As she slept, he crept in and tied a noose around her throat. He dragged her from her bed and choked her, forcing her to perform oral sex on him. He then tied her to the bed, shoving amphetamines down her throat, and stuck straight pins through her nipples before using sex toys to sexually assault her. His victim turned him in, and he ended up in prison.

For Darin, normal sexual intercourse was boring. He was not interested in a relationship, but only in sexually dominating another person. To his interviewer, he stated, "It's difficult to describe something invisible stirring inside your belly, reaching into the muscle-lining of your throat, demanding I do something! Deciding, all right, tonight, I'll cruise and find some morsel to feed you. Leave me be. Festival [his term for sexual attacks] is near."[8]

Professor Lee Ellis agrees that biological variables are the cause of rape. He suggests that men are interested in procreation, and desire to produce as many offspring as possible. To that end, rape is nothing more than the extension of their biological drive to have children. If men have sex with as many women as possible, they have a greater opportunity to reproduce. Because of this, Ellis argues, men who are "pushy" in sexual matters are more likely to achieve this goal. Unfortunately, whenever one man is selected, others lose out in the evolutionary sweepstakes. Some of these losers then commit rape.[9]

The Psychological Approach

To view rape from a psychological perspective, it is important to consider both individual and environmental influences. One psychological model suggests that certain behaviors or tendencies might be indicators of sexual deviance, with rape being the result of some personality attribute unique to the rapist. This idea is not new: Sigmund Freud, the father of psychoanalysis, first viewed sexual deviance as a character disorder, wherein infantile sexual desires continued into adulthood.

According to Freud, there are three integral parts of the human psyche that control behavior: the id, the ego, and the superego. The id holds the unconscious and instinctual parts of the personality, as well as the impulses for sexual aggression, while the ego is the rational part of a person's psyche, serving to control the id from following through on sexual impulses, including the desire to rape. The problem is that the id wants what it wants, and when the ability to delay gratification is not held in check, the need for instant sexual gratification takes over. The superego controls both the id and ego, serving as a moral compass and the mediator between the unconscious and external demands. When the superego is weak, the individual ignores right and wrong, and lives to satisfy his every whim. Essentially, Freud's work suggests that men are born with innate drives to fulfill their wishes, and that when a man's id is not contained, the result may be rape.[10]

Nicholas Groth, an expert in the psychology of the sexual offender, has also examined the psychological factors that predispose a person to sexual violence. He argues that rape serves primarily *nonsexual* needs and is an expression of anger, power, or retaliation. In this sense, rape is not a sexual problem but a symptom of some psychological dysfunction. Groth believed that rapists are neither insane nor crazy, and that rape is simply a product of frustration and rage that the rapist cannot contain.[11]

Still another explanation was proposed by sociologist Eugene Kanin, known for his research on male aggression and date rape. In a survey of approximately 400 undergraduate students, he found significant psychological differences between aggressive and non-aggressive males. Specifically, sexually aggressive males were more apt to have had bad experiences in the past with a significant female, inspiring a hatred for women. Therefore, Kanin concluded that rape is a by-product of psychological scarring at an earlier age.[12]

We can see this dynamic in the case of Corey Deen Saunders, who was dealt a lousy hand in life. He was born mildly retarded, and at an early age his mother told him that she had not wanted him.[13] Moreover, Saunders' older sister, molested by their father, in turn molested Saunders. This level of abuse, in combination with his mental deficiency, set the stage for his future criminal behavior.[14] When he was twelve, the Department of Social Services placed Saunders into a youth treatment center, where a staff person first noticed his predilection for younger children. He started to hang out with younger boys and he made statements to social workers that he was having regular fantasies about them. He began to consistently sexually assault many of the boys living in the facility, growing more persistent as he got older. Three years later, Saunders' level of offending became problematic, and he was transferred to the Stetson School, an institution for children with serious psychological problems. It was here that Saunders confided to social workers that he had 400 sexual fantasies a day involving younger boys, and that he planned on raping a ten-year-old resident at the school.

When he was seventeen, Saunders tried to convince a twelve-year-old boy to have sex with him, becoming quite aggressive in his demand. Once again, Saunders was deemed a danger to the children at the school, and was moved to the Top East Shelter in North Carolina. After he escaped, he was brought back and placed in a foster home in Attleboro, where he could be more closely watched. Seven hours after arriving there, he was discovered molesting his new foster mother's seven-year-old son. She called the police, and they charged Saunders with the attempted rape and abuse of the child. He served four years in prison. When he was released and was able to live on his own, he moved to New Bedford, Massachusetts.[15] On January 30, 2008,

Saunders went to the New Bedford Public Library, known for its extensive collection of children's books, looking for someone to molest.

Moving to the second floor, he spotted a six-year-old boy playing in the children's reading room. The boy was less than ten feet from his mother, who was working on one of the library's computers. Saunders sized up the situation and managed to get past the boy's mother and into the reading room undetected. There, he boldly fondled the child and performed oral sex. As he finished, a librarian came into the room, prompting him to leave. She immediately did an online search, found Saunders' criminal history on the Internet, and realized who he was. She called the police, who picked Saunders up a short distance from the library and placed him under arrest. During his trial, the district attorney argued that Corey Deen Saunders was "not just sexually dangerous, but *very* sexually dangerous."[16] Saunders eventually pleaded guilty to rape, indecent assault and battery and enticing a child.

Chester Arthur Stiles, too, was exposed to both physical and psychological trauma. He was arrested for the sexual assault of a six-year-old girl, but it was not the first time that he had been in front of the court for lewd behavior with a child. In fact, Stiles became infamous when the television show *America's Most Wanted* featured him for the attempted sexual assault of a child under fourteen, ten counts of lewdness with a child under fourteen, and eleven additional counts of sexual assault of a minor.

In a letter to Darren Tuck, his close friend, Stiles blamed his deviant sexual proclivity on the torture he'd endured as a boy. He repeated this to his son, stating, "So much abuse made me numb to it . . . Be ashamed of me, be embarrassed of me, but don't carry the blame or the family curse. I'm a monster, but monsters are made, not born."[17]

Stiles called himself a "diddler" and said that ever since he was fifteen, he had been attracted to prepubescent girls because of their "purity of virtue." He had even made a videotape that featured him sexually assaulting a two-year-old girl. Stiles was convicted of all charges and was sentenced to twenty-one life sentences, with the possibility of parole in 140 years.

The unfortunate product of child sexual abuse is the future offending it tends to provoke. The fact is that as many as 40 percent of sexual abusers were sexually abused as children.[18] Of course, this does not mean that all children who are abused will become sexual predators, nor that all sexual predation derives from early abuse. In fact, many survivors of child sexual abuse learn coping mechanics that keep them from abusing others. (Not all of these coping mechanisms are healthy, however; many abuse victims turn to drugs or alcohol, while others practice self-mutilation or develop an eating disorder.) To fully recover, they must develop adjustment skills, learn to forgive themselves for their inadequacies and shortcomings, and view themselves as people, not simply as survivors.[19]

Focusing on victims who grow up to become abusers, Sandy Lane and Pablo Zamora devised distinct developmental phases to explain why those males who have been victimized could end up abusing others later in life.[20] The *precipitating phase* occurs after the sexual assault. The child feels helpless, disgusted, and uneasy.[21] He is in a situation that he cannot avoid or escape. Although adults can utilize various coping mechanisms that come with life experience, children do not possess this ability, and the sense of fear, dread, and helplessness can overwhelm them. They may harbor anger and fear rather than find healthy ways to cope.

The second phase, the *compensatory phase*, occurs as the abused child tries to compensate for how he feels about himself by abusing others. He believes that taking advantage of another person will help him feel better, or at least in control. In addition, this behavior is an outlet for him to release his stress, frustration, and anger. This can take the form of non-sexual power maneuvers, such as bullying or pushing others around, but in cases of early sexually abuse, retaliation occurs most often in a sexual manner—aggressive advances, molestation of a weaker victim, and sexual assault. The problem is that gratification is temporary at best, and in order to control the anger and rage caused by his own victimization, he must continue to sexually abuse others.[22]

With many offenders, this does not begin as rape. They might expose themselves to others, become voyeurs, rub their genitals against someone else (frottage), force sex on animals (bestiality), peek in windows, or insert foreign objects into their victims. It is common for offenders to run through a progression of behaviors until they reach the pinnacle of the rape cycle's *integration phase*, an actual rape. During this phase, the abused child sexually abuses another person, becoming an abuser, raping for the excitement and thrill of the act. However, as we point out in Chapter 3, such euphoria is fleeting, and so to feel satisfied, the individual must rape time and again.

The Sociological Approach

It has also been argued that rapists are made, not born, and that specific factors in society are to blame. As far back as elementary school, males are trained to treat females as sexual objects and to exploit them to achieve their own goals.[23] This process occurs throughout childhood and into adulthood, making rape the product of male socialization. Thus, sexual violence is a learned phenomenon, neither created through the psyche nor genetics, but through imitation and sufficient reinforcement. This learning can take place with any number of groups, including family, friends, or membership in an organization, such as a sports team or fraternity.

Rapists learn behaviors through close associations with others and through social norms, including how to act toward the opposite sex. For instance, men who hold traditional views—women are inferior and should be housekeepers and stay-at-home moms rather than members of the workforce—are more likely to become rapists. In fact, rape is a trait of male domination in societies where females are inferior. Men are taught to be masculine and tough, while women are taught to deny sexual advances and "act like a lady." As a result, men become angry at being rejected and become sexually aggressive.

Social psychologist Albert Bandura theorized three distinct phases in which rapists learn to rape. The first is the *acquisition phase*, in which individuals absorb the characteristics of others via lifelong observational learning. They learn who they are and how they should behave by checking their impulses and comparing them with others in their environment. By the time the rapist hits puberty, he has developed ideas about how to get the things he wants. This is where violent sexual acts start to form. Children cannot understand why their advances have not brought them what they want, and they start to do what most humans do, which is to go after it aggressively. This aggression may be sparked by insults, verbal challenges, or unjust treatment—an *instigation mechanism*—so it is a learned behavior wherein individuals "medicate" themselves by doing whatever they want. Finally, once the instigation mechanisms are learned, they are maintained. The acts are practiced continually to self-soothe.[24]

Sociologically speaking, rape is learned, and the main models for this learning include culture, the media, and the associations with family and peers. The idea of family and peers is easy to understand, because as we spend more time with people, we tend to emulate and imitate their actions. According to Edwin Sutherland, learning takes place because of our differential associations with others.[25] In his view, the more time we spend with someone, the more likely it is that we will take on their traits and behaviors, as well as their beliefs and justifications for deviant behavior. The argument is that rapists learn their techniques and rationalizations for their behavior from the people with whom they spend most of their time.

In her study of sex roles and conventional sexual behavior, Stevi Jackson stated that rape is closely related to conventional modes of sexual expression. In this regard, men learn to rape based on the culturally proscribed sexual scripts. As an example, in some cultures women are treated equally and given as much power as men. In these cultures, rape rates are low, because the men never learn about sexual inequality. Conversely, where cultural norms proscribe women to be feminine and men masculine, and sexual expectations are built around these definitions, rape is more prevalent. According to Jackson, rape is a learned response to the culturally accepted patterns of male–female relationships.[26]

A slight twist on this is the psychosocial perspective, which states that rape is a response to external factors, a mix between psychological and sociological variables. In this sense, rape is a learned response, but a response to particular conditions. As with Corey Deen Saunders and Chester Stiles, their predatory behavior may be a result of personal experiences, such as childhood sexual abuse. One trait that is common for rapists and child molesters is poor social skills. William Marshall and Howard Barberee, experts in the study of rape and sexual assault, have argued that rapists are unable to have normal relationships with women, and rape is a way to secure their goals of sexual gratification. They learn that they cannot attain their ultimate goal of consensual sex, and rape becomes a satisfactory alternative.[27]

Although learning takes place throughout childhood, learning to become a rapist does not necessarily start at an early age. In fact, sexually predatory behavior can be learned from peers well after puberty. Specifically, the formative years of college offer a perfect arena for such learning to take place. The person who starts to rape once he's in college, as Michael Ross did, is no different than any other in that he is socialized to believe that rape is the way to achieve his ultimate goal, whether it's for sexual gratification or domination over another individual.

The sexual culture of college often supports the notion that male sexual exploitation is an acceptable part of the college setting. In a sense, the concept of men practicing their sexually coercive behavior is a normal part of college life. In her seminal piece about rape on college campuses, Peggy Reeves Sanday describes the culture of a fraternity, explaining that they enjoy superior status on campus, and because of that privileged social position, other young men are drawn to join them.[28] In this context, it's logical to assume that sexually aggressive males will be most attracted to fraternities that are more likely to be aggressive in their sexual exploits and misogynistic in their beliefs.

Male sexual aggression is supported through peer contact, perpetuating a so-called "rape culture." In fact, Walter DeKeseredy, in his study of family violence, stated that rape is the creation and perpetuation of a male peer-support model, where social support for rape and sexual aggression has a strong influence on a person, leading to the eventual sexual abuse of women.[29] It is easy to see how this model can be applied to fraternities, with dozens of men supporting your every sexual exploit, all in the name of brotherhood. Sexual domination is a theme in many fraternity houses, and males who are interested in preying on women by exploiting their status as members of the cool party fraternity is of real concern.[30] These men are sexual predators, not unlike those who prey on children. They inject themselves into an environment that consistently gives them access to potential victims, and they take advantage as often as possible. Just as Peter Norris Dupas hid in the public restrooms waiting for his victims, fraternity rapists ply their victims with alcohol and wait for the opportunity to rape them.

ANIMAL HOUSE

Sexual assault at fraternity houses has become a common occurrence throughout the country. In one case, a nineteen-year-old woman reported being raped inside a University of Washington fraternity house, after attending a party at the off-campus residence. She told police that at approximately 1:00 A.M. on a Saturday night, she was leaving the bathroom when two men whom she did not know forced her into another room and raped her. She tried to push the men away, but they overpowered her. Similarly, at the Kappa Sigma fraternity house on the University of Idaho campus, twenty-three-year-old David Barkdall, a former fraternity member, was accused of forcing a woman into a room on the second floor, holding her down, and forcibly raping her. Finally, at an off-campus fraternity party at Eastern Michigan University, an eighteen-year-old woman told police that shortly after midnight on a Saturday night, she walked into the bathroom to find four men waiting for her. The lights were turned off, the four men molested her, and at least one sexually assaulted her.

The influence that social support systems exert cannot be minimized when considering fraternity brothers as sexual predators. It is not uncommon for men in a group setting to subscribe to the notion that women are inferior to them and that they are useful only for sexual exploits. Stereotyping women in specific social roles and minimizing their value as human beings help to create a dangerous atmosphere for college girls. In fact, after studying fraternities on college campuses, Sanday concluded that these memberships are important factors in the creation of the rapist because they mimic and replace family bonds. In one example, Sanday interviews Sean, a fraternity member who was scared of the newly-found independence that college afforded him. He recognized that fraternity life offered a "new family" that would always provide him with a place to go, a place to help him cope with his anxiety, and a place to work out his anxious rebellion.[31] Predators who feel accepted and even licensed within this atmosphere are emboldened to act out.

In some cases, treating women as nothing more than sexual exploits may be a bonding ritual for a fraternal group. Whether it's a group of fraternity brothers or members of a sports team, gang raping a woman is viewed as an experience that the men can share. In their study of sexual assault on college campuses, Carol Bohmer and Andrea Parrot describe Tanja, an undergraduate student in her first year at the University of California at Berkeley. After attending an unsupervised party, Tanja went to the room of an acquaintance to borrow a cassette tape. She met her friend and his twin brother, who pushed her onto the staircase and forced her to have intercourse and oral sex with him. She was then taken to a room occupied by two other men, and all three took turns raping her. After everyone had his chance, Tanja was allowed to leave. The four men were later identified as members of the school football team.[32] This is just one example of the predatory subculture and its emphasis on physical prowess and sexual exploitation.

It would be unfair to say that all fraternity members are sexual predators, or that men join fraternal groups and sports teams solely for the opportunity to rape women on a consistent basis. Similarly, it would be unfair to assume that all fraternities and sports teams teach men how to become rapists. However, there is a clear correlation between the brotherhood that develops within these groups and their participation in sexual assault on college campuses. The fear is that whatever a young man might learn in these groups could be with him for life; he could become a more advanced and determined predator.

Many serial rapists, especially those who grow addicted to aggression and force, go on to become lust killers; how this develops is the subject of the next chapter.

6

Lust Killers

AQUATIC FANTASIES

Jeff Doland had several online discussions with a person he believed was the mother of two young girls, ages nine and twelve. They talked for a few months, and this married stepfather of two sent his correspondent pictures of children being tortured. He also described his ultimate sexual fantasy—watching young girls being submerged underwater, struggling for air until they passed out and drowned. He was aroused by the bubbles rising to the surface. He offered $550 for the opportunity to fulfill his fantasy in real life. She agreed and they set a date. Then in July 2007, he packed up his scuba gear, told his wife he was going scuba-diving, and boarded a plane bound for Miami.

However, Doland's correspondent had not been a mother but an undercover agent for the Secret Service. When Doland arrived in Miami, he confided his disturbing plan to yet another undercover agent, so the Child Predator CyberCrime Unit moved in to make an arrest. Doland was charged with the selling or buying of minors, a first-degree felony, and with promoting the sexual performance of a child. The Ohio school district, where he had worked on computers, cut all ties with him, and administrators assured worried parents that Doland had had no direct contact with children.

Although authorities labeled Doland's type of fantasy a unique case of sado-masochistic child abuse, it's closer to behavior known as aquatic erotic asphyxial fantasies. Aquaphilia is a sexual fetish that involves water. For some, this features auto-erotic activity underwater, and for others, attacks on other people for the pleasure of experiencing their underwater struggles. (Agonophilia is also possible, as people acquire sexual stimulation from a partner who is struggling to get free.) Some fantasize about underwater murder, and there are Web sites online that cater to all forms of underwater sadism. Although Doland's targets never existed, they might have, and while he was caught, authorities can only wonder how many others have managed to broker and complete such exchanges.[1]

Erotophonophilia—lust murder—is one of the most extreme forms of paraphilic behavior in which the offender is aroused by both the act and fact of murder. When a sexual fantasy is attached to a psychological drive, as we described in Chapter 3, the need to satisfy it becomes both complex and urgent, motivating compulsive and repetitive sex crimes such as lust murder.

Criminologists Stephen and Ronald Holmes state that lust killers typically seek the same type of victim, because certain physical characteristics are part of the arousal process. (Because lust killers receive the most media attention, a myth has been perpetuated that all serial killers have a preferred victim type.) The lust killer combines aberrant sexual practices with murder, typically with the goal of making victims suffer prior to killing them. This includes biting, stabbing, repeated asphyxiation, whipping, psychological torment, and even draining them of blood to drink it in front of them. They might also mutilate the body postmortem, with dismemberment, cannibalism, stabbing, or biting. Typically above-average in intelligence, lust killers develop a solitary existence (even if married) where fantasy plays a strong role, both before and after a murder. They usually plan the murder and move the bodies to avoid discovery. Often the anger they direct at a victim is actually aimed at a primary caretaker, usually the mother, although there is no single causal factor in the development of a lust killer. Each case must be analyzed individually.[2]

Debra Niehoff, a neuroscientist and the author of *The Biology of Violence,* reviewed two decades of research on the interplay of genes and the environment in the development of violent behavior. She found that each factor modifies the other such that any given individual may uniquely mentally process a situation toward a violent resolution. Thus any factor may have different effects on different people, and over the course of a lifetime this effect can be modified positively or negatively. That is, some people with a brain abnormality may become violent, others may not, while others with no such disorder may turn to violence. The same can be said about childhood trauma, childhood abuse, substance abuse, violent role models, violent videogames, pornography, and other factors. What each person does to process and manage his or her situation depends on a unique interplay of external and internal factors. Each environmental interaction is handled via the person's unique neurochemical profile, which is influenced by attitudes that derive from his or her array of encounters and experiences, and those attitudes then affect brain chemistry. After every interaction, the neurochemical profile is updated. The brain adjusts along with the attitudes. Thus, each case of predatory violence has unique factors.[3]

It was a lust killer with a bondage fetish during the late 1950s whose crimes inspired the idea for a centralized database for linking serial crimes. Harvey Glatman lured aspiring models or women seeking romance to his home to "photograph" them bound, ostensibly for a true crime magazine. Once they were vulnerable, he became aroused and they realized they were in real trouble. The photographs he took showed their genuine terror. He raped them and then took them into the desert outside Los Angeles, where he strangled and buried them. However, one woman was lucky. A patrol officer spotted her struggling with Glatman, so he stopped to help. She told him that Glatman had tried to kill her, and her bullet wound was convincing. The police arrested Glatman and searched his apartment, where they found photographs of three missing women. Glatman ultimately confessed, showing detectives where he had buried two. In short order, he was convicted and executed, but his crime spree inspired Detective Pierce Brooks to consider the viability of a nationwide computerized databank for violent crimes. It often took weeks of painstaking work to match crimes from different jurisdictions, so he tried to persuade his chief that a computer—then a huge machine that was prohibitively expensive—would be useful. It would take two more decades before the FBI adopted Brooks' idea and developed the Violent Criminal Apprehension Program.[4]

Psychologist David M. Buss, from the University of Texas at Austin, published an in-depth analysis of different types of murderers. Factors that correlate with criminality and delinquency, he states, include impulsivity, sensation seeking, childhood aggression, a lack of empathy, and deficient moral reasoning. Males score higher on these traits than females. Like other researchers, Buss also discusses the important role of fantasy, which he calls "homicidal scenario building." Any number of mental activities can be involved, including daydreams, internal dialogue, planning, and the simple envisioning of murder. He takes an evolutionary stance, suggesting that there is a benefit to being able to mentally rehearse a murder, which means that our brains have specialized circuits for it. The mental simulation of murder, for example, can relieve tension, but for some people, such fantasies become a rehearsal for action. In searching through a rich archive in Michigan's Center of Forensic Psychiatry of 375 murderers, Buss found that roughly 72 percent showed evidence that the killer had indulged in homicidal ideation before committing the crime.[5]

A study that focused on serial killers in 1989 supports this. Prentky, Burgess, and others found that, prior to each murder, 86 percent described having violent fantasies on a recurrent basis. In many cases, a killer had seen someone at random and had begun to draw that person into his fantasies, or he had been the brunt of behavior he found intolerable. Rather than absorb and deal with it in a socially appropriate manner, he honed his anger into a fantasy to mentally target the person with specific violent acts. With lust killers, the fantasies had specific erotic content.[6] Such was the case for child killer, John Joubert.

IT STARTS AT HOME

When he was just six years old, John Joubert envisioned killing and cannibalizing his babysitter. He was angry at her for suggesting to his mother that she leave her husband, his father. She did so anyway, moving her children to Maine, and Joubert transferred his violent focus to her. Fantasies of cannibalism consumed him, especially after he became a butt of jokes at school. Shy and frail, he had a difficult time fitting in, even when he joined the Boy Scouts. Other kids taunted him for being gay, starting a cycle of self-loathing.[7] This only worsened when he developed a latent homosexual relationship with another boy. During one summer when Joubert was away, the boy's family moved to another town, and Joubert's mother refused to tell him where they had gone. Thus, the stage was set for stress: he grieved the loss of the friend and developed anger toward the person who could have helped but who instead hindered him from assuaging his pain. He hated how his domineering mother controlled his life, growing helplessly enraged when she refused to allow him to see his father. The fantasies failed to relieve his stress, however, so it settled into his psyche as tension that demanded release. Shortly thereafter, thirteen-year-old Joubert found an outlet.

Riding his bicycle one day, he slammed a pencil into a young girl's back. As she cried out, he experienced sexual arousal. When no one questioned him about the incident, he felt powerful. He wanted more. The next time, he armed himself with a razor blade. When he spotted a target, he rode up to the girl and slashed her. Joubert found that he enjoyed turning the tables and being a bully. Next, he armed himself with a knife, stabbing or slashing several more kids. In fact, in the papers he became the "Woodford Slasher," which made him feel quite bold, especially since he was failing at other things.

When Joubert was nineteen, he made one more aggressive attack in the area, this time against a boy. On the evening of August 22, 1982, Richard "Ricky" Stetson, eleven years old, was jogging in Back Cove. He never came home, and witnesses recalled another young man with dark hair riding near him on a ten-speed bicycle. Then a motorist found Ricky's body by the side of a road. He'd been stabbed, his jogging pants were pulled over his hips, and his sweatshirt seemed to have been removed and put back on. The autopsy indicated that Ricky had been strangled and stabbed in the chest, and there were bite marks on him, slashed over with a knife as if to obliterate them. The bruise from the bite revealed a distinctive set of teeth, but the police were unable to find a match.

Joubert joined the Air Force, which placed him at the Offutt Air Force Base in Bellevue, Nebraska. He acquired his beloved true crime magazines, and one issue described the kidnapping of a newspaper boy. Apparently, this gave him an idea.

It was early on Sunday, September 18, 1983, when thirteen-year-old Danny Joe Eberle went out on his bike to deliver the *Omaha World Herald.* Later that morning, his supervisor called the boy's father to tell him that Danny Joe had not finished the job and customers were complaining. His bicycle was located at his fourth stop, but he seemed to have vanished.

The police instigated a manhunt, but it was three days before someone found Danny Joe's body, four miles from his abandoned bike. Lying in weeds on a dead-end road, he was clad in only his underwear. He had been stabbed nine times; front and back, and his ankles were bound with an unusual type of rope. His mouth was covered with the same type of surgical tape that bound his wrists. He'd also been hit in the face and bitten on the shoulder, and his neck was slashed. It appeared that there was some attempt to carve a star-shaped symbol on him over the bite mark.

Special Agent Robert Ressler, from the FBI's Behavioral Science Unit, arrived to assess the situation. He thought it was significant that the perpetrator had left Danny Joe's body where it would be found easily. In addition, the offender had picked Danny Joe up during the early daylight hours. These were high-risk behaviors, which suggested a compulsion that was difficult to control.

Other boys reported that a man in a tan car had followed them recently. From the collection of known facts, Ressler devised a profile: the offender was white and would be in his late teens to early twenties. He was either friendly or Danny Joe had known him. The method of dumping suggested panic rather than experience, but the perpetrator was familiar with the area. He would be local, and in possession of no more than a high school education. He was employed in a job that required few skills. Although the crime had likely been preplanned, it seemed to lack follow-through, as if only one part of his fantasy had been worked out. Because it seemed to have been a sexual crime without penetration, Ressler thought the perpetrator was driven by fantasies but did not have much experience with murder. He was probably single and had a mental imbalance or longstanding emotional problem. He might also be abusing substances. He would be a loner with latent homosexual tendencies who worked in some capacity that brought him close to children, such as a coach or Boy Scout leader.[8]

Two and a half months later, with this murder still unsolved, twelve-year-old Christopher Walden disappeared while on his way to school. Witnesses had seen him get into a tan sedan with a white male. Walden, the son of a military officer at Offutt, lived only three miles from where Danny Joe's body was found. Two days later, hunters came across Christopher's remains. Like Danny Joe, he wore only his underwear and had been repeatedly stabbed. In addition, his throat had been cut so deeply that it had nearly removed his head, and a strange slashing mark on his torso appeared to cover an odd bruise.

The two dead boys had been similar in height and build, so they might have attracted the offender by appearance. Both boys had also been abducted and taken away in a vehicle, both were forced to strip, and neither was sexually assaulted. Ressler viewed this as a killer's anger with himself and a denial of his homosexuality. He now believed they were looking for an enlisted man who did mechanical work. Ressler reiterated that this person would likely be involved in some occupation dealing with children.

On January 11, 1984, the killer made a mistake. A preschool staff member, aware of the dangerous predator, spotted a young man driving around the area that morning, scoping it out. She wrote down his license plate number on a piece of paper, and when he saw her, he demanded that she give him the paper. She got away from him and he drove off, so she went to the police. They traced the vehicle to a dealership that had rented it to John Joubert, a twenty-year-old enlisted man at the Offutt Air Force Base. His own car was a tan Nova sedan.

The police arrested Joubert and searched his quarters. They found rope consistent with the type used on Danny Joe. Joubert's car contained more rope and a large hunting knife. He also fit the profile: He was twenty, local, sexually disturbed, an enlisted man who worked with radar, five-foot six, and slender. In fact, he looked like a boy himself, no bigger than Christopher Walden had been. He was also an assistant scoutmaster who had befriended several of the boys.

Physical evidence implicated him and soon Joubert admitted that he'd killed both boys and would likely kill again. He couldn't help himself. On January 12, Joubert was charged with two counts of murder and held for trial, but on July 3, he pled guilty to both counts.

In psychiatric assessments, Joubert was found to be obsessive-compulsive, sadistic, and suffering from a schizoid personality disorder, but not psychotic. He blamed his overbearing mother for his childhood problems. A panel of three judges decided that, given the level of depravity involved, Joubert should be executed. But then his home state took an interest.

That fall, Ressler was showing slides about the case to a group of police officers and one from Maine recognized the similarity to an unsolved crime in his jurisdiction: the Ricky Stetson case. Since Ricky's killer had bitten him, Dr. Lowell Levine, the director of the Forensic Science Unit for the New York State Police, was able to match the bite mark to Joubert. It took another five years, but in 1990 Joubert was convicted of Ricky's murder and sentenced to life without parole.

In prison interviews, Joubert described how he had approached Danny Joe Eberle. He'd seen the boy rolling the newspapers and had followed him. At the fourth house, he'd approached the boy, pulled out a knife, clamped a hand over his mouth, taped it shut, and forced him into the car's trunk. The boy's terror made him feel powerful. When he reached the seclusion of the dead-end road, he took Danny Joe out of the car, made him strip to his underwear, and told him he was going to die. Then he stabbed the boy in the back and chest several times. For good measure, he bit Danny Joe on the shoulder and leg. On top of those marks, he slashed a star pattern.

Leaving the body, Joubert returned to his room on the base to masturbate. It wasn't long before he felt a strong urge to repeat it. In the case of Christopher Walden, Joubert had left the barracks early that morning, intent on finding a child. He knew where kids in town got on the bus and he'd had his eye on a specific girl. However, she was not there that morning. Joubert cruised over to an elementary school, where he spotted Christopher, so Joubert approached him to ask for directions. This, too, was a high-risk maneuver, since other kids were around. But Joubert was desperate, so he showed Christopher his knife sheath and ordered him to get into the car. The frightened boy obeyed. Joubert drove to an isolated area in the woods. He then ordered Christopher to undress and lie down. Christopher removed his clothing but refused the second order, which surprised Joubert. They struggled, but Joubert had a knife. He overpowered the boy, stabbing him. Christopher screamed and Joubert kept stabbing until his victim lay still. In a final thrust, he sliced through the boy's neck.[9]

Years later, Ressler, too, got Joubert to talk. He learned that Joubert, now twenty-eight, had spent his time drawing renditions of his fantasies about violence with boys. "One depicted a boy by the side of the road, hog-tied," he said, "and the second was of a boy on his knees as a man slid a knife into him."[10] Joubert admitted to having fantasies about murder at a surprisingly young age, and then began acting on them by stabbing and slashing little girls. Ressler described this as "cognitive mapping," a concept from psychology that indicates how certain people may become habituated to viewing the world in a specific manner.

> It determines how the individual gives meaning to the events that happen in his world. Deviants may allow themselves to indulge in fantasies as they develop their cognitive mapping procedures. Antisocial people tend to develop an increasingly more hostile framework for how they deal with others, and others with them. Thus, their map determines the roads they take, and the roads they take tend to confirm their maps. So they get used to this and it becomes the foundation for how they fantasize and/or rehearse for murder.[11]

Joubert offered useful information about stresses he'd experienced before his violent fantasies began, as well as just before each fatal incident. In two instances, he had lost close friends, which had confused and frustrated him. It confirmed Ressler's impression that stress can be instrumental in sexual violence. When Ressler asked about the biting, Joubert explained his fantasies of cannibalism. On each victim, including Ricky Stetson, he had attempted to obliterate the impressions by slashing through them. Thus, he'd left a distinct signature that linked them to him. He admitted to getting excited by detective magazines at an early age, and had simultaneously learned from them how to avoid being caught. The boys who had most attracted him had resembled him at the age when he'd initially been aroused by thoughts of murdering other boys. On July 17, 1996, after many legal difficulties, John Joubert was executed.[12]

Louis Schlesinger, a psychologist and expert on sexual lust murders, states that attempting to predict the development of a person into a lust killer is complicated. There are no clear threats, they aren't psychotic, and they might not even have any violent episodes. However, he finds that there are ten ominous signs that often show up in the backgrounds of serial lust killers. Abuse during childhood tops his list, followed by inappropriate conduct by the mother (usually sexual), and the tendency to lie and manipulate. (The same holds true for the developing psychopath.) The emergence of sadistic fantasies, which are usually secret, may be revealed in therapy sessions or in drawings or writings. Then the well-known triad—fire-setting, animal abuse, and bedwetting—might be evident, as well as the apparent need to dominate other kids. There might also be indications of a developing paraphilia or ritual behavior, and abnormal activities, such as voyeurism. In addition, unprovoked attacks against girls indicate anger and the beginning of misogynist attitudes. These children show lower levels of empathy, like fledgling psychopaths, and were often from chaotic or behaviorally inappropriate homes.[13]

THE SITUATIONAL PREDATOR

A young man entered the apartment of a seventy-seven-year-old woman who lived two blocks from him. He had been watching for his opportunity. He strangled the woman into unconsciousness, bashed in her skull with her alarm clock, and then retrieved a butcher knife from the kitchen before he stabbed her twenty-seven times in the face, chest, and vagina. The viciousness of this attack shocked the investigating officers.

This case was among 128 similar cases included in a study of elderly female sexual homicides. Former FBI profiler Mark Safarik, with John Jarvis and Kathleen Nussbaum, collected detailed information on such investigations from around the country, examining the characteristics of 110 offenders and crime scenes. These murders were generally severe and although not always involving rape (8 percent did not), they did include some type of sexual assault. Those that did include rape often involved oral, anal, and vaginal attacks. There were also cases of foreign objects forced into the victims, anally or vaginally.

The study's intent was to offer local jurisdictions predictive information about offender types in the event of a similar incident in their area. The research indicated that 81 percent of the victims were white, while only 45 percent of the offenders were. Nearly half were acquainted with the victim, usually as a neighbor, but most were strangers, with an average age of twenty-seven. However, they generally lived within six blocks and most arrived on foot. About 20 percent were let in, while the others forced their way in. Some 93 percent were substance abusers, 90 percent had prior criminal records, most were high school dropouts, and 70 percent were unemployed. The typical approach was personal: hitting, strangling, or kicking. Nearly half told someone about the crime prior to arrest, with whites being twice as likely as blacks to do so. Robbery occurred in nearly three-fourths of the crimes, and it seemed likely that offenders who were predatory had made a mental map of the neighborhood, identifying its most vulnerable resident. However, it was clear that "the majority of offenders fully intended to sexually assault and murder these women prior to the initiation of the crime, and this intent superseded their intent to steal."[14]

Although not necessarily repeat offenders as most lust killers are, these criminals bore anger against older women and subjected their victims to such extreme sexual violence that it was clear that sexual fantasies had been part of the planning.

FEMALE LUST

Most data about violent crime and criminal types has centered on males, because males have always been more aggressive, violent, and criminally versatile than females. They seem to dominate the area of sexual crimes, although not entirely. Of the sixty-two female serial killers in Eric Hickey's study for *Serial Murderers and Their Victims*, females accounted for between 400 and 600 victims. Some were nurses, some babysitters, some black widows, and several were outright predators. (Most criminologists include Aileen Wuornos as a lust killer, since she was a prostitute who lured johns, but her motive was actually greed and enrichment.) Collectively, criminologists agree that only the rare female kills for sexual pleasure. However, it does happen, and a few have even been sexually compulsive.

During the nineteenth century, Jeanne Weber was a good example: she strangled young boys during orgasmic rushes and was considered sexually insane. Jane Toppan, a nurse, actually climbed into bed to hold her poisoned victims as they died, because it gave her such sexual pleasure. She said that had she married and had children, she would have killed them all. A pair of nurses at a Michigan nursing home, Gwendolyn Graham and Catherine Wood, included murder in their sexual games. They looked for ways to make sex more intense, including sexual asphyxia, and one day they decided to start killing patients. They identified vulnerable nursing home residents whose initials would help them to spell out M-U-R-D-E-R and then began picking them off. Within three months, they had killed five elderly women. At times, the act of killing so excited them that they went to an unoccupied room for a "quickie." They also washed down the bodies for an added layer of erotic fun, and used personal items stolen from the victims to relive the act.[15]

Sexual abuse expert Dr. Julia Hislop has extensively studied female sex offenders, stating that they have abused an estimated three million victims in the United States. She found that many of the offenders were sexually traumatized as children, and understanding the offender means recognizing the context of the abuser/victim relationship. Among the contexts, Hislop lists a lack of any sense of appropriate boundaries, poor relationship skills, releasing stress or relieving depression, distorted sense of normalcy, lack of self-worth, and sexual preoccupations. "Specific emotions, situations, fantasies, justifications, thought processes, interactions with people and behaviors may all increase the likelihood of offending."[16]

Although many female killers rape and murder as part of a team, a few have been quite sexually aggressive. Among the most depraved was Rosemary West in Gloucester, England. During the summer of 1991, a young girl made an allegation of sexual abuse against Fred West, saying that he had raped her and videotaped it. Since she was too frightened at the idea of going to court against him, no investigation was performed.

However, there were other problems in the West household. A social worker had spotted sexual items around the home where children were present, so she recommended that the youngest child be removed. A check turned up the fact that the highly-sexed Rosemary placed magazine ads for sexual encounters, and among her eight children were some by men other than Fred. Apparently Fred was quite the voyeur, so he did not mind.

Then another item surfaced during the background check: twenty years earlier, the couple had been arrested for a sexual assault. They had invited a young woman to move in to be a nanny for their children. Fred began to make sexual overtures, so the nanny left; however, they apparently watched her. One day they lured her to their car, bound her, and took her home, subjecting her to hours of sexual abuse and rape. Rosemary took the lead, touching her inappropriately, stroking her, digitally penetrating her, and kissing her. Then Fred beat her with a belt while Rosemary laughed. When the desperate girl promised she would come back to live with them, they let her go to get her personal effects, and she went straight to the police. However, at that time, the police had persuaded the girl to forego a trial, so the Wests received only a fine. Still, the complaint was on the record, and when the current investigators read it, something stood out.

The young woman had stated that the Wests had threatened to bury her under the backyard paving stones. This was eerily similar to something the West's children had said during the recent investigation: they revealed that their older sister, Heather, had been gone seven years, and that their parents often threatened them with being buried under the patio stones, "like Heather." When questioned, Fred and Rosemary claimed that Heather had left home when she was sixteen and they did not know where she was.

With reasonable cause, the detectives decided to have a look beneath Fred West's concrete patio. Fred seemed nervous and soon after they started digging, he told them they were digging in the wrong place, possibly because he was afraid they would find more victims than just Heather. When he redirected them, he confessed: he had killed Heather and buried her there. Rosemary reacted in feigned horror. The digging continued until the girl's remains were found, and dental records proved that the female skeleton had once been Heather. However, the diggers had also turned up an extra leg bone. Fred admitted that another girl was buried there—in fact, two of them. Detectives now wondered what they might find if they took up floor boards in the basement, and Fred conceded that they would find more bodies. The West's home was a regular house of horrors, and a major excavation was set up. Eight bodies were discovered, including several in cramped holes beneath the basement floorboards, precisely where the Wests had placed their children's beds.

Fred also confessed that he had killed his first wife, his stepdaughter Charmaine, and two other women, revealing the burial sites. While the remains of three of the four victims were found, the investigators decided that Rosemary had been no innocent bystander. Allegations of rape and sexual abuse had been directed against her as well. In fact, it was questionable that Fred had murdered Charmaine, so a careful forensic analysis was undertaken, proving that at the time of her death, Fred had been in prison. Over Rosemary's protests, she was charged with this murder.

She publicly renounced her husband, but no one believed he could have killed and dismembered so many young women in their home without his wife's knowledge. Although Fred had covered for Rose as best he could, it was clear that she was as sexually depraved as he was. He conceded that he had not told the whole story, stating that there were as many as twenty victims, but then committed suicide on New Year's Day in 1995. He took his secrets with him. Rosemary was detained and charged with ten murders (including one off the property).

At her trial, several survivors of the couple's sadistic teamwork testified, including Fred's surviving daughter, Anne Marie. She had become pregnant by her father and was subjected to repeated sexual abuse by both parents, and she added that when she was a child, Rosemary had helped various men to assault her—not just Fred. It was clear from these reports that Rosemary was an equal member of this sadistic team and equally a sexual predator. Together, the Wests had sexually tortured numerous young women before killing them.

Psychiatric testimony on Rosemary's behalf revealed that her mother had been clinically depressed, going through electroshock treatments when pregnant with Rosemary, and that her strict and abusive father had suffered from schizophrenia. Sexually precocious by thirteen, Rosemary abused her younger brother. She also became an exhibitionist and started sleeping with truck drivers. She was sixteen when she met Fred, a petty criminal with a fetish for female dismemberment and car crashes, and the divorced father of two children. They married after she got pregnant with Heather, and not long afterward, Rosemary strangled Charmaine during a rage episode. This apparently freed Fred to confide that he had also killed someone—a former girlfriend who was pregnant. In addition to all this, Fred told police that he had seen Rosemary having sex with her father during this period.

Rosemary had joined Fred in abusing babysitters and "boarders." They were also a pair of truly cruel parents. Rosemary turned tricks as well, and had a sadomasochistic relationship with a woman in the neighborhood. Fred reportedly told one victim that Rosemary had lesbian tendencies, and he liked to watch.

In the end, it wasn't clear who had actually committed the murders. Despite Fred's confession, Rosemary seemed as culpable, so the jury convicted her on all ten counts of murder and sentenced her to life in prison.[17] A few years later, she issued a statement to the press that she hoped one day to reconcile with Anne Marie.

Even though Rosemary West acted as a sexual sadist within a team, she was as predatory and sadistic as her husband. Other lust killers have also kept company with one or more people as depraved as themselves, increasing the intensity and magnitude of sexual crimes they committed. We'll look at the dynamics of these sexual team killers next.

7

Team Predators

PARTNERS IN CRIME

Child rapist Marc Dutroux claimed that his abduction of young girls was just a minor part of an international child pornography and prostitution ring in Charleroi, Belgium. Although he drove around in a ratty van, he did own a number of run-down properties and managed to support his second wife and three children. His claims were sufficient to launch a significant investigation, largely because, despite his arrests, he seemed always to be handled with kid gloves.

Dutroux was nearly caught once when a police officer failed to thoroughly check an abandoned building where Dutroux was holding two girls in a secret dungeon, and when Dutroux went to prison in 1989 for rape, he served a lenient sentence. He even received a government pension for psychiatric reasons. He would later claim that this was all evidence of how far the pornography ring reached—involving law enforcement and even the highest levels of politics. However, to this day no investigator or journalist has turned up evidence of this supposed international child prostitution ring.

In 1996, the police raided Dutroux's home, locating 300 pornographic videos of children, as well as a concrete dungeon. Inside were two girls, ages twelve and fourteen, and they'd both been sexually abused. One had been there for nearly three months. With his wife, Michelle Martin, and a male accomplice, Michele Lelievre, Dutroux had grabbed these girls off the streets as he drove along in his van. Then he drugged them, locked them into his homemade dungeon, and forced them to pose for his films. He also raped them repeatedly. Yet they were the lucky ones.

Two other imprisoned girls, both eight years old, had starved to death when Dutroux was briefly incarcerated for car theft. On his release, Dutroux killed an accomplice and buried all the corpses in his backyard. Two other girls had also been drugged and buried alive under concrete in a shed next to another house.

At Dutroux's sensational trial in 2004, his surviving victims described their ordeal of rape and starvation, although they had kissed Dutroux as they were led from their prison. The prosecutor stated that this behavior arose from the temporary confusion of Stockholm syndrome, and they had eventually realized how terribly they had been treated. Duroux had convinced one girl that her family would not pay the ransom, so she had believed he was the only person who cared for her.

All during the proceedings, Dutroux continued to claim that he was a scapegoat, a mere cog in a larger machine, and he blamed his wife for the deaths of the two girls who had starved; she had been in the same house with them but had ignored them. In the end, Dutroux was convicted of murder, kidnapping, and rape. He received a life sentence. Michelle Martin was convicted of causing the death of the girls who had starved, and she received thirty years. Michele Lelievre was also sentenced. The people of Belgium believed that the incompetence and lax attitudes among officials were equally responsible.[1]

In a study that included over 1,000 serial killers from around the world, about seventy-five are known to have committed murder in a partnership with one or more accomplices.[2] (It's possible that other accomplices were never identified.) Dutroux had at least two, perhaps more. Some teams kill in a short and violent spurt, some over longer periods. We just saw how Rosemary and Fred West brought victims to their homes, and several other teams have done the same, while others go out looking for victims and kill them elsewhere. Many, like Dutroux, have traveled around in vans, seeking just the right person.

In Chicago, Robin Gecht led a group of three other young men in killing an estimated seventeen women. Hiding in a van, they would grab a woman off the street, sever one or both of her breasts with a thin wire, use it for sexual gratification, and strangle or leave the victim some place to die from her wounds. During adolescence, Gecht had reportedly developed a keen interest in Satanism and its secret rituals, believing that he gained power from them. The killing crew was caught when a woman survived to identify the van. One accomplice offered a full confession, revealing how the team had worked.[3]

About three-fourths of American team killers are white, and one-third involve male/female participants. They most typically target strangers.

Sometimes the team leader or dominant partner sends the others out to do what he wants, but more often he participates. There is one dominant personality who maintains psychological control.[4]

Dean Corll got sexually involved in Texas with a young man named David Brooks, and together they participated in petty crimes. Soon seventeen-year-old Elmer Wayne Henley came into the picture. Henley and Brooks procured young males for the older Corll to sadistically abuse and rape. Eventually he began to kill the boys, many of whom were hitchhikers and transients. After handcuffing them to a board and torturing them with large implements, he'd shoot or strangle them. Sometimes he even chewed off their genitals or castrated them. A few times he killed two together; the youngest victim was only nine.

The end came on August 8, 1973, when Corll threatened to kill Henley, so in self-defense Henley shot him. He called the police and showed them where the bodies of seventeen boys were buried under a boathouse, along with containers of genitalia. At two other sites, investigators exhumed ten more bodies. Henley admitted to his part and went to prison for life.[5]

Researchers have found that many couples, no matter what gender, follow a common pattern: Two people meet, feel a strong attraction, and establish an intimate familiarity that allows them to share fantasies, including violent ones. When eroticized, this approval encourages acting out, and if the partners succeed in committing a violent crime without getting caught, they grow bolder. The dominant person, often a psychopath, is generally charismatic and maintains psychological control: his or her erotic preferences set the tone. The weaker partner may have an unstable personality that makes him or her easily manipulated.[6]

After a successful assault, dominant partners often feel arrogant and alive, but submissive partners may experience guilt, anxiety, or regret. However, they are often too weak or afraid to resist. The dominant offender then wants to repeat the crime and his control over the weaker person (or people) heightens his thrill. Short of arrest, there's no stopping the escalation. Their chemistry seems to thrive on the tension. "Such relationships," says Eric Hickey, "tend to be built on deception, bravado, and intimidation."[7]

Although most teams operate on this unequal hierarchy, some balance a co-equal partnership and these teams are usually the most criminally diverse and aggressive, because both participants realize that the other person is as depraved as he (or she) is. With no moral boundaries and no incentive to hold back, they work together to affirm and expand their range of criminal creativity. The other person provides a mirror, which can have an erotic effect that instigates even more villainy. This latter category appears to apply to Fred and Rosemary West.

Several females have lured victims for their male companions or supported the male's penchant for rape and murder in some other way. One woman lived in a home that held wall-to-wall shackles and torture implements, and she assisted her partner, David Parker Ray, with the victims. When the police answered a 9-1-1 call at this home, they were astounded. They soon realized that a young woman who had just run nude into nearby Truth or Consequences, New Mexico, had escaped this very place. Hysterical, she claimed she'd been abducted and held for several days of torture and rape, certain the couple had planned to kill her. Burns and cuts on her body confirmed her story. She also described a twenty-minute tape the man had played to inform her about what was in store: she was their sex slave and she could expect a great deal of abuse. Among other things, she would have sex with animals, be forcibly raped with dildos, have her nipples fully stretched, and provide oral sex on demand. The man told her that other women who were once in her place had died.

Next to the trailer was a smaller one, generally used for moving cargo. It was fifteen-by-twenty-five feet and the space was entirely devoted to sexual torture. Ray had drawn pictures of what he planned to do to the victims, and to accomplish it he had gathered a number of surgical instruments that could inflict different types of torment. He also utilized medical manuals, specifically devoted to female anatomy, and made an electrical device that was clearly intended for inflicting pain. Then there were obvious sexual implements, such as large dildos, belts, and whips. There was also a home video of the couple applying these implements to a woman, who screamed in agony and terror.

Ray had the whole place rigged with a series of chains, shackles, and pulleys. He also had drawings of things he wanted to do, as well as photographs of bound and tortured women. In addition, he had a series of dolls strung up in various states of bondage. Among his texts was a copy of *American Psycho* by Brett Easton Ellis, a novel that details the violent bloodbaths a man inflicts on victims whenever he needs to blow off steam from his high-stress life. Like its lead character, Ray thought of his victims as expendable pawns; they were his "packages."

Among the more interesting items, supposedly based on his years of experience, was a page of directions that Ray had apparently written for how to handle a sex slave. Bondage was a must, and the neck collar was considered permanent. He included methods of psychological torture, including a blindfold. Verbal abuse was part of every move, including putting the slave in the right positions as he told her what he was going to do, and it was important to prevent her from thinking too much. "Keep her off balance," the list read, as well as emphasizing the importance of keeping both her mind and body in a state of stress. He had a list of sixteen techniques for brainwashing someone, which included isolation, fear tactics, abuse, and occasional small favors.[8]

Researchers Lisa Shaffer and Julie Penn spell out what sadism entails. They indicate that it may or may not involve consent; for some offenders it's definitely more exciting to inflict pain on nonconsensual victims. Most sadists begin as masochists, who are aroused by the infliction of pain or humiliation. They then move into a dominating role and find that they prefer it. Some even develop such a hunger for arousal that they become rapists and murderers. The types of activities sadists enjoy include whipping, handcuffing people, hanging them, choking victims into unconsciousness and then reviving them, stomping on them, using substances to induce altered states of consciousness, electrocuting, piercing, raping, cutting, and keeping them imprisoned. Although there are differing opinions on this condition and its causes remain vague, this predilection appears to form during certain associations in adolescence. Even so, more than one-third of people with this condition report discovering their perverted desires well into adulthood; they enjoy the feeling of power and authority that arises from having their way with a vulnerable and submissive human being.[9]

The police arrested fifty-nine-year-old David Parker Ray and his girlfriend, Cindy Hendy. When the incident was reported in newspapers, a second woman came forward with a similar story of abuse at their hands, and police soon identified a third. Hendy was willing to deal. In exchange for a reduced sentence, she told what she knew about Ray's alleged murders, which totaled fourteen. She claimed that Ray had disposed of many of the bodies in the lake and in ravines around south-central New Mexico. Authorities followed leads in ten different states, using ground-penetrating radar and cadaver-sniffing dogs, but failed to locate any bodies. Hendy also revealed that Ray's daughter, Glenda, had participated, as well as a man named Dennis Roy Yancy. Investigators soon brought Yancy in for questioning. He offered information about the sadomasochistic acts he had witnessed and in which he sometimes participated. Eventually, he admitted that they had tortured his former girlfriend in the Toy Box, killing her. Yancy received two sentences of fifteen years each. Soon Glenda Jean "Jesse" Ray was arrested and charged with kidnapping women for sexual torture.

David Parker Ray went through several trials, and after the jury convicted him in one, he said, "I feel raped." He seemed to believe that what he did to his victims was what they wanted, that he had given them the pleasure they craved. He made a deal to plead guilty to other charges in exchange for leniency for his daughter. Glenda Ray pled no contest to a kidnapping charge and received a sentence of nine years for second-degree kidnapping. Six years were suspended, and she was to serve five on probation.

Although Ray faced spending the rest of his life in prison, on May 28, 2002, just as he was about to be transferred to the general prison population, he suffered a heart attack and died. Since there would be no one to charge, the expensive investigation fizzled out.[10]

WILLING TO LEARN

It's not always clear just how involved a partner is: some are full participants while others go along with what the dominant partner wants, because they're afraid not to. During the 1990s, Robert R. Hazelwood, a former FBI Special Agent with the Behavioral Sciences Unit, undertook an extensive study with Dr. Park Dietz and Dr. Janet Warren of twenty wives and girlfriends of sex offenders. He designed the study because he believed that these women would be more truthful than would the primary offenders. The study explored their sexual preferences, the preferences of their partners, their background, their level of education, and other factors. He was surprised to learn that these women all seemed normal and came from mostly middle-class backgrounds, although most described early episodes of incest or familial abuse. Without exception, they said the males were the instigators. "These men have the ability to recognize vulnerable women and they manipulate them," said Hazelwood. "The behavior gets reinforced with attention and affection, gifts, and excitement. Eventually they [the men] are doing things that isolate them and further lower their self-esteem. All they have is this guy, so they cooperate."[11]

Hazelwood and his colleagues found the motives to become "compliant" in these situations to be complex and diverse. In part, it was to keep their lovers' attention. It also involved some degree of assimilation, i.e., the women grew used to the deviant demands and activities, and eventually failed to view them in the light of reality. The researchers identified a five-step process that turned these women into accomplices:

1. Identification: Identifying a vulnerable, easily-controlled person.
2. Seduction: Getting the woman to fall in love.
3. Reshaping the woman's sexual norms: Introducing her to sexual images and acts that may offend or frighten her but which she must do to please the man and keep him involved.
4. Social isolation: Cutting her off from family and friends.
5. Punishment: Physical, verbal, and sexual abuse which further erodes the woman's self-esteem and ability to act on her own.[12]

In short, it's a relationship of dominance and submission, which means that one person is assertive and the other submissive as a means of achieving intimacy or greater sexual satisfaction. (This dynamic is different from, but often coincides with, sadomasochism.) Such conflict reportedly magnifies physical sensation. The partners exploit the illusion of forced captivity and intensify it to make it edgier. The dominant person finds pleasure in mastery while the submissive one enjoys the surrender and loss of responsibility. They help each other to explore their fantasies by each playing the role that the other needs to achieve the desired feeling. The experience reportedly pushes both closer to primal needs, which creates a flow of energy that neither can experience alone. Oddly enough, when it works, a paradoxical equality can be achieved.[13]

It might happen that someone who gets involved with a sadistic person would not have committed the crimes he or she did; however, these relationships are so rare, with no certainty about honest responses, that we simply cannot say. With the following couple, the female partner seemed eager to get involved, and then went on to kill on her own. Still, she's the one who finally called the police. But during her confession, she waffled between truth and lies.

This case occurred in Los Angeles, California, in 1980, when the bodies of murdered females were found in various places. They weren't immediately connected, because two were just hitchhiking girls, while two were prostitutes. One was missing her head, but the head was soon discovered inside an ornate box; its decomposing flesh was partially frozen. When a fifth victim was found in the Valley, the papers linked them all and dubbed it the "Sunset Strip Murders." No one yet included the body of a man, beheaded and stabbed in his van that August. He was identified as small-time country singer John "Jack" Murray.

On August 11, Carol Bundy, thirty-seven, told coworkers that she was involved in murder, so they called the police. When officers arrested her, she handed them three pairs of panties that she said had been taken from victims, as well as a photo album of her boyfriend, Doug Clark, having sexual contact with their eleven-year-old neighbor. Bundy admitted that although she had only assisted with the other murders, she had killed Jack Murray herself. Another team arrested Clark at work; when the guns he had stashed were found and linked, he was charged with five murders.

Bundy told police, with whom she openly flirted, that she had met Clark in a bar in 1979 and they became lovers. Eventually Clark confided his fantasies of torture, captivity, necrophilia, and murder. He persuaded Bundy to entice young girls for him. Then in April 1980, he came home covered in blood and told her about committing a double homicide. Bundy was intrigued, so Clark took her to a ravine and pointed out where he had dumped a woman after shooting her. Soon, Bundy lured a young prostitute to the car. While the girl performed oral sex on Clark, Bundy was supposed to shoot her, but she hesitated, so Clark did it in front of her.

Next, Clark brought home the head of a dead woman. He placed it in the freezer to preserve it as a sex toy. Bundy put make-up on it, and Clark penetrated the mouth for necrophilic oral sex. When it decomposed, they put it into a box and discarded it. Bundy had murdered Jack Murray because she had confided some of this to him, and then feared he would go to the police. However, during her three-hour confession, Bundy admitted to police that killing Jack and removing his head "was really fun to do." She compared the experience to an amusement park ride and said she would probably do it again. Still, she was offered a plea deal that spared her from the death penalty in exchange for testifying against Clark. Her interviewers believed she was just a homely woman so grateful for male attention that she would do anything for it.

Clark disputed everything that Bundy had said. He insisted that she and Jack Murray had killed the victims before Bundy turned her wrath on Murray. However, the police had already collected plenty of physical evidence that pointed to Clark.

Bundy was the chief witness against Clark at his trial. Dressed like a prim housewife, she spoke about being under Clark's spell, stating that he had bragged about committing murders since he was seventeen—to the tune of about forty-seven. Bundy claimed that she was hesitant but afraid that if she did not go along with him, Clark might reject her. She had found him to be quite controlling. He demanded that she do whatever he wanted and said he would leave her unless she complied. He wanted a sex slave, someone who would see to all of his needs, mundane and bizarre. She gave in, expecting that in return he would be true to her. But he soon told her that he needed something new and exciting. He brought prostitutes home, and to please him Bundy went along with it. She even watched him assault an underage girl.

Clark was found guilty of six counts of murder and one count of attempted murder. On March 16, 1988, he received six death sentences. Bundy pled guilty to killing Jack Murray. Her deal gave her life in prison but spared her the death penalty. [14]

FORCED TEAMING

In a few rare cases, the rapist has employed an unexpected accomplice—one of his victims. While it's understandable that people will act under coercion if they believe they or their family might otherwise die, this case of a compliant accomplice was rather unusual. There was no time to have brainwashed her, and yet that's how she acted.

In 1984, contractor Christopher Wilder, thirty-nine, came under suspicion in Florida in the disappearance of several women, so he fled across the country. Along the way, he stopped long enough to lure several young women into his clutches, killing them, but he also kept one of them alive to obey him.

A chance survivor told the police about Wilder's modus operandi. He followed young women in malls or parking lots to tell them he was a photographer looking for a model. He'd lure them with flattery about their beauty and the promise of a career, and then show them his photograph portfolio. Once they were lulled into trusting him, he would force them into his car, often killing them quickly after raping or torturing them. This survivor said that Wilder had told her to undress while he masturbated. Then he'd made her perform sexual acts, and finally he raped her twice. All during this activity, he watched television. After a few hours, he pulled out an electrical cord, which was cut in the middle, with a switch attached. He then applied the open copper wires to her feet and painfully shocked her. Once this activity bored him, he used Superglue to force her eyes shut, drying them with a blow dryer. He found an aerobics show on the television and ordered her to mimic the movements of the exercising women, and when she did not perform as he wanted, he shocked her. This appeared to arouse him. When he was not looking, she locked herself in the bathroom and screamed so loud that he fled. Yet he continued to pick up other girls.

At one point during his cross-country spree, Wilder abducted a sixteen-year-old girl, "Marie," from a store. He raped her and then ordered her to help him lure others. When Wilder selected a girl who was filling out a job application, Marie introduced herself as Tina Wilder and learned that the girl's name was Dawn. Marie asked Dawn to step outside the store to speak to the "store manager," who was actually Wilder. He forced Dawn into his stolen car, making Marie drive as he placed duct tape over Dawn's eyes and mouth before raping her.

They stopped at a hotel in Ohio, where Dawn was treated to Wilder's electric torture device, and then they all drove to New York State. Marie and Wilder took photographs together at Niagara Falls before they went to Rochester for the night. Wilder warned both girls that if they tried to escape or draw attention to themselves, he would kill them. The next day, he took Dawn into the woods and tried to suffocate her, but she fought him off. When he stabbed her, she pretended to be dead, so he left. She managed to get out and find help.

Near Victor, New York, Wilder had Marie persuade a woman driving a Pontiac Trans-Am to come over to their car. Wilder grabbed her car keys and ordered Marie to drive the Trans-Am, following him. At a deserted gravel pit, he shot the woman in the back. Then, inexplicably, he drove the Trans Am to Boston's Logan Airport, gave Marie enough money to fly back home, and they parted.

Oddly, when she arrived in Los Angeles, she did not call her family or go to the police; instead, she directed the cab driver to a lingerie store. She spoke to the sales manager and told her that Wilder had cut her hair short to make her look like a character from *Flashdance*. It was not until her friends spotted her that she finally went to the police.

At this time, Wilder was killed in New Hampshire in a struggle with a state trooper who had recognized him.[15] Found in his possession were handcuffs, rolls of duct tape, rope, a sleeping bag, the specially-designed electrical cord, and the 1963 novel by John Fowles *The Collector*. Therapists who had treated Wilder over a period of time knew that he had practically memorized this book as a slave manual. *The Collector* features Frederick, a lonely entomologist who abducts a beautiful woman named Miranda, to hold her captive in a locked dungeon he has prepared on his isolated property. He has the delusion that he can make her love him just as he can make her wear certain clothing. He has decided that she belongs to him and will obey him perfectly. While Frederick did not take pains to brainwash Miranda in this story, he relied on a technique known to sadists: gestures of kindness mixed with the torture will elicit the slave's affection, even adoration. Eventually Miranda grows ill and dies, but Frederick dismisses this unfortunate "accident" and looks for another captive.

Some mental health experts might view Miranda's eventual acquiescence as a classic case of Stockholm syndrome, which occurs under conditions of severe stress in captivity, especially where there's torture and/or uncertainty about the outcome. The captive appears to become involved to some degree with his or her captor, even to the point of consenting to the abuse and captivity. This person may express feelings of sympathy and affection for the person who imprisoned him or her in a way that surprises outsiders and makes them wonder just how abused the person really was; the captive's confusing response derives from the malleability of the human psyche. What appears to occur is that the person "freezes" in defense and then, over time, yields to appease the captor, which may then decrease the abuse and even curry some favor. If the captor takes care of the captive's basic needs, the captive may feel grateful and thus become more susceptible to suggestion. Some may finally cease looking for a way to escape.[16]

While Marie's quick compliance remains a mystery, Wilder is more of an open book. His childhood was fairly stable, although he did some window-peeking in early adolescence. He was also arrested with a group of friends for the gang-rape of a girl on the beach. He pleaded guilty and received a year of probation with counseling and electroshock therapy. This apparently fueled his fantasies, for shortly after the treatment he began to envision shocking girls while having sex. Therapists who saw him for various court-ordered sessions noted his need to dominate women and his desire to turn them into unwilling sex slaves.

Quite a few lust killers start injecting violence into their fantasies while young, and it's often incidents in their lives that provide the frame. Research on juvenile predators is essential for understanding the formative development of adult serial offenders.

8

Boys Gone Bad

STARTING YOUNG

Wayne Mallette was only seven when he was lured into the deserted exhibit grounds in Toronto on September 15, 1956. He was strangled, bitten, and undressed, and the killer had defecated near the body. The wrong person was picked up for questioning, giving Peter Woodcock, seventeen, more time. He found that he enjoyed the experience of choking a child to death; it was erotic and afterward he felt at peace. He would later say that it was the only thing that gave him pleasure. Three weeks later, he strangled, bludgeoned, and bit a nine-year-old, and then decided that since he had killed two boys, he would now try a girl. His next victim was only four years old, and her body was found in a ravine. Her clothes had been pulled off and she had been choked. She had also been vaginally penetrated with a tree branch, and her eyes were poked in.

Witnesses had seen a teenage boy on a bike, which sent police, who knew Woodcock, in his direction. He was arrested and he confessed, but his crimes were so shocking and his manner so distant that he was declared legally insane and committed to a psychiatric facility in Ontario. He changed his name years later to David Michael Krueger. Going through numerous treatments, he charmed the staff until they finally gave him a one-day pass in 1991. Within hours, he murdered an inmate who had jilted him, mutilating and sodomizing the corpse. He nearly made it a double homicide, and after he turned himself in, he masturbated continually for hours.

Woodcock is a good example of someone who was disadvantaged before he could even talk. His young mother kept him for a month before he was shunted around from foster family to foster family, one of which physically abused him. He cried all the time and it was not until he was three that he finally got into a stable home, but by this time he had grown quite defensive. He screamed when anyone came near him and he had difficulty walking. Withdrawing into his own world, he made strange animal noises. Understandably, he was a lonely child and this did not improve as he grew up. In fact, he became a target for neighborhood bullies. He soon became aggressive himself, killing a family pet.

When Woodcock's foster mother sustained a head injury, she grew mean, often beating him. Much as he loved her, she scared him. Woodcock looked around for ways to control his world, memorizing the streetcar system. He also found solace in anger, imagining ways to kill other children. By the time he was thirteen, he was molesting them. Despite being exceptionally bright, Woodcock just did not fit in, and he paid a price for that. He soon began to fantasize how he could get children alone and cut them up. He started to choke children into unconsciousness, removing their clothes to examine their bodies.[1]

It is difficult to believe that a child is capable of committing a sexually predatory act. When we think of a sexual predator, we picture a male in his late thirties or early forties, who preys on children at the playground. However, the sexual predator can be a child, committing sex offenses against other children at an early age. The problem is that little research has been done on this type of sexual predator, so it is difficult to intervene before the child offends against another.

When we take a look at the juvenile sex offender, we see that certain attributes tend to be prevalent, which are not seen in non-offenders: specific individual, cultural, and familial characteristics. The important thing to remember is that just because an adolescent falls into these categories does not mean that he or she will become a sex offender. Just as it is impossible to accurately predict which adults will commit a sexual offense, no predictive profile can be applied to every sexually abusive youth.

NEVER TOO YOUNG

When a mother leaves her children in the supposedly capable hands of her boyfriend, the last thing she expects is that the children will be sexually abused. However, this is exactly what happened when seventeen-year-old John Price was asked to watch his twenty-four-year-old girlfriend's children. After she left to visit a neighboring apartment, Price bit, beat, and raped the two-year-old daughter. On returning to the apartment, the mother noticed bite marks and bruises on the girl, and Price offered a story. She did not believe him. Police originally investigated the incident as a case of physical abuse, and with the help of doctors at Hasbro's Children's Hospital, they determined that the little girl had been raped as well.[2] Originally deemed incompetent to stand trial, Price was eventually found competent, and was indicted on three counts of first-degree child molestation and nine counts of second-degree child abuse.

Even younger was Trevor Reizenstein, age twelve, from Nampa, Idaho. He was caught running from the scene when a group of kids on bikes came across his victim on January 24, 2007: a half-naked little girl who had been raped and beaten within an inch of her life, dumped in an alley. She was only five. The boys saw Reizenstein running and went to grab him. They detained him while one went for the police. After a thorough investigation, doctors found that the girl had been deprived of oxygen, either through chest compression or by being strangled. In addition, she had been beaten, sexually assaulted, and left for dead in the alley.[3] Reizenstein was eventually charged with attempted homicide, battery, and forcible sexual penetration of the little girl, and has been in custody for more than two years. He is set to stand trial as an adult in August, 2009.

DEMOGRAPHICS

The main roadblock in determining the characteristics of a typical juvenile sexual predator is reporting and documentation. Many cases go undetected, others are never brought to the attention of the criminal justice system, and still others are referred to diversion or social service programs for treatment. Often, their cases are sealed, even from researchers. In essence, the problematic behavior is not given the attention it deserves. However, if we examine the statistics we do have, which include the FBI Crime Index and self-report surveys, we can draw some general conclusions.

First, the National Crime Victimization Survey shows that almost 11 percent of all forcible rapes were committed by someone under the age of eighteen.[4] Their victims can even be infants. However, when we look at the total number of sexual offenses committed in the United States, these numbers can be disturbing. More specifically, crime reports say that offenders under age eighteen account for about 16 percent of the forcible rape arrests in the United States.[5]

With such a high number of active juvenile sex offenders, at least a general typology can be constructed to provide psychologists and criminal justice practitioners with an idea of the differences between offenders. One typology is based on victim type and modus operandi.

The first category is the *juvenile pedophile*. This individual is between the ages of six and twelve, and has an unnatural desire for sexual relations with other children. This offender tends to molest younger children, often because he is lacking confidence in his ability to engage in social interaction with boys. He feels socially isolated from the popular group, and uses verbal coercion, threats, and manipulation to gain compliance for his sexual acts.

The second type, the *sexual assault offender*, is male, thirteen to fifteen years old, who attacks mainly female victims. They can be of varying ages, but nonetheless are victims that he can overpower. (In the same vein, some juveniles target elderly women for sexual assault.) The problem with this type of offender is that he is often seen as "just experimenting" rather than being dangerous: it's considered normal sexual curiosity. This is not totally false, since such crimes can be the result of sexual experimentation, but these offenders become enthralled with sex itself, regardless of the level of force needed to complete the act. They often have numerous early experiences from playground encounters.

Finally, the *mixed offense offender* is between the ages of six and fifteen, and commits his crime on an ongoing basis, but generally only has one victim. He generally knows the victim as a friend of the family or acquaintance from school. These types of offenders tend to branch out; their victims will become younger, and they will not discriminate between boys or girls. This is very similar to a power rape, done to feel powerful or control over another individual.[6]

The mother of Christi Blevins believes that knowledge of Robert Rotramel's juvenile sex offenses may have been enough to save her daughter's life. In fact, she claims that she would have watched Christi more closely had she known that a sex offender was living in her neighborhood. But the boy was only nineteen. In August 2000, two days after starting the second grade, seven-year-old Christi and her twelve-year-old friend were playing in Christi's front yard. It was 8:45 P.M. on a Saturday evening in Oilton, Oklahoma, and Rhonda Blevins sent Christi's friend home and told Christi to come in the house. Before the child made it to the door, a man grabbed both girls, covering their mouths and taking them to an abandoned house. Rhonda called the police. They found the perpetrator, standing over his victims with a penknife, but not before he had raped the twelve-year-old and strangled Christi to death.

The perpetrator was Robert Rotramel. He performed lewd sexual acts on Christi, and then took her friend to another room and forced her to perform oral sex on him before he raped her.[7] He was charged with murder, rape, kidnapping, lewd molestation, and forced sodomy. Rotramel had a long juvenile history of criminal behavior, which included forcible sodomy and the molestation of a relative when he was thirteen.[8] Yet his motive for murder remained a question. It was possible that he was trying to rape the older girl and while detaining Christi, he simply applied too much pressure to her neck or chest, causing her to asphyxiate and die. It is also possible that killing her aroused him, leading him to have oral and vaginal sex with the older victim. Given his background, and the sudden bold aggression that night, escalation to murder seemed inevitable.

Unfortunately, while juvenile offenses are generally perpetrated by youths in their late teens, there also are reports of sexual abuse perpetrated by children as young as four or five. Not surprisingly, similar to sex offenses committed by adults, the vast majority of offenses are committed by males, usually around the age of fourteen.[9]

At first glance, these juveniles seem like normal kids, and people who know them have difficulty believing that they could commit the sexually predatory crimes of which they are accused. At the time of an offense (or series of offenses), the offenders are most often living with parents, both of whom are in the home.[10] Although an argument has been made that criminal behavior arises from single-parent households, the statistics fail to bear this out. In fact, many of the preconceived notions that we hold about sexual criminality do not apply.

Juvenile sex offenders rarely have any previous convictions for sexual assault. However, the incident in which they're accused is often not their first offense, or even their first victim. They most likely have been committing predatory acts for a while, but have not yet been detected. In fact, the average number of victims of juvenile perpetrators is seven, although some have reported having thirty victims or more.[11]

Several variables have been considered as explanation for the behavior of child predators. For instance, mental illness has been considered, but the studies fail to make a definitive link. The fact is that few juvenile sex offenders are ever identified as suffering mental illness or psychosis.[12] External factors have also been considered, including poverty, education, and ethnicity. If we look at the juveniles committing these predatory crimes, and accept the notion that, with most serious crimes, they come from lower-income households, we would expect that juvenile sex offenders have a lower socioeconomic status (SES), and are therefore at greater risk to commit these offenses. The argument is that having no money means that the family tends to interact differently, and that the resources to decrease stress are absent. However, the statistics paint a different picture.

The alternate point of view, and the one that is revealed in a large number of studies, is that juvenile sex offenders come from all levels of family income, and that there is no difference by social class. In a sense, we cannot categorize an offender as poor or wealthy, because there is no discernible pattern that points to either one, or any specific status in between.[13]

One variable that seems to have no relevance is the ethnicity of the offender. When we think of sex crimes, thanks to media stereotypes, we tend to think of a black man, mid-twenties, preying on a white woman. In the case of juveniles, the offenders and victims are of similar race; juvenile sex offenses, like most other crimes, are intraracial in nature.[14] This is not a surprise, since these crimes are often committed not by a stranger jumping out of the bushes, but by juveniles targeting people they know.

Although many variables have been examined, none contributes to a definitive profile of the juvenile sex offender. As we pointed out in Chapter 3, it's not just the environment that matters, but also how any given person interacts with it. In some instances, the offender has been abused, in other cases he has not; some have been deemed mentally ill, while the vast majority have not. Some are impulsive, others are angry, and others just find sexual assault interesting or amusing. Still, the study of juvenile sex offenders, although not an exact science, yields valuable insight into the creation and evaluation of a predator. We must consider not only the offender himself, but the totality of circumstances surrounding the event, including the relationship between the offender and the victim.

In Townsville, Australia, a fifteen-year-old boy was sentenced to five years in prison for repeatedly raping a disabled girl, as well as forcing her to perform oral sex on him. Though the victim was sixteen years old, the court deemed his behavior "contemptuous and aggressive," as her handicap prevented her from resisting his advances.[15] In this case, something about the victim's condition encouraged the boy to abuse her; he might not have been so freely aggressive if she'd been able to fend for herself.

RED-HAIRED DEVIL

On August 2, 1993, Derrick Robie, age four, was on his way to a summer recreation program one block from his house. It was the first time his mother allowed him to go off on his own, without her. In Savona, New York, with a population of 970, no one would imagine that Derrick would be in any sort of danger. In fact, most people in town knew the sweet boy who liked to wave to everyone.

However, when thirteen-year-old Eric Smith saw Derrick walking down the block that morning, he decided that sexually assaulting and killing the little boy was on his daily agenda. Somewhere between Derrick's house and his final destination, Derrick was lured into the woods. Once Smith had

Derrick alone in a secluded spot, he strangled him, rendering him unable to fight back. Smith repeatedly terrorized the child, digging up rocks and sticks to use as weapons. Removing one large rock and one small rock from the dirt, Smith repeatedly hit Derrick on the head, knocking him unconscious. Finally, Smith poured red Kool-aid on the boy and sodomized him with the small stick, both as the child was dying and after his lifeless body lay in the leaves. Investigators determined that Smith had continued to "enjoy" Derrick's body, even after he was dead, repeatedly sodomizing the corpse.

Smith, a red-headed kid, had been a bullied loner, prone to temper tantrums at home. When the police talked with him, he eventually confessed, and seemed as if he enjoyed the attention. There was no attempt on his part to show remorse or act as if he could not control what he'd done.

Sexual assault on another child is one thing, but trying to figure out why a child would sodomize and kill another is mind-boggling. In the case of Eric Smith, extensive medical testing and psychological examination allowed doctors to conclude that Smith suffered from explosive rage disorder, where he could be violent one minute, normal the next. However, nothing in his hormone levels indicated anything out of the ordinary in his brain function. The best they could determine was that there was something wrong with him, but they could not pinpoint what it was.[16] Based on the brutal nature of the sexual assault, some questioned whether Eric had been sexually assaulted at some point in his life. However, he repeatedly denied this took place. In sum, it is difficult to determine why Eric Smith raped and killed Derrick Robie.

Despite a defense that took account of his uncontrollable rage episodes, he was found guilty of second-degree murder. The jury believed that he knew what he had done, appreciated that it was wrong, and chose to do it anyway. These days, as he comes before parole boards, he insists that he would be a good counselor for bullied boys, but has consistently been denied parole.[17]

FAMILY STRUCTURE AS A FACTOR

The real question, when dealing with juvenile sexual predators, is whether the activity is influenced more by nature or nurture. Is the child a born criminal or has he been socialized to become one? Does the child learn these actions from the parents or is it in the genes? Studying the family structures of juvenile predators offers insight into the type of families these offenders grow up in, and reveals the influence that families can have on the behavior of juvenile sex offenders.

Research indicates that there are several characteristics common to families of juvenile sexual predators. Besides having dangerous secrets that they keep from the rest of the world, these families are generally guilty of emotional impoverishment. They lack the appropriate affect in real-life situations, often not behaving as "normal" families would, in either happy times or times of sadness or crisis. They have a distorted attachment to each other, an attachment most other families would consider uncomfortable or too close, which may include unique sleeping arrangements (a grown son sleeping in his mother's bed, for example) and seemingly-incestuous methods of comfort. In these families, the juvenile's role is often to act as a receptacle for negative feelings within the family (shame, guilt, anxiety), and the sexual abuse may become the presenting symptom in a long history of problematic behaviors.[18]

Characteristics within the families themselves may also enhance the prospect of sexual offending. For example, juveniles may be more apt to commit a sexual offense if there is a parental history of abuse. In fact, abuse within the family can increase the likelihood of predisposition to offending. This is the concept of the Cycle of Violence, where the abused individual eventually becomes the abuser. Parental substance abuse could play a role in a juvenile's proclivity to sexually offend. However, there seems to be no clear-cut correlation between parental drug or alcohol use and a child's sexual offending.

SEEKING EXPLANATIONS

Taking into account all of the possibilities that familial and parental characteristics may offer, the fact is that the juvenile sexual predator is still responsible for the deviant choices and behaviors, so an explanation for it is needed. Like all criminological theories, each has its own positives and negatives in explaining juvenile sexual offending.

The most comfortable explanation for rape and child sexual assault is psychosis. It is easy to say a child "has serious issues," "must be crazy," or "must be sick in the head," because it deflects blame from the child.[19] No one wants to believe that a person, much less one under eighteen, would willfully and in their right mind commit a sexual offense against a child. "Psychosis" is possibly the oldest and most widely accepted theory for explaining juvenile sexual offending, and yet in the vast majority of cases, there is little basis for a diagnosis of such an extreme mental illness. In actuality, truly psychotic sex offenders account for less than 8 percent of the total population of perpetrators, and there is little evidence that psychosis leads to sexually exploitative behavior. Predators usually plan in a way that requires the type of linear thinking and careful logic that psychosis defies. Although some psychotic individuals have been predatory, it's quite rare.[20]

As mentioned previously, physiological disorders, such as post-traumatic stress disorder (PTSD), attention-deficit/hyperactivity disorder (ADHD), mood disorders, obsessive-compulsive disorder (OCD), and dissociative disorders, have been examined as reasons for juvenile sexual offending. One way to determine whether this is a viable explanation is to determine whether treating for these reduces the amount of offending or the feelings that precipitate it. However, this makes the assumption that these disorders actually cause predatory behavior. Although such children often masturbate excessively and often publicly, and also display multiple paraphilias, there is little evidence connecting these deficiencies to predatory sexual behavior.[21]

As with most other criminal behavior, learning theory is a more plausible explanation for the behavior of juvenile sex offenders. Learning theory states that an individual will act on his desires if it makes him feel good. Psychologist B.F. Skinner argued that all behavior is the result of the individual receiving positive rewards with no negative consequences.[22] Specifically, crime results when people receive pleasure without being punished for their actions. In this case, if a child sees his father assaulting his mother without repercussion, he will eventually learn that sexual assault can be gratifying, as long as there are no negative consequences. If he copies his father's assaultive behavior and receives gratification without punishment, chances are good he will continue until he is stopped.

Similarly, because our behavior is modeled after others, we learn not only by watching but also by experiencing. In this sense, if a child is the victim of sexual victimization, he may learn that this is the proper way to behave with others. As an example, if a child is molested and becomes aroused during the assault, he may associate sexual assault with sexual arousal, eventually assaulting others for his own sexual gratification. Ultimately, exposure to deviant models might result in the practice of deviant behaviors, regardless of the level of reward or punishment.

Michael Gottfredson and Travis Hirschi also believed that reinforcement was the key to behavior, but argued that all behavior was a conscious choice. Their theory, the *general theory of crime*, states that individuals commit crime because they have no self control. According to this theory, juveniles molest and sexually assault other juveniles because they want to. They consider the possible consequences of their actions, and decide that they simply want to assault another child. Gottfredson and Hirschi believe that humans seek pleasure and avoid pain whenever possible, and that juvenile sexual predators simply have no self control, doing whatever they please.[23]

Finally, some have argued that juvenile predators are simply different from non-offending juveniles. According to cognitive theory, criminal offenders think differently from non-offenders, and virtually all sex offenders, regardless of age, demonstrate some patterns of distorted thinking to support and excuse their behavior. They have a faulty set of beliefs and impaired thinking, creating a distorted view of the world. Their desire for sexual deviance becomes an addiction, and their sexual behaviors become out of control because of a preoccupation or compulsion to commit sexually deviant acts.

Ultimately, each theory has its deficiencies, and any characteristic or behavior can have alternate explanations. It seems apparent that juvenile sexual predators are created in an environment that perpetuates deviance, with familial relations that are sexually damaging and devoid of love. At some level, juvenile sexual predators have learned their behavior; maybe not explicitly, but in the various environs and relationships that have shaped them throughout their years of adolescence.

9

Erotomania

S.W.A.K.

In 1949, baseball player Eddie Waitkus was the leading National League first baseman for the All-Star Team. He had played for the Chicago Cubs before being traded in December 1948 to the Philadelphia Phillies. By this time the "Lithe Lithuanian" was a popular media figure, in part because he was a well-educated, decorated veteran of World War II. Among Waitkus' many fans was a dangerous stalker.

On the evening of June 14, 1949, Waitkus received a note to meet him on an urgent matter. "It is extremely important," the note said, "that I see you as soon as possible. We're not acquainted, but I have something of importance to speak to you about. I think it would be to your advantage to let me explain this to you as I am leaving the hotel the day after tomorrow. I realize this is out of the ordinary, but as I say, it is extremely important." In a mix-up with another message, Waitkus believed the note had some connection to his fiancée, and he went to room 1297, as directed. When he knocked, a tall woman whom he did not know opened the door. Waitkus thought he had the wrong room, but the woman said she was a friend of Ruth Ann's and that Ruth Ann would be right back. He went inside to wait. He could not have known that his hostess, Ruth Ann Steinhagen, had been there for two days, preparing for her ultimate moment. She went to a closet and removed a .22 caliber rifle.

"For two years you've been bothering me," she said, "and now you're going to die." Before Waitkus could react, she shot him in the chest and he fell to the floor. Steinhagen watched him for a moment before calling the front desk to report that she had just shot Eddie Waitkus. Help arrived in time to save him from bleeding to death. Although there seemed to be no reason why Steinhagen would commit such a violent attack, it was in fact the result of a fixation that had developed over several years.

Steinhagen had followed Waitkus' career from its beginning in 1941, when she was just eleven years old. She'd gone to a ballgame and then started collecting clippings and pictures of Waitkus. Sometimes she even set a place for him at the family table in her hometown of Chicago. Her parents indulged her, believing her hobby was harmless, although she had taped blown-up photos of her idol over her bed and would spend hours looking at them. Between 1946 and 1948, her obsession grew worse. When her parents suggested she get help, Steinhagen moved out, transferring her Waitkus paraphernalia to her apartment. She went to every game she could, but watched her idol only from a distance. Apparently she told her mother, "I'm going to get a gun and shoot Eddie and myself. I can't help it. I'm crazy about him." Since he was from Boston, she adopted a bean diet and even tried learning Lithuanian.

Finally Steinhagen agreed to see a psychiatrist, but this failed to alter the intensity of her obsession. When Waitkus was traded to the Phillies, she grew upset, because it meant she would be near him for fewer games. Her mother hoped the change would help diminish the obsession, but around this time Steinhagen complained of a "funny feeling" at the back of her head, and said she was going to do something about it.

Steinhagen learned the date when Waitkus would next play in Chicago. Then she discovered in which hotel the team would stay and used the name of a former classmate of his to book a room for herself. She stored a knife and a rifle there and on the fatal night, she paid a bellhop five dollars to leave Waitkus the note that lured him to her room. However, his roommate received it instead, giving Waitkus the impression his fiancée was in town. Steinhagen's plan had been to stab him, but when he came into the room so quickly, she resorted to plan B, shooting him. He would later say that she'd had the "coldest looking face I ever saw. No expression at all."

Waitkus survived, and Steinhagen was taken to his hospital room so he could identify her. He asked why she shot him and she replied, "I don't know." However, she told the state attorney, "I had to relieve the tension that I've been under the past two years. The shooting has relieved that tension." She had planned to kill herself as well, but told police she did not have the courage to do it. She was arraigned in criminal court, claiming, "I've never been so happy in my life," but was found to be legally insane. Throughout the proceeding, she talked happily with the media and posed for pictures. Then she was hospitalized. In 1952, after a series of electroshock treatments, Steinhagen was pronounced cured, and released. This was one of the first modern examples of a criminal stalker with deadly intent.[1]

DISTORTED PERSPECTIVES

Erotomania is a rare disorder in which someone develops a delusional belief that another person—usually a celebrity or someone of higher social status—loves him or her.[2] Also referred to by some experts as de Clérambault's syndrome, the symptoms include a perception of "secret gestures" from the target person that "confirm" the delusion and a persistent need to contact or see the inamorata. Up until the eighteenth century, it was thought to be a disease produced by unrequited love. Then it was associated with hypersexuality, especially (and sometimes exclusively) in women, before the diagnosis evolved in the twentieth century into viewing "love sickness" as a mental disorder bordering on a compensatory paranoid psychosis. Currently, it is viewed as a delusional belief, close in quality to schizophrenia or dementia. Secondary erotomania piggy-backs on another psychoses, such as schizophrenia. It generally resembles a schizoaffective or bipolar condition.[3] Cases have been described as far back as Plutarch and Hippocrates.[4]

Primary erotomania is a subcategory of stalking, and about 10 percent of stalkers are considered erotomanic. In legislation, a stalker is defined as "someone who willfully, maliciously and repeatedly follows or harasses another person and who makes a credible threat with the intent to place the victim or victim's immediate family in fear of their safety." There must be at least two incidents to constitute the crime and the stalker must show a "continuity of purpose" or credible threat. They may send unwanted letters or packages, make numerous phone calls, or take up a determined pursuit. The object of affection can be a complete stranger, as Waitkus was to Steinhagen. Efforts to contact the love object are common, but stalkers may also keep the delusion completely private. Sometimes they will set up a rescue episode by endangering the object of their affection, staged or real, so they can be a hero. Those with erotomania generally believe that they and their target person are "meant" to be together. No matter what the other person says, and even if that person is married, the erotomanic stalker "knows the truth." Although 75 percent of stalkers in general appear to be male, there are more documented cases of female erotomanic stalkers. The average age differs from one study to another, but they tend to be older and more educated than other types of sexual offenders. They are also isolated from a support system and have unstable employment histories. Often, before an outright assault, there is another significant stressor in their lives.[5]

In 2008, the U.S. Department of Justice Bureau of Justice Statistics relied on the largest survey undertaken thus far to update information about victims of stalking. In a twelve-month period from 2005 to 2006, an estimated 3.4 million Americans experienced such disturbing contact. The most common forms are phone calls, letters, e-mails, or becoming the subject of rumors. More than one-third reported being followed or monitored, and more than 75 percent knew their stalker, usually from a romantic association. The most vulnerable age range was eighteen to twenty-four, especially if divorced or separated. Nearly 10 percent believed they might be murdered. Many had to give up their current job—even their residence—to escape the unwanted attention. It's estimated that at least one in twelve women has been or will be stalked, and one out of every forty-five men.

Many stalkers threaten harm, and the latest study indicates that nearly 25 percent who threaten actually carry out their threats—including damage against property or harm to pets. The targeted people most likely to be murdered have been in a relationship with their stalkers, although there are more than a dozen celebrities who have had stalkers with fatal intent.

One method of categorizing stalkers comes from members of the team that wrote the FBI's comprehensive *Crime Classification Manual*:

1. Nondomestic stalker, who has no personal relationship with the victim
   a. Organized (based in a calculated, controlled aggression)
   b. Delusional (based in a fixation like erotomania)
2. Domestic stalker, who has had a prior relationship with the victim and feels motivated to continue the relationship.[6]

Stalkers are often unemployed or underemployed, but seem to be smarter than most other types of criminals. With the added element of erotomania, they tend to have close relatives who have suffered from psychiatric disorders, especially mono-delusional conditions. They have a history of failed intimate relationships and tend to idealize certain people, imagine motives and actions that have no basis in truth, and rationalize that a target person deserves to be harassed and violated. Many view their actions from within a delusional framework and therefore see no need to get help.

Sometimes (but less often than commonly believed) only violence can end the attachment: erotomanic stalkers might attack their target (as Steinhagen did), attack themselves, or even attack someone else. Ralph Nau stalked actress Olivia Newton-John for a decade, writing hundreds of love letters and camping out near her home in Australia before returning to the

United States. Subsequently, Nau beat his younger brother to death with an axe.[7] One stalker even committed mass murder when his "beloved" failed to respond as he desired.

During the 1980s, Richard Farley wrote more than 200 love letters to coworker Laura Black. Both worked at a California-based company, ESL. Farley, a thirty-five-year-old electrical engineer, left the letters on Black's car or placed them in her mailbox. When she returned one unopened, he sent it again, with a warning that she had better read it. He'd followed Black and knew where she lived and took evening courses. As his obsession intensified, he developed a belief that she belonged to him. If he could just get a few moments, face-to-face, he thought, he was certain she would find him so compelling that she would soon feel as he did.

At first Black tried to be nice but firm in her resistance, but when Farley failed to get the message, she moved several times. But the persistent Farley always found her. She filed a sexual harassment suit against him, which resulted in the company firing him. Farley, a navy veteran and gun collector, did not take this lightly. He spent even more time keeping Black under surveillance, but now he was angry: she had challenged his sense of authority.

When Black filed for a restraining order, Farley decided enough was enough. He armed himself with a gas mask, an assault rifle, two shotguns, ammunition, a knife, and several cans of flammable liquid, then went to ESL. Inside, he shot seven employees on his way to Black's office. Confronting her there, Farley shot her, but despite her critical wounds, she survived. The police responded quickly, surrounding the building as Farley barricaded himself into an office. To negotiators who communicated with him by phone, he indicated that he had just wanted to take Black out on a date. He had not meant to kill anyone. He requested a sandwich, a soda, and a priest, and then turned himself in.

At his trial, Farley was convicted of seven counts of first-degree murder and given the death penalty. He claimed that he'd gone to ESL that day to kill himself as a way to make Black feel guilty. Instead, as a result of his obsession, he had killed seven people he did not even know.[8]

Anthropologist Helene Fisher, one of the most renowned experts on romantic love and human behavior, took brain scans of eighteen people who claimed to be "madly in love." She found that, similar to the way dopamine fuels addiction, it was also implicated in fixations that developed into erotomania. The initial attraction triggers euphoria, encouraging impulsive and risky behavior, but when frustrated, the brain pushes the person to try harder to satisfy the craving.[9] Perhaps this is why stalkers can be so unrelenting.

The first anti-stalking laws in the United States would not be in effect until 1991, after John Bardo shot and killed actress Rebecca Schaeffer. She had played a kid sister on the popular 1980s television sitcom, *My Sister Sam*, and had starred in a movie. As her popularity grew, she received increasingly more fan mail, but she faithfully responded.

In Tucson, Arizona, nineteen-year-old Robert John Bardo was among her devoted fans. When he received a reply from her to his adoring letter, along with a signed photograph, he believed that Schaeffer had feelings for him, too. He built a shrine to her in his room, and then hired a detective to find out where she lived.

In 1987, Bardo went twice to Warner Brothers Studios in Los Angeles, but he could not get past the gate. This frustrated him. In his diary he wrote, "I don't lose. Period." Then he saw the movie in which Schaeffer had appeared and was shocked that she would play a character with loose morals. Angered over this perceived betrayal, Bardo drew a diagram of the young actress' body and marked spots where he planned to shoot her. Then he went to Hollywood once more.

On the morning of July 18, 1989, he arrived at Schaeffer's apartment building to watch for her. After a courier delivered scripts to someone, he decided to ring the buzzer, himself. To his delight, Schaeffer was there. She'd been getting ready to meet with director Francis Ford Coppola to audition for his film, *Godfather III*. Since her voice intercom system did not work, she had opened the door. Bardo could hardly believe his luck. Breathless, he pulled out the photo that she had sent to him and claimed he was her biggest fan. A little disturbed, she thanked him, asked him to leave, and closed the door. He walked a short distance away, enraged, and then returned. She wasn't at all the nice girl he had believed, and he had brought his gun, just in case. He buzzed again, but remained hidden in the bushes. When she saw no one there, Schaeffer stepped outside. Bardo burst forth and shot her in the chest. Schaeffer screamed in shock, "Why?" and fell to the ground. Bardo bolted. He returned to Tucson, but since he had told his sister about his intent to visit the actress, and she knew how obsessed he was, she called the police to turn him in. He was extradited to California, where he was convicted of first-degree murder and sentenced to life in prison.[10]

Schaeffer's murder, along with an earlier assault of another actress, provoked Governor George Deukmejian to sign a law that inspired the Los Angeles Police Department to create the nation's first Threat Management Team. Stalking soon became a serious national issue, and by 1993, all states had introduced some version of an anti-stalking law.

FOREVER MINE

Most people believe that to get rid of a persistent admirer, it is sufficient to tell them their affection is not returned. However, this is not the way stalkers operate, especially those with an erotic delusion. Any acknowledgment from the target person, positive or negative, offers the stalker hope, which intensifies the feelings and the belief that something will happen between them. This, in turn, supports the predatory behavior. Dr. J. Reid Meloy says that pathological attachments most often occur in males and follow a predictable progression. There is an initial sighting or contact, after which infatuation develops. The love object is deified and is thus considered perfect and unattainable. The stalker then begins to approach the object, but also sets himself up for rejection (because he's not worthy), which triggers the delusion through which he projects his own feelings onto the object. He may develop intense anger to mask his shame, which fuels a desire to control the object, even through harassment or injury. Violence is most likely to occur when the love object is devalued—when his or her behavior defies the ideal or appears to be a betrayal.[11] Rebecca Schaeffer apparently fell from grace when she played a character in a film who was willing to do something that Bardo considered immoral.

Dr. Michael Zona and his colleagues from the University of Southern California School of Medicine make a distinction between the "simple obsessional" stalker, the "love obsessional" stalker, and erotomania. The first one describes the most common form—a male who has been sexually intimate with a female, and after she breaks it off, he cannot let it go. He believes he should be in control, so he cannot abide her making this decision. A love-obsessed person idealizes someone from afar and fantasizes about a relationship, while erotomania takes it a step further with the stalker's false delusion that he or she in fact is loved by that person. At different times, Bardo would fall into the second and third categories.[12]

Psychiatrist Doreen Orion experienced a terrifying ordeal when a female patient developed an obsession with her. In fact, psychiatry, counseling, and psychology are among the professions most vulnerable to this kind of victimization. Orion had agreed to see "Fran" as a referral and for the next eight years became entangled in a nightmare.

It began in 1989 in a psychiatric institute in Arizona, just a few months after Bardo had murdered Rebecca Schaeffer. Fran, thirty-eight, was sedated when Orion met her, suffering from a psychotic breakdown. She remained in the hospital for sixteen days, admitting that she'd had several failed lesbian relationships. While under Orion's care, Fran developed a fixation. When released, she began to show up in places where Orion went, trying to get her attention. Orion soon discovered that Fran had been diagnosed with erotomania.

Through their session, Orion realized with dismay that Fran had stalked half a dozen women before her. According to what she learned about the disorder, the typical person suffering from this delusion is single, immature, unable to sustain close relationships, and generally has a history of obsessive attachments or addictions. In particular, they are prone to fixations on unattainable objects or people, and they rely on fantasy to assure themselves that they could surmount any hindrance. They project their own feelings and needs onto the other person, and nothing can dissuade them. If the person they desire ignores them, they have a ready rationale for that, which fits into their delusional framework, and their predatory behavior gives them the feeling of control. They'll resort to devious means to collect information. They will accept any form of acknowledgment, including restraining orders and prosecution, because it confirms the connection. Often these delusions develop or intensify after the loss of a meaningful connection.

Orion received letters and poems from Fran spelling out their "psychic connection." Disturbed, she had no idea what to do. Fran seemed to take hope in a variety of "signs," viewing everything as a means to remain attached. Orion failed to respond, hoping that would discourage Fran, but it didn't. Fran even sent a huge Valentine's bouquet.

After a year, the messages became more violent, including a picture of a woman with her face severely beaten. After two years and several instances of trespass, Orion took out a restraining order. That only meant that when Fran was arrested for violation and then appealed, she managed to have a face-to-face confrontation in court. The legal process merely ensured that the stalker fulfilled her fantasy.

Orion learned that, short of putting them in prison, the behavior of stalkers cannot be controlled. Even if stalkers like Fran get prison time, their predatory stalking often resumes on release. Some of them move on to a new object, but some never quit until they die. Orion also learned from her research that few people take the harassment seriously, unaware of its terrorist nature. Although laws are getting better, the best that many victims can hope for is to learn how to protect themselves.[13]

The unrelenting harassment causes great emotional stress in the targeted victims. Some people lose their jobs or have to change their identity and move. They may suffer from extreme anxiety, sleep disorders, and depression, and may develop a reliance on medication. Some consider suicide. If they have family members, they suffer from guilt and fear for the others. Even if these incidents get reported, restraining laws can do little against the verbal harassment. In fact, some laws require that there be a genuine risk of danger or a pattern of incidents before formal protection is offered.

There is no easy way to predict who might become a stalker: It could be a former boyfriend, girlfriend, or spouse; a fellow employee; a neighbor; a store clerk; and even a stranger who spotted the victim on the street. Even people who were not abusive prior to their obsession can become so in the throes of it, because they gradually exchange reality for an imaginary world that feels more empowering.

INTERVENTION

It is difficult to determine the percentage of specifically *erotomanic* stalkers who are male. Some researchers believe it's rare to find a male in this category, but another has said that males constitute at least 20 percent of cases. The scientific basis for estimates is lacking, given how difficult it can be to document these cases, making predictions unreliable.[14] However, two cases of erotomania that caused significant changes in the practice of forensic psychology both involved male stalkers: John Hinckley, Jr. and Prosendjit Poddar. One affected the wording of the insanity defense nationwide, and the other made some form of risk assessment part of clinical treatment.

John Hinckley, Jr. was obsessed with the film *Taxi Driver* and particularly its young actress, Jodie Foster. He watched the film over and over, using it as a guide for his actions. Robert De Niro starred as Travis Bickle, a disturbed taxi driver who decides to assassinate a presidential candidate as a way to attract the attention of a female political worker. However, he fails and becomes involved with Iris, a young prostitute (Foster). He rescues her by killing three people and thus, with criminal violence, becomes her hero.

Hinckley, a failed songwriter with an imaginary girlfriend, eventually moved to be near Yale University, where Foster was enrolled, and decided to win her attention by shooting President Ronald Reagan. On March 30, 1981, outside the Washington, DC, Hilton Hotel, Hinckley emptied a revolver, wounding Reagan and three men before he was wrestled to the ground.

At Hinckley's insanity trial, Dr. William Carpenter, Jr., described how Hinckley had identified with Travis Bickle, imitating him in a variety of ways. He'd isolated himself and lived largely in his fantasy world, coming to believe that he *was* Bickle. As the movie was shown to the jury to help them understand how Hinckley "became" this character, Hinckley strained to see his hero. Found not guilty by reason of insanity in 1982, Hinckley was confined to St. Elizabeth's Hospital in Washington, DC. This verdict upset the American public, so the federal government, along with several states, revised the laws regarding insanity. Three states abolished it as a defense altogether.[15]

Mental health experts bear another burden as well: seeing into the future. Prosenjit Poddar, a native of India, attended the University of California at Berkeley and met Tatiana Tarasoff at a dance. He developed a strong romantic interest in her, and when they shared a quick New Year's Eve kiss, he thought this meant they were engaged. Yet Tatiana had no such interest. Poddar felt desperately obsessed, suffering an emotional breakdown, so he attempted to end all contact. Then Tatiana called him and his obsessions returned. He believed he might have to kill Tatiana to end them.

Poddar sought outpatient psychiatric services at a hospital in Berkeley. The treating psychiatrist prescribed anti-psychotic medication, and then referred Poddar to a psychologist, Dr. Lawrence Moore, for counseling. Despite their sessions, Poddar persisted in his delusion that Tatiana would eventually love him. He purchased a handgun to orchestrate a life-threatening situation from which he could rescue her. Alarmed, Dr. Moore said that he might have to take steps to restrain Poddar, resulting in Poddar's angry exit from his office.

Moore discussed this with colleagues and mentioned to the campus police that Poddar was threatening to kill a girl. Officers located him and thought he appeared rational, so they let him go. Eventually Poddar's delusions reached a breaking point. He went to Tatiana's house, armed with a knife and pellet gun. She realized something was wrong when she answered the door; she ran from him, but he shot her and then stabbed her fourteen times, killing her. Then he turned himself in. He was convicted of second-degree murder and after five years, he was released.

Yet this case had an impact on the relationship of psychiatry to violent stalking obsessions. Where once whatever was said between doctor and patient was considered privileged, that was about to change. The Tarasoffs instigated a civil case of negligence against the Regents of the University of California. In 1974, the California Supreme Court found that, despite confidentiality, a duty to warn a potential victim exists when the therapist determines that a warning is essential to avert a danger rising from a patient's condition.

The mental health profession quickly responded that they have no inherent ability to predict violence and that such a ruling violated their "special" relationship. It would also hinder patients from trusting them, as well as generate false positive predictions as a means of diverting liability. In the big picture, this would be a detriment.

The court then issued a second opinion. They still found that therapists have a duty to potential victims, but they need only use "reasonable care" to protect the person. That is, the therapist may have to civilly commit or voluntarily hospitalize the patient to avoid the potential for harm, rather than actively warn a potential victim. Most jurisdictions now recognize a Tarasoff-type duty. Standards vary from state to state. However, there is no automatic duty to warn a potential victim, because more violence has been shown to result after a warning than if no warning is issued.[16]

In terms of risk assessment, certain traits and behaviors are common to stalkers who have become violent: an unhealthy level of obsession, clearly delusional expectations, anger about something the target person did, a plan for assault, and access to a means of carrying it out. They also have a history of other types of antisocial behaviors. Growing tension signals an internal conflict that could erupt in homicidal violence; what these individuals often lack is insight about themselves and the explosive nature of their personal issues. Risk assessment is always tentative and short-term, but the research in this area has greatly improved over the past decade. Still, some researchers believe that, utilizing the above factors, it is possible to predict with nearly ninety percent accuracy whether someone will actually commit an assault. In a court-referred cohort of erotomanic stalkers, Meloy and Gothard reported that about one in four physically assaulted someone, although only 2 percent had committed a homicide. A non-forensic sample of thirteen men offered a 23 percent incidence of assault, with the love object being the most common target.[17]

There is currently no single explanation for the emergence of erotomania, in part due to the lack of clinical details about the inner lives of these people. However, a narcissistic character pathology and a borderline grasp of reality appear to be central components, with rage at some perceived insult fueling the rare assault. There might also be a biological factor, and in cases of foreign-born stalkers, culture shock might be a contributor. The best strategy for any victim is to cut off all contact with a stalker and to document any and all incidents, which will support police or psychiatric intervention.

Next we turn to another unique population, which has received little research, the female teacher predator. The degree of fixation some of them evince suggests kinship with both stalkers and pedophiles.

10

Female Teacher Predators

REVERSE LOLITA

Jennifer Rice, a trusted elementary school teacher in Tacoma, Washington, was convicted in April 2009 of having sexual relations with two underage boys, a ten-year-old and his brother. Rice, thirty-one and a married mother of three, was found guilty of kidnapping with sexual motivation, first-degree child molestation, and third-degree child rape. She had lavished so much attention on the child that his parents finally asked her not to come to the house. She had then taken the ten-year-old from his home, driven him 100 miles away, and had sex with him at a highway rest area. Court documents indicate that they'd had intercourse on several previous occasions as well. In a separate incident, Rice had also molested his brother, then fifteen. It came to light that at an earlier job, Rice had been placed on leave for inappropriately fraternizing with students, raising the alarm of parents who wondered how she had been hired. Because one of Rice's crimes was ruled to be predatory, she qualified for a longer sentence.[1]

That same month, a teacher in Chandler, Arizona, also got involved with two students, and one ended up dead. Tamara Hofmann seduced Sixto Balbuena after meeting him in her math course. Their relationship grew serious and he believed she was his girlfriend, although he was twenty-eight years younger. He graduated and joined the Navy, remaining involved with her, but when he arrived at Hofmann's home one day, he discovered someone else there—Samuel Valdivia, currently her student. The two young men got into a scrap and Balbuena stabbed Valdivia with a knife, killing him. He called the police and turned himself in.[2]

Just a month earlier, two junior high school teachers in Utah were accused of assaulting the same thirteen-year-old boy. One was thirty-nine, the other forty-six. Both confessed to having sex with him, and both admitted it began with intimate personal discussions that soon grew romantic and then overtly sexual.[3]

The number of these incidents has risen over the past decade, especially with the popularity of social Web site fraternization and cell phone texting that occurs between teachers and students. A study of these female offenders reveals that they are generally self-centered, insecure, and aggressively needy. These predators prioritize their own goals. After getting caught, they often describe how good it felt to be so admired by a boy. They fail to recognize a child's inherent vulnerability, immaturity, and inability to make adult decisions about sex. They also fail to grasp the unfair power differential, except to exploit it, which can have negative repercussions for the child in later life. But the child is not the sole victim. Most of these teachers are married at the time they decide to sexually abuse a minor, thus harming their families. They also damage the relationship between a school system and a trusting community.

Most targets are boys, but several female teachers have been caught having unlawful sexual contact with girls. Amy Gail Lilley, thirty-six, got involved with a fifteen-year-old in Florida, receiving house arrest and eight years of probation. In Michigan, Elizabeth Miklosovic pled no contest to assaulting a fourteen-year-old girl, whom she apparently "married" in a pagan ceremony in 2004.[4]

Females represent roughly 10 percent of sex offenders, and many of these are mothers molesting their children or female relatives of the victims. Other offenders include babysitters and acquaintances. In California, for example, a thirty-year-old female had sex with three underage boys. She was the mother of one of their friends.[5] Yet the number of reported female teachers targeting students has increased. Psychologist A. J. Cooper points out that the reasons why some women become sex offenders is incompletely understood, but he thinks that it might result from a combination of hypersexuality, associations with early sexual experiences, and imitation of abuse perpetrated on them (although only a few of the teachers have said they were abused). Most are immature, dependent, and sensitive to rejection, so they gravitate toward younger people who are not their peers. The risk of rejection is less likely and they create situations in which they can be in control: The child follows their lead, sometimes even when he or she doesn't want to.[6]

Many of these offenders suffer from anxiety or depressive disorders, have troubled relationships with their fathers (and, by extension, husbands), and have a grandiose image of themselves. They believe their husbands fail to give them the type of attention they crave, so they turn to hormonally charged boys who will tell them how beautiful and desirable they are. Being with a boy, some have said, makes them feel younger. Teachers who become erotically entangled with their students have described the allure of having a secret, their feeling of entitlement, their false belief that the student is "mature for his age," and the naïve notion that there are no victims. As the situation progresses, it becomes easier for them to revise reality to serve their own needs. These women often initiate the activity with a flirtatious overture or feigned concern over the boy's problems, taking advantage of a boy's developing hormones to provoke sexual attraction. Some have only one victim, but many have several.

In California, serial predator Sarah Bench-Salorio, twenty-eight, had numerous sexual encounters with an eleven-year-old student at Santiago Charter Middle School before he ended it. She went on to a new school and took up with a thirteen-year-old, but this boy confessed the whole thing to his mother. She informed the police, who caught Bench-Salorio before she could complete the conquest of yet a third young man, age thirteen. Even though the second victim testified against her, she reportedly mouthed "I love you" to him in court. Her modus operandi was to send the boys numerous e-mails, have them to dinner, and gradually get them under her power. On September 29, 2005, facing a possible sentence of more than sixty years, she pled guilty to twenty-nine lewd acts with the three boys and received three to six years. She will also be required to register as a sex offender.[7]

Despite their protests to the contrary, these women are sex offenders, having sexual relations with an underage child. Often these case become high-profile when the offender is attractive. Pamela Ann Smart (who still claims to be innocent), is serving a life term for being an accomplice in first-degree murder. She was accused of seducing a fifteen-year-old boy at the school where she was a media services coordinator, getting him so involved that when she threatened to end their liaison if he did not kill her husband, he agreed to do it. On May 1, 1990, he enlisted three friends and they carried out the crime.[8]

The case that has caused the most media flap was that of Mary Kay Letourneau, a teacher at Shorewood Elementary School in Burien, Washington. She first noticed seven-year-old Vili Fualaau when he was in the second grade. By the time he was twelve and she was thirty-four, she was ready to make her move. Despite being married and having four children at home, Letourneau offered Vili a reward for good grades by taking him to a restaurant—the type of deception a predator will often use. It wasn't long before they were meeting secretly to have sex, and soon Letourneau became pregnant, revealing the situation. A relative reported them to child protection services. On February 26, 1997, Letourneau was charged with child rape.

Letourneau pled guilty to two counts of second-degree statutory rape. The judge accepted her interest in getting psychological help, so he suspended Letourneau's sentence on the condition she take medication, attend a sex offenders treatment group, and have no further contact with Vili. She agreed, but quickly violated the order. She was soon pregnant again and back in court.

Psychiatrist Julie Moore diagnosed Letourneau with bipolar disorder: she showed periods of intense energy and activity—including hypersexuality—coupled with periods of depression. This condition can induce inappropriate behaviors, impulsivity, and impaired judgment, so she could enjoy high-risk behavior but fail to appreciate the gravity of the consequences. A specialist on sex offenders, Susan Moores, disagreed. She stated that Letourneau showed a deviant sexual arousal pattern, not a bipolar disorder. Moores placed the responsibility for the inappropriate relationship squarely on Letourneau's shoulders: The teacher had made a decision that she knew was wrong.

Letourneau kept in touch illegally with Vili as she served her sentence, and when she emerged from prison, she married him in 2005. He and his mother sued the school system for allowing the situation to happen, but they lost. The couple then had a high-profile wedding and published a book together about their love. In an interview a year later, Mrs. Fualaau stated that she would like to get another teaching job. In this interview, Vili slipped when he compared her to a male rapist who has served his sentence. That same year, Vili was sentenced for driving under the influence of alcohol.[9]

I'M NOT A SEX OFFENDER

Some sex researchers believe there is no such thing as a female pedophile, even if females commit child abuse. However, according to a Department of Justice list of twenty-one characteristics and behavioral indicators of a pedophile, at least two-thirds apply to some of these cases, including the following:

1. Usually married
2. Relates better to children than adults
3. Prefers children in a specific age group
4. Usually prefers either males or females
5. May seek employment or volunteer in programs that allow them to be near children in their preferred group

6. Pursues children for sexual purposes
7. May furnish narcotics or alcohol to child to lower inhibitions
8. May go to great lengths to conceal their activity
9. Is usually intelligent enough to recognize there is a problem
10. Often rationalizes the illicit activities, emphasizing the positive impact on the victim
11. Talks about children in the same manner one would use to talk about adult lovers
12. Is usually nonviolent and has few problems with the law
13. Access to pornography

Psychiatrist Janet Warren and psychologist Julia Hislop researched female sexual offenders to offer the following generic typology, which includes teacher-offenders:[10]

- Facilitators—women who intentionally aid men in gaining access to children for sexual purposes
- Reluctant partners—women in long term relationships who go along with sexual exploitation of a minor out of fear of being abandoned
- Initiating partners—women who want to sexually offend against a child and who may do it themselves or get a man or another woman to do it while they watch
- Seducers and lovers—women who direct their sexual interest against adolescents and develop an intense attachment
- Pedophiles—women who desire an exclusive and sustained sexual relationship with a child
- Psychotics—women who suffer from a mental illness and who have inappropriate sexual contact with children as a result

There are cases in which the sexual contact is a form of revenge against a male partner or inappropriate male relatives. Female perpetrators generally come from chaotic homes, which can influence the traumatization of others. As they were seduced, so they seduce, transforming themselves from victims into predators.

It was the victim's mother in Temple Terrance, Florida, who discovered the inappropriate relationship between her fourteen-year-old son and Debra Lafave, a twenty-five-year-old reading teacher at Angelo L. Greco Middle School. She notified the police and they set up a sting. After recording incriminating phone conversations, authorities moved in as Lafave went to the boy's home. She was placed under arrest. Lafave's husband, Owen, who divorced her shortly thereafter, indicated that she had cultivated the relationship for several weeks until she finally had a chance to get her target alone. She took him to her home and performed oral sex on him. Soon they were fully engaged in a sexual relationship, apparently choosing her SUV as the liaison vehicle. Stories emerged of how the boy's cousin drove the vehicle around while they had sex in the back.

In her defense, Lafave claimed that she had been raped when she was thirteen and that during high school she had undergone therapy for being involved with another girl. She described the manic phases of her bipolar disorder, which skewed her judgment, and thus she acted inappropriately. For these reasons, she claimed it was not her fault.

The prosecutor offered her a deal, but it included prison time, so Lafave turned it down. The boy's mother, wishing to keep her son's name and likeness out of the press, reluctantly agreed to a plea deal that took a prison sentence off the table. On November 22, 2005, Lafave pled guilty and received three years of house arrest and seven years of probation. However, she had made the mistake of having sexual contact with a minor in two different jurisdictions; the judge in the other county set a court date, but then the prosecutor dropped the charges. Lafave basically got away with her crime. On September 13, 2006, she did a televised interview on *Dateline,* to explain her side of the story.

Lafave admitted that she was a troubled woman and that the long string of problems she had experienced over her lifetime influenced poor decision-making. She revealed that she had experienced anxiety disorders ranging from panic attacks to obsessions. A boyfriend had also raped her when she was in eighth grade. Over the next couple of years, she developed a substance abuse problem, became suicidal, and experienced the effects of an eating disorder. At college, she had bouts of depression and then her beloved older sister was killed in a car accident. Finally, Lafave graduated and became an eighth grade teacher.

Lafave said she had associated sex with sin and filth, and had a difficult time being a wife. Nevertheless, she appreciated her husband's friendship, especially during recurring periods of bipolar disorder, with stretches of deep depression and periods of exuberant mania. Her energetic periods caught the attention of many of the boys in her class, and she was considered "hot."

When she chaperoned a field trip to Sea World, the boy with whom she got involved was in her group. When he flirted with her, she enjoyed the attention and the sense that she was on equal footing with these children. She claimed that she felt confident and beautiful, and she wasn't about to stop. In her own classroom, she kissed the boy. Not long afterward, he approached her with a friend and forced her against the wall, exposing her breast to the other boy. She claims she tried to stop him, but his story was that she willingly flashed him. In support of his version she did not report it. It wasn't long before she had a sexual encounter with the boy after school was over. They carried on sexually in her car, with the boy's cousin driving. By now her husband suspected her of having an affair.

Lafave thought that other rape victims—and only rape victims—would understand. She blamed her father for not being emotionally engaged with her, and said she had been "in a fog" and never considered the possibility that other boys who knew about this affair were telling people; she was their peer, she thought, so they would not betray her.

Lafave mitigated her offense by stating that fourteen-year-olds today are different than when she was fourteen. Her lack of insight was revealing, and many viewers were probably relieved to learn that she had to register as a sex offender and was barred from working with children. Even so, her final words in this interview were, "I am not a sex offender."[11]

Because Lafave was a pretty blond, the Internet was rife with comments from many young males who wished they had such a teacher. One Internet site even invites visitors to vote on which from the long list of female teacher-predators is the "hottest." The double standard in judgments on these cases is pronounced, but sometimes it comes from influential sources.

EROTOTOXINS

When an adult male gets sexually involved with a child, especially a female child, he is immediately charged with a crime, jailed, and if convicted, labeled a sex offender. The community is outraged. When stories of females committing the same crime began turning up, there was less collective anger, due to a perception that boys were willing accomplices while girls were victims. Even some officials in the court system accept this notion.

When thirty-eight-year-old Robin Mowery was sentenced in Massachusetts in June 2009 for felonious sexual assault of a fifteen-year-old boy, Judge Robert Lynn was merciful. He gave Mowery a two-to-four year sentence, stating, "Like it or not, an underage boy having sex with an older-aged girl is viewed differently than the other way around." Citing the fact that the boy himself had been aggressive, he said, "Young men have raging hormones." Lynn seemed disinclined to accept the father's victim impact statement, in which he described how the assault had "changed" his son and worried about the boy's future emotional problems.[12]

Journalist Cathy Young calls attention to this double standard and notes the case in Clifton, New Jersey, of forty-year-old Pamela Diehl-Moore. This teacher had entered into a sexual liaison with a thirteen-year-old male student. She met the seventh-grader at the Woodrow Wilson Middle School, and during the summer of 1999, Diehl-Moore took him to her home for sex. After her arrest, she blamed depression for her lapse in judgment. She pled guilty to sexual assault, a second-degree crime punishable by up to ten years in prison. Bergen County Assistant Prosecutor Martin Delaney argued that Diehl-Moore had egregiously violated the trust of a teacher-pupil relationship and should therefore receive the most severe sentence possible. But Diehl-Moore tearfully promised to change her ways. Her attorney entered her history of mental illness: a suicide attempt by medication overdose since her arrest and two hospitalizations. She had a lifelong history of depression and had suffered through a divorce and her mother's recent death.

Superior Court Judge Bruce A. Gaeta was apparently persuaded. "What good is it sending her to state prison, where she's not going to get any help for her problems?" he queried. "This is an exception where society is best served by having her treated." He noted the lack of a victim impact statement, since the boy's father had declined to subject his son to the proceedings, and changed the terms of the deal by sentencing Diehl-Moore to five years' probation, with intensive counseling.

More controversial were his concluding statements: ""I really don't see the harm that was done here," he said, "and certainly society doesn't need to be worried. I do not believe she is a sexual predator. It's just something between two people that clicked beyond the teacher-student relationship, that evidently the help was lacking in his own family." The judge also noted that he had seen no evidence that the boy suffered any psychological damage from the liaisons. "Maybe it was a way for him, once this happened, to satisfy his sexual needs," Gaeta said. "People mature at different ages. We hear of . . . newspapers and TV reports over the last several months of nine-year-olds admitting having sex." He noted that the affair had evolved from mutual consent, although he conceded that, by law, the boy was too young to actually give it. Still, he added, "Some of the legislators should remember when they were that age. Maybe these ages have to be changed a little bit."

A number of people involved with the case were upset. The Advisory Committee on Judicial Conduct received a complaint and its members found that the judge had violated the code of conduct by "making statements expressing a bias that indicated lack of impartiality in the course of a sentencing proceeding in a criminal case." The judge had expressed stereotypical views regarding the sexual nature of young boys, as if "a young boy's feelings about sex equate with a 'need' that should or must be met; that such needs may acceptably be met through sexual acts with adults; that a young boy has maturity, experience, and understanding intelligently to consent to sexual acts with adults; that a young boy is not vulnerable or prone to psychological or emotional harm from sexual experiences with adults, and, further, that an adult participating in sexual activity with a young boy could be behaving naturally and normally."[13] The committee found such a view contrary to the impartiality, open-mindedness, and objectivity necessary to determine whether the boy in question had been sexually victimized. Such views were also inconsistent with the meaning and policy of the law that criminalizes sexual activity between adults and children. Gaeta's sentence was thus determined to have been erroneous. While noting that he was attempting to be fair to the defendant, the committee decided that his attitude about the victim was an inappropriate basis for a decision.

Traditional stereotypes support a bias against the idea that males can be victims. Young points out that, before the 1970s, seduction by a female of an underage person did not even qualify in most states as statutory rape. However, repeat offenders will get a judge's attention, if for no other reason than their brazen insult to the court.

A pretty physical education teacher who inspired a lot of media coverage was former beauty queen Pamela Rogers, in McMinnville, Tennessee. Her marriage ended early in 2005, by which time the twenty-eight-year-old had already seduced a thirteen-year-old basketball player. She had told him via a text message that she thought he was cute. They met secretly for three months, but the affair was revealed and in February 2005, Rogers was in court. She faced fifteen counts of sexual battery by an authority figure and thirteen counts of statutory rape. She initially pled not guilty but then agreed to plead "no contest" to four counts of sexual battery and to serve nine months in the Warren County jail (she was out in six). With a suspended eight-year sentence, Rogers had to serve the rest on probation, wherein she could not profit from her crimes, she had to register as a sex offender, and she had to refrain from contact with her victim. In addition, she had to give up her teaching certificate.

Defying the court, Rogers sent a video image of herself in black lingerie to the boy's cell phone, and communicated with him via his sister's MySpace Web site. When all this was discovered, Rogers was arrested again. Although she pleaded for mercy and said she was willing to change, the judge ordered her to serve the rest of her sentence at the Tennessee State Prison for Women. He added two more years when Rogers pled guilty to sending nude photos of herself to the boy.[14]

EXCUSES, EXCUSES

Some boys turn against their seducers. In Australia, Bridget Mary Nolan was convicted in December 2005 on three counts. A victim impact statement from the boy and his family indicated that as a result of the encounter, the boy had been mercilessly teased at school and the family had undergone an extensive ordeal; the mother had difficulty entrusting her children to anyone. The relationship had begun with a kiss from teacher to student on a school bus, which then turned into a full-blown sexual affair. Nolan was caught, and she reportedly told authorities that she had agreed to the sex so the boy wouldn't feel rejected. Her attorney said that Nolan, too, was a victim, because she had been depressed over a cheating boyfriend.[15]

The excuses these predators use are common from one case to another, similar to the way male offenders try to mitigate their crimes, although with more emphasis on mental illness. Among them are:

- The boy pursued me.
- Boys are more mature these days.
- It was true love and I couldn't resist.
- I was depressed and it made me feel better.
- I was on medication.
- I felt inadequate.
- I suffer from bipolar disorder.
- My husband was too controlling.
- I was getting revenge for being abused/betrayed.

What many people fail to realize, however, is that these cases are not just about the perpetrators and *their* issues. The boys and their families are victims, and they may suffer much longer and more profoundly than the predator ever will. In some cases, the predator even allowed others to watch, which compounded the psychological issues.

In Wilmington, Delaware, Rachel Holt, thirty-five, received a ten-year sentence. Alluding to incidents in 2006 involving a thirteen-year-old boy that resulted in twenty-eight counts of first-degree rape, Holt told the court, "I know what I did was wrong." Not only did she involve the boy in a week-long affair but also gave him alcohol and let him drive her car illegally. She supposedly allowed a twelve-year-old boy to watch her with the victim. Her attorney protested the sentence, saying that his review of forty other such cases resulted in sentences that averaged from eighteen months to two years. Nevertheless, Holt escaped the maximum of twenty-five years. She read a three-page letter of apology to the victim's family. However, the family refused to accept this resolution and sued the school over reports that officials might have known that Holt had repeatedly been inappropriate with students. The results of this suit are unknown.[16]

According to the Child Molestation and Research Prevention Institute, sexual abuse causes harm that carries over into the child's adult life. Statements made on the Institute's Web site indicate that this includes:

- difficulty in forming long-term relationships
- sexual risk-taking that may lead to contracting sexually transmitted diseases, including AIDS
- physical complaints and physical symptoms
- depression, suicidal thoughts, and suicide
- links to failure of the immune system and to increases in illnesses, hospitalizations, and early deaths.

"A thirteen-year-old boy will seldom grow up thinking how cool it was that he had sex with his teacher," says sex crimes researcher and criminologist Eric Hickey, "especially as they begin to understand terms such as sexual assault and child rape. Sexual violation of a child is traumatic, regardless of who commits the act."[17]

In a 2004 study commissioned by the Department of Education, author Charol Shakeshaft indicates that nearly 10 percent of U.S. public school students have experienced sexual advances from school employees. Students have reported unwanted sexual innuendo, as well as groping, inappropriate invitations, and outright rape. Shakeshaft insists that educator misconduct is "woefully understudied." Among the seductive behaviors teachers utilize are deception, gift-giving, isolation, and friendship, gradually moving on to inappropriate touching and methods that will make the student feel complicit. It's a desensitization process common to pedophiles, which works quickly with boys and includes tests to see if they can keep a secret. Often the teacher will provide additional "help" that leaves the child alone with them, creating the aura of a special relationship. They might also get the child to feel indebted.

When children go to authorities, they might find they are not believed, which adds another level of harm. Now they'll really feel isolated. The 2004 report states that this fear is top on the list of reasons why children say they did not report abuse.[18]

Dr. Frederick Mathews states that many adolescent boys abused by women become rapists and sex offenders, targeting girls. "There is an alarmingly high rate of sexual abuse by females in the backgrounds of rapists, sex offenders, and sexually aggressive men." He cites one study finding 59 percent, another sixty-six percent, and a third from 1993 stating that it is 80 percent. The implication is that they are expressing rage against women for being at least psychologically violated themselves.[19]

Warren and Hislop, mentioned earlier, agree: "A number of researchers have found that children who have been abused by females have often experienced significant difficulties."[20] In one study, the boys said that the immediate effects of being molested by women were devastating. Other studies indicate that they experience adjustment disorders and have problems in later relationships or with parenting. Many also experience sexual identity issues.

Sarah Jayne Vercoe pled guilty in 2005 to fourteen charges, including eleven counts of having sexual intercourse with a person under seventeen. Once a science and math teacher at Rose Bay High School in Tasmania, she lost her teaching privileges, and parents of two of her victims spoke publicly about the impact of her crimes. They said the boys had been unwilling participants, contrary to the stereotype about what boys want, and they were outraged that some people discounted the boys as victims. One boy's parents had noticed how sullen and moody their son had become, alarmed that he barely ate and that he stayed in his room most of the time. In addition, they said, they have had a great deal of difficulty coping with the fact that someone to whom they had entrusted their children had violated that trust.

Married a short time, Vercoe claimed she had experienced stress in the relationship, so she had sought other sexual encounters. She picked a boy she was supervising at a school camp, calling him and leaving text messages, then inviting him to her home when her husband was away. She urged him to lie to his mother so he could spend the night. After a few weeks, the boy decided there was something wrong with the situation and he ended it. When Vercoe wrote him a letter to persuade him to protect her, he told his parents and they went to the police.

Just before she was arrested in May 2005, Vercoe also took four students, ages fourteen to sixteen, to a party, drank with them, and engaged in sexual activities. She apparently threatened them if they told. The judge called her a predator and the education minister in Tasmania instituted a new code of ethics for teachers, which specifically included prohibitions against sexual violations.[21]

Although we may yet learn more about long-term effects when researchers take the issue more seriously, there is little doubt that the situation can also be dangerous. Aside from kidnap and rape, a few cases have involved more serious crimes. For example, Sean Powell believed that his thirty-year-old teacher, Erin McLean, an intern at his high school, loved him and wanted to marry him. He obsessed about her and finally could stand being apart no longer, so on March 10, 2007, Sean showed up at her home in Knoxville, Tennessee. Her husband, Eric McLean, was there, and he saw the boy sitting outside in his car. McLean called the police to report an intruder on his property, but seven minutes later, Erin phoned to report that her husband had just shot Sean Powell, killing him. McLean fled, but he was soon under arrest. He claimed he did not know exactly what had happened, saying it had been an accident. He had wished only to scare the boy off and save his marriage. McLean had a reputation as a good father and a good neighbor. The sudden violence seemed uncharacteristic, and many who knew him believed his story. However, he had stolen the rifle and ammunition from his parents two weeks earlier, which suggested premeditation.

Powell's birth mother, Debra Flynn, told reporters that Erin McLean had "led him on." She had discovered the text messages that Erin had left on Powell's cell phone, urging the boy to come to see her. To Flynn's mind, the teacher was a predator, teasing the impressionable young man with the possibility of marriage. He had admitted the affair to Flynn, telling her that he had asked Erin to marry him. The affair allegedly began when Erin started teaching English as part of a graduate internship at West High School. She met Sean there. Like most of these female offenders, she was married and had two young children.

Erin had asked her husband to help Sean when his adoptive parents kicked him out of their home, and Eric had tried to persuade his own parents to take the boy in. They had declined. Afterward, Eric began to suspect there was more to Erin's interest than merely helping a boy in trouble, and he may have felt betrayed and exploited. Sean went to live with his birth mother in another town, dropping out of school. However, he returned to Knoxville to see Erin.

McLean's attorney stated that McLean, charged with first-degree murder, was docile and had little comprehension of his situation. Since the victim was shot on the defendant's property, this would be a key factor, as would McLean's state of mind. At trial in September 2008, McLean took the stand in his own defense. He explained that he had felt powerless to stop his wife's affair and had been angry that Powell had shown up at his home. He said he had taken the rifle and three bullets with the intention to commit suicide, but when Powell arrived, the gun was handy, so he had pointed it at him. Powell had grabbed the barrel, causing McLean to react. The shooting was an accident. The jury considered all of this and convicted McLean of reckless homicide. He was sentenced to ninety days.[22]

The debate on the issue of whether boys can be victims of female predators often divides communities, influenced by a deeply entrenched double standard. (In 2009, Vili and Mary Kaye hosted a "Hot for Teacher" event at a nightclub in Seattle.) Only research that will convincingly prove that boys can be harmed will change future policies. However, there is no debate that female teachers who exploit their position of authority to seduce students for their own self-centered purposes should pay a price. Given the number of cases over the past decade, it's clear that this area deserves more attention from sex researchers. The same might be said about our next category of predators: pedophilic priests.

11

Thou Shalt Not Prey: Offenders in the Clergy

CORRUPTION OF THE SPIRIT

After completing theology studies in New Orleans, Gilbert Gauthe became a seminarian. Popular and well-respected, he became active in several youth organizations, including the Boy Scouts of America. Once he was ordained in 1971, he had the opportunity to serve in several parishes in the diocese of Lafayette, Louisiana. What people in his congregations did not realize about the personable priest was that behind his religious garbs, he was secretly a child molester. This was the first case of repetitive sexual child abuse by a Catholic priest brought to trial in America, and it was a shocking one.[1]

While serving as an associate pastor in Broussard, Louisiana, from 1971 to 1973, Gauthe molested at least four boys. Caught, he agreed to counseling, and eventually submitted to several sessions before moving to a new parish. However, the attempt at therapy had not addressed his problems, and he had no intention of stopping. He merely went through the motions to keep his standing in the church, and he continued to look for opportunities with altar boys. If anything, being under suspicion merely made him more careful, and after transferring to a church in New Iberia, he sexually molested sixteen more boys. The church caught on, but despite the fact that he was committing crimes as an active predator, they decided to take care of matters themselves. One laughable "fix" was to move his quarters from ground-level to the second floor. Rather than removing him from the dioceses altogether, the elders thought it best to change his environment, so in 1976, Gauthe was transferred to a church in Abbeville.

Here, he molested even more boys before he was caught again. He was moved once again, this time to a church in Henry, Louisiana, where he kept up his deviant activity before the church finally suspended him from pastoral duties in 1983. Overall, it is estimated that while serving as a priest, Gilbert Gauthe sexually molested close to 100 boys. Some people believe there were even more.[2] Gauthe had a method, akin to other predators of children. As he went through his duties, he watched for boys that fit a specific type and befriended them when they were nine or ten years old—the age group that aroused him.[3] In many cases, the boys had no father figure in their lives, many being raised by a single mother or having a disinterested father. Additionally, the mothers of his victims looked up to Gauthe and his position as a priest. To them, he was above reproach, incapable of doing anything inappropriate. Gauthe was an authority figure, with special status before God, and these women believed that he was a good role model for their sons to emulate. They had no issue with how much time Gauthe wanted to spend with the boys. He even had slumber parties at the rectory for as many as six boys together, assuring their mothers he was taking good care of them.

Gauthe's modus operandi was consistent: After befriending a boy and his mother, and ensuring that the mother trusted him, he would get the boy alone. In many instances he would invite the child to his house or take him on a camping trip. The mother typically thought this was great, because the boy now had the attention of an adult male figure who was also interested in his spiritual growth. It seemed a match made in heaven—and Gauthe realized his advantage. He could not have found a better cover.

After getting a boy alone, he would get them comfortable with him. Then he would start some "innocent" physical activity, which he knew the boy would enjoy. Tickling, wrestling, and being playful eventually led to subtle touching, which turned into outright sexual molestation. Afterward, he would buy the boy something he liked, and made him feel special. Thus, he rewarded the boy for allowing him to trespass, as well as making him feel complicit, which opened the door to a repeat episode with ever bolder activities. In most cases, Gauthe was able to move on to rape. He also took pornographic photos and showed the boys explicit adult films. This was all possible because the boys trusted Gauthe. Although they realized that what he was doing was wrong, he was their priest. He was a father figure to them, and someone that they could trust. If they had to trade sexual discomfort for his love, support, and companionship, they were willing. Most kept the secret, just as he had manipulated them to do. But one boy finally broke down and told his father what was happening. In the past, whenever Gauthe was unmasked, officials had settled with families in private, allowing the predatory priest to move on. However, the situation had become truly scandalous, in part because it became clear to parishioners that the Church had knowingly harbored a sex offender for over a decade, letting him continue to be near his prey.

One family retained an attorney and decided to make the situation public, because the Church could not be trusted to correct the situation. Gauthe was arrested and the case was reported across the nation. It divided a community, many of whom refused to believe it even after the priest confessed the extent of his crimes. "Neighbors stopped speaking to neighbors," one reporter wrote. "Faithful Catholics stopped going to church." A few families who challenged the church lost their business and some fathers used alcohol to buffer the horror of what had happened to their sons. The first boy who reported the abuse ended up in a psychiatric institute, and the lawyer who defended Gauthe, himself a staunch Catholic, "became an alcoholic, was diagnosed with bipolar disorder, got a divorce, and stopped practicing law." Some families were incensed that the Church never asked them how they were or how their sons were getting along.[4]

The problem of sexual abuse by Catholic priests—more widespread than anyone yet realized—was now out in the open.[5] Gauthe was charged with sexually molesting thirty-seven boys and two girls. As part of a plea bargain he accepted his guilt and received a sentence of twenty years in prison. In addition, more than twenty-five civil suits were brought against the diocese of Lafayette, with millions of dollars paid out to the victims and their families.

But Gauthe's story was not over. He served less than half his sentence and got out to commit another offense. He moved to Texas, where he was arrested for fondling a three-year-old boy. He got probation in a deal that reduced the charge to a non-sex crime. Eight years later, when a journalist looked into Gauthe's case, he found that Gauthe was arrested for not registering as a sex offender.[6] He is now properly registered.

It turned out that Gauthe was no anomaly. Around the country, more victims were emboldened to come forward and accuse their abusers. The issue of sexual deviance and the clergy is no small problem. In this country, approximately 60 million people practice Catholicism, or about 26 percent of the population.[7]Assuming that each Catholic family has two children, approximately 30 million children are possible targets for priests with a predilection toward sex with kids.

In December 2007, the archdiocese of Los Angeles reached a $60 million settlement with forty-five victims whose claims dated as far back as the mid-1950s. More recently, fifteen trials involving 172 alleged victims were scheduled to be heard beginning July 2008 but a settlement was reached, with $660 million being split among the 508 people who claimed to have been abused by catholic priests in the Los Angeles area. However, this is just the end of a problem that started decades ago. Allegations of sexual abuse by Catholic priests go back as far as the 1950s. Between 1960 and 2002, there were approximately 94,000 priests in the Catholic Church; the total number of priests with known allegations of child sexual abuse over that time period is 4,127, which is slightly more than 4 percent of all of the priests in the Apostolate.[8] The majority of predatory priests were ordained between the 1950s and 1970s, and many showed a history of psychological and behavioral problems, discovered after they were ordained and serving the Catholic Church.[9] However, although the problem festered for years, it did not come to the forefront until the arrest and sentencing of Gilbert Gauthe.

COVER STORY

In 1962, Father John Geoghan graduated from the Cardinal O'Connell Seminary, with the goal of being a priest in the Catholic Church for the rest of his life. However, there is some question as to whether his secondary goal was to obtain access to young children. On being ordained, Geoghan's predatory behavior began when he became a priest at the Blessed Sacrament Church in Saugus, Massachusetts. After allegations that he was bringing young boys into his bedroom, Geoghan was transferred to St. Bernard's Church in Concord in 1966.[10] Though no allegations came to light at that point, Geoghan was transferred a year later, this time to Hingham's St. Paul's Church. Finally, in 1968, the father of a boy claimed that he caught Father Geoghan in the act of molesting his son. The diocese ordered Geoghan to undergo psychiatric treatment at Baltimore's Seton Institute, in the hopes of stopping his predatory behavior. Although they were aware of the numerous complaints against him, the Church made no attempt to report Geoghan's alleged sexual assaults to the authorities.

After completing his mandatory treatment, Geoghan returned to St. Paul's and continued to molest boys. Joanne Mueller, a mother of four boys in this parish, reported that Geoghan had abused each of them. To gain their trust, he took them out for ice cream, gave them baths, and read them bedtime stories, before sexually assaulting them and sending them home. This mother was understandably enraged, but rather than deal properly with the issue, the Church once again moved Geoghan. This time he went to St. Andrew's in Jamaica Plain. Serving this church throughout the 1970s, Geoghan acted like a model priest, paying attention to the parishioners who needed help, caring about the families' concerns, and saying the things that parishioners want to hear from their priest. However, closer observation revealed that he was lavishing attention on specific families—those with poor home lives, little fatherly guidance, or suffering from recent tragedies. In other words, boys that were vulnerable and who would allow a priest to spend time with them and get close to them.[11]

Geoghan was soon accused once again of sexual molesting boys—six of them—and all were members of the Doussard family. Geoghan reportedly admitted his transgressions to the Auxiliary Bishop Thomas Daily, who concluded that the abuse did occur, but that it was not a serious problem. Once again, Geoghan was required to undergo psychotherapy, being relieved of his duties as a priest until he was "cured" of his sexual predilections. After completing treatment once again, Geoghan was transferred to St. Brendan's in Dorchester, his fifth parish, allowing him to use the guise of religion to molest more children.

Between 1980 and 1989, several parents wrote letters to the Archbishop of the dioceses, accusing Geoghan of molestation and, in one case, the rape of a child. The Church assured the parents that the issues would be dealt with in an appropriate manner, but no one stopped Geoghan from continuing his behavior as a sexual predator. In one incident that allegedly took place in 1986, Father Geoghan paid a visit to twelve-year-old Patrick McSorley, whose father had recently committed suicide. In a veiled attempt at consoling the boy, the priest offered to take him out for ice cream. After they got into his car, the priest slid his hand down Patrick's shorts and started to fondle him. At the same time, Geoghan slid his other hand down his own pants, fondling himself as well. This incident was reported.

In another incident, a witness saw Geoghan put his hand down a boy's swim trunks at the pool, playing with the child's buttocks. On at least one other occasion, Geoghan was accused of forcibly raping a child, assaulting a fourteen-year-old boy in the changing room of the Boys and Girls Club. This was no surprise to Joanne Mueller, who stated that Geoghan orally and anally raped all four of her boys. The reports came across the archbishop's desk.

Finally, in 1989, Geoghan was ordered to check in to St. Luke's Institute, where doctors diagnosed him as a pedophile. He admitted to molesting several boys while serving as priest at St. Andrew's. Yet he was eventually "cured" and allowed to resume his duties as a priest. In 1991, he was appointed to his final parish, St. Julia's in Weston, where he continued molesting and raping children. One mother asserted that Geoghan molested each of her sons and made obscene phone calls to them. In 1995, Geoghan was forced to retire, but he still managed to molest a boy while attending the christening of the boy's older sister.

Eventually, the police were notified, resulting in charges. Geoghan was indicted for several counts of rape and molestation, found guilty, and sentenced to ten years in prison. In total, some 150 individuals have come forward to speak out against Father John Geoghan, claiming that they were either fondled or raped by the priest.[12] In prison, Geoghan was murdered by Joseph Druce, a white supremacist inmate serving life for killing a man who had made homosexual advances toward him.

What many people fail to realize is that, while this issue dies down in the press, it remains a painful trauma for the families who have suffered through it. Besides having to deal with the betrayal of trust and the psychological damage to their children, they must also grapple with faith that can be bruised or irreparably lost. It's difficult to accept that a priest could do these evil things to children, but it can be even harder to accept that the official stance of the Church itself is to create a cover story and just move the offender to a new place. Adding insult to injury, some of the families face ostracism from former friends and neighbors—even relatives—who believe they were morally wrong to humiliate a priest. Their stories have been told and retold in various public mediums, and yet the problem has continued to surface elsewhere.

DIFFERENT DESIRE, SAME STORY

From the time he became an ordained priest, Father James Porter was molesting children. Starting in 1953, before he entered the priesthood, Porter was accused of inappropriate behavior with a twelve-year-old boy at a church camp. Between 1956 and 1960, Porter molested several others there, which were either undetected or covered up. Once he was ordained in 1950, Porter was assigned to St. Mary's Church in North Attleboro, Massachusetts, where he took young children under his wing to offer them guidance. However, it was here that the complaints about his predatory behavior became a significant issue.

Porter was not subtle in how he went after children. As is common with serial rapists and child molesters, he began luring children back to his office as soon as he perceived that he had gained their trust. In one instance, he offered cake and soda to an unwitting victim, and asked the student for a massage, claiming he was sore from moving furniture. Then he made his move. In another incident, he invited a ten-year-old girl to his office to help him with the roster for the school's basketball team, and he fondled her. He continued to invite her and she continued to come, in a deviant relationship that went on for years.

With some children, Porter quickly graduated from fondling to rape and forcible sodomy. In one instance, he forced an eleven-year-old girl into the bathroom and sodomized her, keeping her quiet by claiming that he had "the power of God on his side." On field trips to his Rhode Island beach house, he would invite families to spend the weekend, and then take turns roaming from room to room, molesting and sodomizing children he found alone. Ultimately, he found various ways to rape his victims, employing both trust and force, whatever it took to get what he wanted.

During his time at St. Mary's, it is estimated that Porter molested and raped close to forty children. Complaints were registered, but the Church took no legal action. When his predatory behavior became a problem, they sent Porter to a hospital for electroshock therapy treatments, with the hope of curing him. The doctors who performed the procedure pronounced him cured, but within twenty-four hours of his release, Porter molested two more boys.

Porter received probationary assignments in Texas, New Mexico, and Minnesota, all of which allowed him to work with children. More complaints reached the ears of his superiors, but nothing more was done. Porter finally retired in 1974, got married and had four children. He might have quietly faded into anonymity but for a man who decided to make the person who had abused him pay for what he'd done. That abuser was James Porter.[13]

In 1990, Frank Fitzpatrick claimed that Porter had sexually abused him when he was a boy. He reported this to the state police, the FBI, and the media. Soon other victims came forward, with over 200 individuals accusing Porter of sexual molestation. The result was dozens of charges and lawsuits being filed. After a thorough investigation by the *Boston Globe*, it was determined that at least 130 victims had formally named Porter in allegations of sexual abuse. The former priest eventually pleaded guilty to forty-one counts of child molestation, and received a prison sentence of eighteen to twenty years. After being denied parole on several occasions, Porter died of cancer in a Massachusetts prison.[14]

The Archbishop of Boston, Cardinal Bernard Law, made a public statement to the effect that Porter was an aberration, and that the media was overgeneralizing from his case to other priests. However, he came under heavy criticism, both personally and as a representative of a church that had badly handled sexual predators in its ranks. A group of specialists on sexual abuse claimed they had met with Law in 1993, at his invitation, but he had dismissed the advice they gave him to instigate a zero-tolerance policy and to turn the cases over to civil authorities. Law did finally implement such a policy, but too late. The appearance was that Church officials were more interested in protecting priests than children. Archbishop Law resigned in 2002, and was given a post in Rome.[15]

At this point, more than 400 Catholic priests in North America have been accused of molesting children between 1984 and 1992.[16]

Unfortunately, that does not mean that there are only 400 victims; the patterns of the typical molester suggest that the average pedophile priest abuses numerous children, and in the most egregious instances, hundreds. The Catholic Church has paid out over $400 million in settlements, and the total is expected to reach $1 billion before all is said and done.[17]

WHAT MAKES THEM DO IT?

There are many theories as to why priests are prone to predatory crimes against children. Of course, the fact that it happens is troubling, but with 60 million Catholics in America, this problem deserves proper attention. To this point, it has been argued that the church has failed to understand the seriousness of the problem or the magnitude of the offending behavior.[18] The goal should be to figure out where the problem lies and address it with certainty and swiftness. However, there is some confusion as to why the problem exists.

Philip Jenkins, author of *Pedophiles and Priests*, states that priests may be nothing more than homosexual deviants who have been separated from society and placed into a situation that allows them to prey on children.[19] This theory is disturbing, because it makes the assumption that homosexuals go to seminary and become priests just so they can prey on young boys. It is true that Roman Catholic priests reportedly abuse mostly males. In fact, almost 80 percent of all of the allegations of abuse have been brought by males.[20] However, it would be unfair to make the connection between homosexuality and this form of sexual abuse. In fact, in a report on the problem of sexual abuse, researchers have stated that they don't place blame on the sexual orientation of Catholic priests, as there were many chaste priests who had not acted inappropriately in any way.[21] It is more appropriate to view predatory priests as pedophiles rather than homosexuals, with a different set of motivations and rationales. In either case, however, it would be a stretch to make the assumption that people would join the priesthood just to gain access to children.

A more likely theory is that the church is nothing more than a highly sophisticated bureaucracy, not unlike many governments, and that the nature of bureaucracy itself has allowed pedophile priests to continue their criminal behavior unchecked and unpunished. Most corporations and governments will act in their own best interests, and the Church is not any different. In some ways, this theory is more disturbing than the first, because it suggests that the Church is nothing more than a conglomerate that looks out for itself first, its people second. If this is true, the Catholic Church recognizes the level of depravity of these pedophile priests, and to protect itself, allows them to continue under the shroud of secrecy, similar to a company that turns a blind eye when its products cause harm. The Church knows that some of its priests are preying on children, but chooses to ignore it in the hopes that the problem will go away.

A third possibility is that the structure of the church itself creates pedophile priests. In a sense, the training that priests go through—the perpetuation of the notion that priests are above reproach and should not be questioned about any moral or ethical circumstance—may encourage certain priests to express their sexual craving inappropriately. Similar to learning traditions and behaviors from our parents and friends, it is possible that priests learn the traditions and behaviors of a sexually naïve lifestyle and become more prone to touching the boys with whom they are in close contact. A.W. Richard Sipe, an ordained Roman Catholic priest who has written on the crisis in the Catholic Church, argues that because of the limitations placed on how they are allowed to live their lives, as well as the seemingly unchecked freedom within their own parish, they do whatever they want with whomever they can.[22] For example, they take vows of celibacy, so any and all sexual activity is strictly forbidden. But this does not drain them of all desire. Coupled with the fact that they are surrounded by males who experience the passion of religious ceremony and belief, the argument can be made that the rules and regulations of the Catholic Church could create a sexual preference for boys. It is the result of circumstances, practices, and certain types of temperaments.

A fourth view, not wildly popular, is that Catholic priests are the product of a patriarchal value system, and boys are favored over girls.[23] We have seen throughout history that in patriarchal systems, the male has been the dominant figure in the family, in government, and in culture. In many cultures still, the father makes the rules and the wife and children are expected to be obedient and subservient. Similarly, Catholic priests are the dominant figures of the Church and some may come to believe they should be allowed to do whatever they want. Again, as the Church father of an extended congregational family, he makes the rules but does not necessarily have to follow them. In this sense, acting on his sexual predilection for young children might seem both allowable and acceptable to him. It's not difficult for the boss to convince himself whatever he does is permissible.

The best option is probably some combination of these theories, because as we discussed in Chapter 3, each case of sexual offense has its own variables. It's possible that someone might believe that the priesthood is a viable place to exercise his pedophilia, but there are easier ways to accomplish this. As well, few experts believe that the patriarchal make-up of the Catholic Church causes priests to become predators. To be sure, the Catholic Church has perpetuated and exacerbated the problem, by hiding the crimes and moving such offenders from parish to parish. Additionally, insisting on vows of celibacy, which many people think is a relic from the past, during an era of constant sexual focus, can place extreme pressure on self-control. Altar boys are accessible, while females are forbidden, and some people find their physical need overpowering their desire to be spiritual. Close contact during spiritual ceremonies can also ignite the wrong kind of flame.

One point of interest is the number of cases that have occurred in the Catholic Church compared to other religious denominations. The first obvious difference is the confusion between confidentiality and secrecy. Priests exploit the concept of confidentiality to protect admissions of guilt by parishioners and find it easy to carry this over to their own behavior. It is something that Catholics have come to understand as an advantage of the religion, and one that even the courts have ruled to be untouchable (except in cases of threatened violence).

However, there is a difference between confidentiality and secrecy. The stance of secrecy is often used to shield power, control, or manipulation. Confidentiality is merely keeping to oneself what someone else has said. The Church seems to conflate them to play off the ambiguity in order to rationalize their handling of the predator problem. In the case of sexually abusive priests, their behavior is not—and should not be—covered by the sanctity of confidentiality. In a sense, the Catholic Church has created its own definitions of confidentiality to hide abhorrent behavior. It's a peculiar way of practicing deception, especially since its primary victims are its own members.

12

Cyber-Predators

PREDATORS.NET

John Edward Robinson always believed he would be important. Full of himself, he was often in trouble. Despite his background as an Eagle Scout and wannabe priest, he initiated his criminal career with white-collar crimes before moving on to darker acts. After he learned how to use a computer during a prison stint, he developed ideas for how to lure vulnerable women online to become his sexual slaves. He had a knack for finding women who willingly walked right into his trap.

Serving time for another petty offense, Robinson seduced the prison librarian, Beverly Bonner, and when he was released in 1993, she left her husband for him. Then she disappeared—the fourth woman who knew him who had vanished in the past decade. He hadn't been charged in any of those cases, but he was racking up a few too many such associations. A mother and daughter also fell into his net, and Robinson fraudulently collected the daughter's disability checks to the tune of more than $150,000.

On the Internet, Robinson entered bondage-oriented chat rooms as "Slavemaster." This moniker proved powerful for women who wished to be dominated, and Robinson soon had them meeting him offline and signing sexual slave contracts that granted him total control. In 1997, he developed a relationship with a student at Purdue University named Izabela Lewicka, who was interested in exploring sadomasochism. At Robinson's invitation, she went to Kansas City, Missouri, and filed for a marriage license. Then she disappeared. Something similar happened to Suzette Trouten, but Trouten's family wanted a thorough investigation.

Thanks to their tips, the authorities put Robinson under surveillance. In April 2000, they had reason to arrest him when Vickie Neufeld, who had moved to Kansas City to pursue a relationship with Robinson, filed a complaint. The police finally had a case against Robinson for sexual assault, as well as for theft. Items in his possession linked him to the missing women, providing sufficient cause to have a computer expert examine his files and e-mail. At this time, computer forensics was a primitive field, but not many cyber-offenders were protecting their systems with the sophisticated processes available today. Certainly, Robinson was not.

Detectives learned that he owned storage units there in Missouri, as well as vacant property at La Cygne, Kansas. They took a team of cadaver dog handlers to La Cygne and the dogs led them to two eighty-five-gallon drums next to a pole barn. They were the right size for a body, and when police opened them, that's exactly what they found: the remains of Suzette Trouten and Izabela Lewicka. Three more barrels from Robinson's storage units back in Missouri were opened, yielding the remains of Beverly Bonner, Sheila Faith, and her daughter Debbie. That was five murders, and counting, with three more missing women.

A Kansas jury found Robinson guilty of the murders of three women and sentenced him to death. For the Missouri charges, to avoid the death penalty there, Robinson acknowledged that prosecutors had enough evidence for five murder charges in total, although he did not actually plead guilty. He was fifty-nine at the time, among the oldest serial predators ever convicted.[1]

Robinson is the first serial killer who utilized the anonymity and wide-ranging facility of the Internet to prowl for victims. His case brought attention to the dangers of meeting strangers offline, especially within the type of sexual context that Robinson proposed. It turned out that Robinson had covered his tracks by faking letters from the victims to their families, so at the time there was no clear way to prove that he was responsible for their disappearances. He's not the only predator to have found Web connections useful.

In 2009, a German man, "Christian G.," who had met over 150 women via online contacts went on trial for killing two of them. One murder, he said, was the result of uncontrollable rage. He stabbed the woman twenty-six times. The other one had been an accident in the midst of a heated argument.[2]

Craigslist, an online marketplace for goods and services, has been exploited by several murderers. In 2007, Katherine Olsen answered an ad for a nanny and walked right into the arms of her killer, who thought taking a life "would be funny." He was nineteen. A sexual encounter arranged through Craigslist ended the life of a radio reporter, stabbed fifty times, and a massage appointment trapped Julissa Brisman in a hotel room with a thief who shot her three times. The latter incident led to the arrest of a Boston

University medical student, Phillip Markoff, who was about to get married. This murder was linked to the armed robbery of another woman who had advertised masseuse services on Craigslist. Markoff, twenty-three, was traced by his e-mail contacts with the victims, from an address he appears to have created for his predatory activities. Physical evidence that implicates him was found in his apartment. He tried to hang himself in jail, and told his family to "Forget about me," alluding to more allegations that they would soon learn. Despite his charm and good looks, he had a dark side that his loving fiancée never saw. But his victims did.[3]

The Web, or cyberspace, is an information and communication highway that connects millions of homes and offices around the world, and offers numerous opportunities to meet people from all over the globe. Since it's easy for participants to present themselves in whatever way seems attractive, including sending false photos, cyberspace has become a playground for predators. They can be a friend, a potential spouse, a business connection, a client, even a fellow-deviant. People desperate for love or connection may accept whatever they're told and are often willing to meet strangers offline. Even if they're cautious at first, predators know how to win them over. Sometimes this results in conning them out of their money or property, sometimes in rape, sometimes in the initiation of stalking, and sometimes in murder.

Dr. Robert Lloyd-Goldstein describes the case of a man and woman who communicated on *America Online* and arranged a meeting. The man immediately raised the subject of marriage and children, which frightened the woman. She backed off, but he didn't. He sent e-mails, letters, and packages, and made numerous phone calls. When she still did not respond as he had planned, he became a cyber-bully, threatening to make details about her public online. Then he began to show up where she worked, insisting that he was the perfect man for her and that she was turning his love into something "dark." When he sent an e-mail telling her quite specifically how he had stalked her, she was able to get the intervention of law enforcement.[4]

California's first successful prosecution of cyberstalking involved a fifty-year-old man who had erotomanic delusions. A former security guard, he had used the Internet to punish a woman, twenty-eight, who had resisted his advances. He went into various chat rooms and impersonated her, putting out the message that she desired to be raped and offering her phone number and address. Men came to her door in the middle of the night to "fulfill her fantasy." The stalker was arrested and pleaded guilty in April 1999 to one count of stalking and three counts of soliciting sexual assault.

These victims were all adults who were accepting a certain amount of risk, but more worrisome are predators who seek out children. With the rise in popularity of social networking sites, it has been quite easy for predatory pedophiles to "befriend" their future victims. Children are especially vulnerable to a predator's encroachment, because they spend hours in chat rooms talking with strangers, tend to miss the signals of deception, and may be seeking what they believe will be an innocent adventure. Often they're unaware of the true danger. The most perilous areas are chat groups, message boards, and personal e-mail boxes; the most common forms of harassment online are threatening e-mails, sending a virus, and trespassing in live chats. Cyberstalkers can spread rumors, post false information, screw up a hard drive, send damaging e-mails to everyone on this target's contact list, or even lure someone into an offline encounter.

KIDS SEEKING FUN

Kids who utilize social networking Web sites, such as Myspace and FaceBook, seek a place of their own, where they can exercise self-expression and a certain amount of independence. Generally more savvy about computers than their parents, they can also explore things and talk with strangers in ways their parents might try to block. (In fact, about 50 percent of parents fail to even monitor what their children do online, and most have no clue about encryption tricks kids devise and pass around to hide information.) What these children fail to realize is that when they make their personal information freely available, they're as vulnerable in such places as mice to hawks—and often just as oblivious to the danger. Prowling among them are men, fueled by a strong craving, who mean to exploit them for self-gratification, and perhaps even to kidnap, harm, or kill them. Even seemingly safe places can attract this type of evil, and not just from adults. Some are teenagers.

Sexual predators looking for children are generally male, between thirteen and sixty-five. Many of the adults are married, although most are single, and they have been classified into four operational types:

1. Collectors—predators who start on "static" sites by collecting photos and pornography but who generally graduate to "dynamic" sites, i.e., real-time chat rooms, where they can meet potential victims and devise ways to entice them.
2. Travelers—these men are the most dangerous type and will go great distances to meet their prey (even to other countries) to get what they want, generally sending gifts and using other enticements to draw their targets into their nets. They are quite persistent as well as skilled and look for vulnerable, lonely children who crave attention. They can get a relationship going within two to four chats.

3. Manufacturers—they distribute pornography to others and sometimes partake themselves, but are mostly in it for the money; their danger lies in luring kids for films they might make, but most are merely distributors.
4. Chatters—they like to engage children in chat rooms and talk about sex but don't often graduate to meeting offline.[5]

At least 50 percent of kids go online every day, and many are watched or contacted by predators seeking a viable contact.[6] Most predators have a number of fetishes and paraphilias, so for some, almost any kid who responds with curiosity or interest will do.

For many kids, the appeal of online socializing is its anonymity and the opportunity to present a façade that might have little basis in reality. The Internet also provides a forum for kids to admit to things they don't want to say to people they personally know, especially their parents. For example, a child who believes she's a lesbian may not want to tell friends, but she can easily find someone online with whom to discuss her feelings (using a screen name, which allows her to "hide"). This kind of interaction can help kids figure out who they are and what they want to do about it. Unfortunately, it also gives predators informational bait for their hooks.

Detective Joe Pochron, involved with the Southeastern Pennsylvania Computer Crimes Task Force, conducts general investigations and pro-active examinations of identity theft, online chats, and peer-to-peer connections. For a community demonstration about identity theft, he went into MySpace and selected a random participant. Since her personal controls were not set for privacy, he was able to extract information that allowed him to go to public databases and retrieve her cell phone number, her home address, her previous address, where she went to school, where she worked, and who all of her family members were. "I got much more information from her MySpace site," Pochron said, "than she would ever want me to know. If I wanted to stalk her, I had what I needed."[7]

Cyber-offenders generally target multiple victims, and they're looking for kids who seem to have low self-esteem, family troubles, uncertainty about their sexuality, and other issues common to the transitions of adolescence. These predators will go where they are likely to encounter a large pool of kids and remain undetectable. Sometimes they will pose as adults who offer kids a "mentoring" relationship; other times they act like kids the same age as their contactee (although one study has found this occurs less often than media hype suggests). Online, predators can achieve a faster sense of intimacy than they can face-to-face, especially if they're self-conscious or unattractive, because they have more time to calculate and can use clever phrases to convince a kid they actually care. In other words, before they make their move, they study children to get the right phrasing so they can come across as an equal in the child's cadre of friends. They also develop a relationship prior to any visual interactions, which can establish a degree of trust that undermines basic gut instinct: kids who meet them already view them as friends or mentors.[8]

In June 2006, Katherine Lester ran off to the Middle East to meet a man who had contacted her on Myspace.com. Only sixteen at the time, she was on her way to Tel Aviv, Israel, to join twenty-year-old Abdullah Jimzawi when authorities intercepted her in Jordan. They sent her back home, where she faced a hearing in court. Judge Wallace Kent, Jr. ordered her to surrender her passport and go to counseling. The two had interacted online, falling in love and making plans, but Jimzawi wasn't thinking clearly; he still lived with his parents, was a high-school dropout, and had no job. But this story ended well for Lester and her family. Other young people have fallen prey to predators who had no intent to marry or otherwise assist them in life.[9]

Christina Long, thirteen, was an honor student, altar girl, and cheerleader in Danbury, Connecticut. She was also actively seeking adults with whom to have a sexual encounter, hiding her true password from her aunt, who had temporary custody. In late May 2002, Christina's aunt dropped her off at a mall, and the girl disappeared. A search of her home computer revealed that she had exchanged sexually explicit e-mails with "Hotes300," or Saul dos Reis, a married twenty-four-year-old Brazilian man from nearby Greenwich. They had initially met online, and had already met face-to-face a few times for sex. After dos Reis was arrested, he confessed to having sex with Christina, but insisted that he did not know she was underage. He said her heart gave out during rough sex, which involved asphyxiation, so to avoid a mess for himself he had dumped her body in a nearby ravine. He showed police the spot, and they found Christina face-up, lying in a stream. She had been strangled. Dos Reis received a thirty-year sentence for manslaughter.[10]

This fatal relationship began, according to dos Reis, as a simple Instant Message (IM) communication, wherein people can seek out others, real time, who share the same interests, and have quick and easy conversations: they're linked via the profiles they fill out with their personal information. This was not the first man with whom Christina had hooked up. Christina's aunt had warned her about strangers in chat rooms, but the girl had ignored her. Yet her aunt still believed she was safe because she was on her computer at home. "You don't realize that a computer predator is practically in the same room as your child," the aunt said.[11]

Christina is an example of a young girl who went willingly into a risky sexual relationship from an online contact; she was not duped or mislead. Not many parents want to believe this about their children, but the Internet allows kids of all ages much more access to sexually charged subjects, and more opportunities to talk about sex and explore what they want. In such cases, the adult is still the offender, no matter what the child does or wants, but with more children exploring sex through online resources, a greater onus lies with the parents to recognize what their child might be doing.

Investigators and psychologists who specialize in Internet predation offer a series of red flags for parents to be aware of, such as:

- gifts sent to a child from someone the parents do not know
- phone calls from unknown adults for the child
- a child who spends a lot of time online but doesn't say much about it
- a child who tries to hide what he or she is doing online
- a child who begins to behave differently, especially more aggressively

Although the laws governing cyberspace are just catching up to this problem, law enforcement has devised some ways to help protect kids. Many jurisdictions have devoted significant resources to special teams. One predator trolled the Web as "Dr. Evil," seeking young girls. He finally persuaded a child to meet him in Virginia. When he arrived, however, it was no thirteen-year-old he met, but agents from Operation Blue Ridge Thunder. Its members, like many other cyber crime units, spend hours in chat rooms looking for such pedophiles and posing as children or potential buyers of child pornography to trap them in an illegal act. In this case, they were successful. Such units have also cracked extensive international pornography rings.

Still, Internet predators are posing more challenges to public safety officials, because they remain a step ahead and they far outnumber law enforcement resources. They seem to hover and wait for anyone posting his or her age, then move right in. One agent who posed as a fourteen-year-old boy received a query within a couple of hours, asking if he was "really fourteen." Despite the many sting operations now in place, the bad guys have multiplied and become more savvy. In the past decade, arrests for underage soliciting have quadrupled to over 3,000 nationwide, but the agents still feel overwhelmed, as if they're trying to trap a dragon with a butterfly net. In 2008, the National Center for Missing and Exploited Children received more than 94,000 reports of predators in the cyberworld, most for child pornography, but about one-tenth were about online solicitations. Predators know that cops are overwhelmed, and the odds are in their favor.[12]

PREDATORY AGENDAS

Kids' online chats range from having someone to talk with about the topic of their choice to relieving loneliness. While this can be a healthy way to work through pressure and relieve frustration, as well as to exercise ideas they aren't brave enough to express with parents or in class, kids often freely agree to anything. They offer personal information, such as their age, address, and phone number, and they can easily be lured into talking about sex. Unmonitored sites attract more males than monitored sites, and warnings seem to have little effect.

Parents trying to protect kids may forbid them from talking with strangers in chat rooms, but the kids are no match for wily cons on the make. One study indicates that children below the age of twelve cannot quite grasp what it means that strangers circulate in this arena and may contact them. Their awareness of the potential peril is vague at best, and with the typical adolescent sense of invulnerability, they believe they can tell who's dangerous from who's not—but they can't.

Predators initiate the enticement process with "real time" conversations, often an IM posting. Because participants post profiles that list things about themselves, such as their gender, their favorite movies, their hobbies, and what they like to do for fun, this gives predators a way to introduce themselves. Kids may also include their photos or use webcams to show themselves in action. They may offer a cell phone number, which gives sophisticated predators a way to connect in and get all the information they need—as well as the ability to send text messages whenever they want and to listen in on private conversations. Through one child, they can find out plenty about others who may not even go online.

When sexual predators find what they seek, they hone in. If a child expresses conflicts with adults, depression, an experience of abuse, loneliness, or the need for love, that's all a predator needs to start manipulating. They offer emotional support and gradually work their way into inviting the child to meet them offline. They make certain the child keeps "the secret" and they use specific tactics to isolate the child from friends and family. Often they will send gifts, particularly webcams or paid phone cards, and they will do whatever they sense it takes to seem trustworthy to the child. It's the old "candy" ploy.

Detective Richard Peffall, from Pennsylvania's Montgomery County Major Crimes Unit, has been involved in a long-term sting operation that utilizes officers who look for these predators in teen chat rooms.

> The Internet predators of today are the same guys that we would catch standing outside of school yards thirty years ago when I started in police work. These criminals are the same sick deviate individuals that preyed on children in the past; the Internet has just created an entirely new avenue for them to find victims. With "travelers," the most common initial excuse we hear is, "I was just coming to warn them about how dangerous it is to meet

> strangers from the Internet." When asked to explain why they came with a pocketful of condoms, and when confronted with evidence of their chats, they quickly give in.[13]

In *Investigating Child Exploitation and Pornography,* attorney Monique Ferraro and forensic examiner Eoghan Casey discuss how the Internet has impacted every significant human endeavor, including how predators operate. They specifically focus on the online exploitation of children. The Internet, they state, has created a trade in child pornography that stays several steps ahead of law enforcement and legislative regulation. It has even encouraged communication among child molesters who might otherwise have remained solitary wolves. They pass around ideas and describe new opportunities, as well as support each other in criminal activity. The child porn networks have grown enormously, expanding internationally.[14]

To ensure their child's safety, parents must set up clear rules about Internet use and remain firm, engage in regular periods of monitoring, keep open communication with children, and discuss the reality of Internet dangers. There will still be enticements for children determined to defy their parents or try something "dangerous," but other kids, when educated, may be deterred.

The fact is, sexual aggression is a persistent crime, and cyber-predators have found a viable avenue for tapping vulnerable children. Travelers are determined to satisfy their needs, but they will avoid children who clearly are protected if easier targets are available.

MYSPACE/THEIRSPACE

One in five adolescents with a regular online presence report an encounter with a person they don't know who sexually solicits or harasses them. Of those, certain behaviors act like bait, and kids can thus make themselves unwitting victims. A team of researchers from Internet Solutions for Kids ran a study in 2005 in which they phoned kids nationwide between the ages of ten and seventeen. Most subjects were white and the pool was evenly split between male and female. When they posted their initial results, the team had nearly 1,500 kids in their sample population. They then did another survey with an equal number of participants, as well as talking with over 600 people in federal, state, and local law enforcement who dealt with these crimes. In this combined study, they found that there were five specific behaviors that stood out among those who had reported an encounter with a sexual predator:

1. Making contact with people in a wide variety of online venues
2. Talking specifically about sex with strangers

3. Allowing strangers to be part of their personal buddy list
4. Making rude comments online
5. Intentionally visiting x-rated sites

The above activities are erotic markers to sex offenders trolling for child victims. Often, the child participates in these behaviors while in the company of peers, and a high percentage of those experiencing unwanted sexual attention online reported having serious problems with parents, incidents of sexual abuse, and difficulty with bullies at school. They generally realize they're speaking with an adult, rather than being duped by an adult posing as a person of the same age, and they willingly meet new online "buddies" offline. Youth who engaged in at least four of these risky behaviors were most likely to become victims of sexual predators.[15]

In Pennsylvania, the Attorney General's Child Predator Unit arrested a sixty-two-year-old man who used Internet chat rooms to try to meet underage girls. He believed he was on his way to engage in sex with a thirteen-year-old when he was caught; he had flown all the way from Texas to consummate the deal. His approach had involved initially asking the "girl" about school and her friends, and then he told her he was looking for a young girlfriend. He offered to give her sexy lingerie and a digital camera, and told her he could teach her about sex. He asked her for the names of hotels in her area where they could meet and gave her his cell phone number. He then flew to Pittsburgh, rented a car, and set out to meet her, cautioning her to make sure no neighbors saw her leave home. He carried with him a laptop computer, digital camera, and a webcam. He had also purchased a birthday card for the girl.[16]

When the problem of these clandestine meetings between adult and child drew media attention, Sentinel Tech Holding Corporation, the leading online background verification company, entered into an agreement with MySpace in December 2006 to help identify registered sex offenders (RSO) who were listed as participants on the social-networking site. Sentinel estimated there were several thousand. When law enforcement officials learned about Sentinel's numbers, the attorneys general from eight states jointly sent a letter to MySpace. They insisted that allowing sex offenders onto MySpace placed them in proximity to children, a violation for many of them of the terms of their probation or parole. They demanded that MySpace provide the exact number of RSO profiles that Sentinel had collected and to describe their procedures for dealing with these criminals. They also contacted authorities from all fifty states to join them in applying pressure on MySapce to take protective action.

At first, News Corp, which owned MySpace, resisted because the attorneys had not pursued the proper legal channels via the Federal Electronics Communications Act. So, the attorneys acquired the necessary subpoenas. This time, MySpace complied. It turned out that Sentinel had removed the names and profiles of over 7,000 MySpace participants from the site after identifying them as RSOs or other types of violators. The list was turned over to the authorities, and presumably each state official sent the information to officials in local jurisdictions who could best decide if violations had occurred: Some sex offenders are prohibited from using the Internet for any purpose, while others may not contact children. The problem, however, is that this process of ferreting out sex offenders affects only those who have honestly registered with their actual information. Those who are determined to pursue their criminal goals will find ways around it. And some just get right back on until they're caught again.

On June 15, 2007, there were two significant announcements about online sexual predators. Texas Attorney General Greg Abbott told reporters that six convicted sex offenders were found to have violated parole by posting their profiles on MySpace. All six had been prohibited from using the Internet, and yet they'd ignored the rules. He presented Patrick Blevins as an example of why it's urgent to keep certain offenders from participating in social networking sites that attract kids. Blevins had been arrested for sexual offenses in two different states and had served eight years in prison. Instead of recognizing he had a problem, he was online trying to meet kids.

MySpace had turned over the data, facilitating police efforts. As part of the Cyber Crimes Units' efforts throughout Texas of protecting children from online predators, the six men were arrested and their profiles removed. It was the first crackdown in the country, and it's hoped that more states will be reporting similar enforcement. A seventh offender in Texas was also arrested, according to Computerworld.com, because he'd failed to register as a sex offender, as required by his parole terms.

The second announcement came from the United Kingdom. Home secretary John Reid offered the results of a study, "Review of the Protection of Children from Sex Offenders," that took into account what other countries have done about these offenders. The report proposes twenty specific measures that will strengthen efforts in Britain to keep the one in five recidivists away from children, including satellite tracking for high-risk offenders, compulsory polygraph tests, broadening the type of information required when offenders register, allowing the public to pro-actively request information about possible sex offenders, and stepping up community awareness campaigns. While the United Kingdom already has some of the strongest post-sentence restrictions on sex offenders, this plan will make those measures more stringent.

Ideally, authorities would like to see mandatory registration of sex offenders' e-mail address registrations. Reportedly, it would expedite the identification process and thwart sex offenders in at least some of their online movements. Thus far, this has not occurred nationwide.

A computer "edugame" being sent to schools may help to teach children about the dangers: *Missing* features a boy who establishes a relationship with a stranger online, and then goes missing. Players look for and offer clues to help find him, and in the process, they learn about how they could be vulnerable to such situations. Yet again, this aims at children who are not actively looking for sexual experiences; those who are will ignore it.

However, a behavior that appears to be gaining popularity is putting even more children at risk—"Sexting," or sending sexually explicit images of themselves via their cell phones. One study found that one in five teenagers are participants.[17] These images can be sent to others or posted on the Internet on sites such as YouTube. But some kids are tangling with child pornography laws. One high school senior in Vermont was arrested for allegedly forcing two girls to send videos of themselves performing solo sexual acts. They were willing accomplices, but they were underage, so it was a crime. If convicted, he faces having to register as a sex offender. His life will be ruined.

Kids tend to think of the Web as a way to be connected with people when they're not in the same room. They seem to lack any notion of how their information, photos, and videos can end up where they would never want them. But once the photos are posted or sent, they have no more control. The same is true of cell phone technology. They think it's private, like a land phone. However, predators can use software to tap into a cell phone and download images, listen in on conversations, and acquire a lot of personal information. In addition, despite being erased, the images remain in the memory.

The practice of posting sexually graphic images in public venues is a crime. These laws are aimed at child pornography rings, but they're catching kids all over the country as well. In January 2009, six boys in Massachusetts passed around a photo of a thirteen-year-old girl on their cell phones. She was partially nude. They were caught and sent to court on charges of distributing child pornography. Their ages ranged from twelve to fourteen.[18] Many jurisdictions are trying to come to terms with this activity among teenagers by adjusting the pornography laws for certain age groups, but even if kids are protected from arrest and prosecution, they're still vulnerable to techno-predators. Raising awareness is still the best idea.

13

Catching Lies

THE PREDATOR'S BEST TOOL

Bobby Joe Long developed a successful method for getting inside the homes of vulnerable women to rape them. He scanned papers for ads that listed items for sale. Then he made calls until he found the right situation. In particular, he was looking for mattresses and beds, because he could ask a homeowner to show him into the bedroom, to "try it out" before a purchase. Once he spotted an ad he liked, he would arrange to look at the item during the day, when husbands were unlikely to be home. In the event he was mistaken and a man was present, he could always decline to buy the item and walk away; nothing lost and no one the wiser. Besides looking at ads, Long also went up to houses that had "For Sale" signs outside and posed as an interested buyer. If he did this during the day, most often, a woman alone answered the door, or she had a child or two in the home. (Young girls were fine with him as well.) For his presentation, Long would shave, dress up in a suit, and act like a "nice young man," to disarm his potential victims. Already gregarious, he knew how to turn on the charm. He would describe the item in the ad, lie about why he wanted the item, and act as if he was prepared to make a purchase. They often let him in because he came across as trustworthy and respectable.

Long practiced this maneuver in a number of different neighborhoods in counties surrounding Ocala, Miami, and Fort Lauderdale. Once a woman closed the door behind them, Long would pull his knife. Then he would bind the victim and rape her (and possibly her daughter), often robbing the home as well. While he raped them, he made them talk to him. Most did not resist, but those who did received a punch in the stomach that showed he meant business. He would later claim that some had enjoyed it. In his narcissistic opinion, he was doing them a favor, because he figured they had miserable sex lives with their husbands. Getting away with this activity for years, Long believed he could have kept it up indefinitely. He got a kick out of seeing himself described in the newspapers as the Classified Ad Rapist or the Ad-man Rapist. Even when the police figured out his method of operation, they were unable to catch him. For Long, the challenge was thrilling, and it appears that he raped at least fifty women and girls, probably more.

However, this activity apparently grew less interesting to him, and he moved to the Tampa area and began to commit murder. He would pick up women alone in high-risk areas, focusing on exotic dancers, drug addicts, or prostitutes who needed a ride or who willingly got into cars for their occupation. He then bound them and beat them up before he killed them. Dumping most of the bodies along highways, he alerted law enforcement to the presence of a serial killer. Within a year, he was caught, and with solid evidence he was convicted in 1985 of nine murders.[1] Long was also suspected in a tenth murder.

The point is that this predator had figured out an easy way to deceive people into believing they could trust him. As a psychopath with no feeling for his victims and an interest only in himself, he lied easily and without remorse. Despite some claims that people can learn to "read" deception for self-protection, predatory con artists are usually several steps ahead. It takes both concentration and awareness of certain aspects of their manner to actually spot their cache of lies.

Long was caught, not because someone suspected him of a crime, but because he made a mistake and let a rape victim go. He had taken her in his car to his home, so she had a way to take the police to him. Under interrogation, he lied again and again. First he claimed to be innocent, but faced with physical evidence, he confessed. Then he said he had freed the survivor because he wanted to be stopped, but this time no one believed him.[2]

Sexual deviance is developed and practiced in secrecy, and people whose fantasies victimize others are usually skilled at hiding their intent and behavior. We even see cases in which a predator dupes other predators. It's much easier to spot these behaviors during interrogation than in normal life situations. Yet as difficult as it may be to recognize them, they give off signals through certain behaviors that betray either specific emotions or the attempt to control these emotions. This can help targeted victims spot the danger. People who understand how offenders "groom" potential victims (gain their trust and gradually seduce them) are better prepared.

There is no simple formula for catching a liar, not even for professionals with repeated exposure to deception. To make a mistake in one direction—to miss a lie—can be a matter of life or death, while to mistake the truth as a lie can result in injustice against another person. A popular notion holds that lying requires more effort than truth-telling, so it produces physiological signals, but this idea misleads: truthful but anxious people may also display these signals, while lying psychopaths may not.

The psychology of deception has been studied for over a century, starting in the first psychology labs in Germany, and it has been the subject of some of the earliest court cases involving forensic psychology. (A psychologist in one case claimed he could spot deception in a rape victim, but the jury did not believe him—and they were right. He had overestimated his ability.) The initial attempt to invent a machine that detected lies preceded what we now know as the polygraph, and there have been numerous methods for studying the manner and content of a suspect's statements. Although no one has yet devised a method or machine that offers a high degree of reliability, many scientists are working on it. There are no hard-and-fast rules, but the types of behaviors that can signal the discomfort or over-thinking that shows up in deception include:

- overgeneralizations, deflections, and increased vocal pitch
- speech hesitations and pauses, a lack of spontaneity
- an increase in number of shrugs, blinking, and nervous habits
- changes in the eye pupil
- venting the clothing
- feet pointed toward an exit
- blanching, flushing, sighing
- reduced use of hand gestures

These behaviors occur more often in those with motivation to deceive—possibly because they are trying to plan and control what they say. Some researchers think that liars take slightly longer to start answering questions, or show a rehearsed quality, as if they've already thought about what they might say when questioned. If they've planned well, they might actually jump in more quickly than a truth-teller, because they have their act in a nice package. Yet they're generally more negative and say less than truth-tellers. They'll also repeat phrases more often, and appear to be trying to manage the interviewer's perception of them.[3]

Researchers Granhag and Strömwell suggest that the accurate detection of deception should be separated from the skill of discriminating between truth and lies, and from the accuracy of detecting truth tellers. These skills are often confused, but they rely on different criteria. "One should acknowledge that a group of lie detectors can achieve high deception detection accuracy but poor truth detection accuracy."[4] They say that, with few exceptions, the accuracy rate of tested observers in over 250 studies falls between 45 and 60 percent—not an impressive number. Influencing factors in accuracy include preparation (knowing in advance the need for a lie versus lying on impulse), diverse mediums (audio versus video or face-to-face), mere observation or interaction, familiarity with the subject (the more the better), the subject's degree of motivation to lie, and the degree of generalizability from the research setting to a real situation.

MEASURING LIES

Certain psychological tests can pick up a specific type of deception: feigning a mental illness, or malingering. The Minnesota Multiphasic Personality Inventory (MMPI-2), which picks up "faking bad" and "faking good," and the Structured Interview of Reported Symptoms (SIRS) specifically detect malingering. However, these sessions require a clinical professional for administration and interpretation. They might be given to someone as part of a court-ordered assessment before trial.

The most common form of detection deception, used for witness statements and interrogation, is Statement Validity Analysis (SVA), or just Statement Analysis. SVA was developed in Germany to assess the credibility of statements that children made during accusations of sexual misconduct. It appears to be useful for other applications. Many detectives use a form of Statement Analysis, or semi-structured interview, for both witnesses and interrogatees. The investigator asks an open-ended question and leaves the subject to fill in all the blanks, usually in the form of a recorded oral or a written statement. The questioner refrains from exerting any influence or guidance. Because the subject picks both the starting and ending point, this method provides a better medium for psychological interpretation.

Statement analysis focuses on several things: what is said about events leading up to a crime, how the crime itself is described, and any statements made about the aftermath. Investigators watch for the distribution of detail in each area, and note whether subjects provide more information than requested or skip something crucial. Also, a change in tone or speed of delivery can reveal their comfort (or not) with what they're saying. Another clue is a change in language regarding another person, or sensitivity about some item, which might be apparent in a shift from first- to third-person. Information that is left out, about which investigators know the individual has some knowledge, is a good source for follow-up questions.[5]

A similar method, called Criteria-based Content Analysis (CBCA), examines how an incident is retold, comparing it against the typical truthful method of recall versus fabricating a supposed recollection. Psychologist Aldert Vrij of the University of Portsmouth, England, is among the leading figures in developing this method. Accordingly, analysts look for nineteen specific features of a narrative that seem truthful: coherent and consistent, but not strictly chronological; detailed, with superfluous elements; accurately reiterating dialogue and personal interactions; including feelings and theories about a perpetrator; self-deprecation, and spontaneous corrections. In truth-telling, people easily admit to memory gaps and wonder if they're recalling it correctly. Although useful, with an error rate of up to 30 percent, this method alone is unlikely to reveal a skillful liar, especially a pathological one who can easily add details.[6]

Reality Monitoring (RM) also examines verbal differences between truthful and deceptive statements. The assumption, which is not well-supported by memory research, is that describing the memory of an actual event differs in quality from describing a fabricated memory. (A common myth—shifting the eyes left or right during recall—is no indication of which type of tale is being told.) Memories of real experiences supposedly contain more perceptual details, as well as more cognitive operations and more context-specific details. Questioners look for clarity, affect, manner of story reconstruction, and realism. In studies, the accuracy rate is slightly under 70 percent.[7]

Computer software known as Linguistic Inquiry and Word Count (LIWC) analyzes written content, derived from the statement analysis approach, and looks for three markers: fewer first-person pronouns, more words that convey negative emotion, and fewer exclusionary words (e.g., except, but). The software has been more effective than human judges, but the accuracy rate is still only about 67 percent.[8]

Many investigators swear by the polygraph, a compact device that measures three or four key involuntary physiological responses to questioning: skin conductivity, abdominal and chest respiration, blood pressure, and heart rate. Some questions are designed to establish baseline responses, some are neutral, and others attempt to register "guilty knowledge," or at least a sense that the person knows something that confirms him or her as a suspect. Although practitioners vouch for its accuracy, and investigators rely on it to at least "spook" people into giving up information, it falls short as a sure thing. In research, skin conductivity increases when subjects see or think about information they're trying to conceal, but in such experiments, the stakes are low because there are no real consequences.[9]

The wave of the future for deception detection is brain research—measuring how the brain reacts to information. Psychiatrist Lawrence Farwell developed the Brain Fingerprinting process, based on the notion that the human brain stores all experiences. In that case, the electrical activity of a suspect's brain should indicate if he has a memory of a specific crime. His brain is monitored with sensors on a headband attached to a computer, while the subject is exposed to words or images that are both relevant ("probes") and irrelevant to the crime. Certain information would be meaningful only to the actual perpetrator and would include such items as what was done to a victim, where the victim was taken, items removed from the victim, and items left at a scene. The subject would not see this list until the test was performed. Irrelevant stimuli might include a different type of weapon than the actual weapon used, items in the landscape that were not there, a different modus operandi or location, or acts that were not performed during the commission of the crime.

Relevant items, or probes, are known only to the investigators, the test-maker, and the perpetrator. If the brain activity shows recognition of the probes, it will manifest as a distinct spike called a MERMER (memory and encoding related multifaceted electroencephalographic response). This means the subject has a record of the crime stored in his or her brain. Innocent people will display no such response to probes. If the suspect has offered an alibi, the brain fingerprinting device can check that as well.[10]

Farwell is not alone in devising a machine-based measuring system for the brain's response. At the University of Texas Southwestern Medical Center, fMRI scans are used to detect differences in neural activity between lying and truth-telling. In the experiments, participants perpetrated a "theft" of one of two items (either a ring or a watch) and were instructed to conceal this information from the researchers. Each was asked neutral questions while being scanned, as well as questions about minor wrongful deeds commonly committed. This way, the researchers could identify typical neurological patterns during truthful responses. Then each subject responded to questions in a way that was truthful about an object he or she did not steal, but was deceptive about the stolen object. The rate of accuracy for the fMRI was around 90 percent. Apparently, the trick lies in scanning brain regions that activate to suppress information and resolve internal conflicts; these regions are quiet when the person is telling the truth.[11]

Similarly, researchers at the Max Planck Institute for Human Cognitive and Brain Sciences in Leipzig, Germany, had subjects make decisions about adding or subtracting numbers before the numbers were shown on a computer screen. Bursts of activity in the prefrontal cortex—"thought signatures"—signaled what the results would be. Although the set-up is simplistic, more disturbing possibilities are on the horizon. Scientists might one day be able to tell, without consent, what a person is thinking or feeling—including the intent to deceive.[12]

It is clear that the frontal lobe activates when someone wishes to conceal information, as if additional brain resources are needed. However, whether these responses are exclusive to deception is not yet known. There is as yet no "one size fits all" signal in the neurocircuitry that a person is lying, but it does appear that brain scans are better at revealing "tells" than is watching someone fidget and sweat under questioning. Identifying the right combination of brain signals for a high rate of accuracy when a person lies or hides the truth is still in the future, but possibly not far away.

However, these methods all require that a subject be brought in and questioned, whether hooked up to a machine, writing out a statement, submitting to a written assessment, or taking a polygraph. The real skill for avoiding a predator lies in spotting lies or deception in a natural setting.

SEXUAL CONS

Raymond Fernandez had swindled more than 100 women who had placed lonely hearts ads during the 1940s. They were looking for husbands and he posed as an interested suitor, often moving in with them, having sex, and acting as if he intended to fulfill their every need. Then he would get control of their bank accounts, take the money, and run. Among his marks was Martha Beck, a grossly overweight woman. While Fernandez merely expected to scam her and depart, she had other plans. Sexually abused as a young girl, she had learned to fend for herself. She fell hard for Fernandez, and when he finally confessed how he supported himself, she wanted to team up with him.

Beck used her considerable libido and sexual prowess in kinky matters to keep his interest. She persuaded Raymond, who believed in black magic, that together they could not only enrich themselves, but also acquire sexual partners to satisfy their needs. During 1947 and 1948, with Beck posing as Fernandez's sister, they engaged in the fraud and deception of numerous trusting women.

However, Beck was a possessive lover and she did not want Fernandez to consummate his faux relationships. She had sex with one woman, herself, to thwart the developing affair. Yet Fernandez was a hopeless philanderer, so he ignored Beck's demands for fidelity. For him, these conquests proved his supernatural powers, and he was not about to give that up.

They murdered some of their victims, fatally bludgeoning one woman in Long Island, and shooting another in Michigan, as well as drowning her child. Arrested, they quickly confessed, and Fernandez admitted to seventeen murders. They were tried in a sensational proceeding in New York that included Beck's detailed descriptions for the press of her bizarre sexual practices with Fernandez. On August 18, 1949, they were both convicted of first-degree murder. Despite Beck's attempt to appear to have fallen under a con man's spell, they were executed on the same day in 1951. They were suspected in at least twenty deaths.[13]

Some researchers believe that certain people with high levels of emotional intelligence have a knack for spotting a liar: they can perceive certain signals that others cannot. In other words, they would not have fallen for Beck and Fernandez's ploys. Paul Ekman from the University of California, San Francisco, and Maureen O'Sullivan at the University of San Francisco claim that some people are "naturals," highly accurate at instinctively spotting a liar. When the stakes are high, such as with a violent crime or a threat assessment, they're even better at it, because they're more vigilant. Ekman has pioneered a technique called the Facial Action Coding System (FACS), which he is automating for law enforcement. He claims an accuracy rate of 90 percent, when combined with measurements for voice stress and speech factors. He believes the best cues are found in the voice and face for lies about feelings, and he locates the best "hot spots" in gestures and words when a person lies about beliefs and actions. Extremely slight gestures can "leak" emotional states that a person is trying to hide, providing a "tell" to a skilled and observant detector.[14]

Challenging the notion about naturals, Charles Bond, Jr. and Bella DePaulo ran a large-scale study and found that lie detection is not about the observer but the *observee.* A person's perceived credibility plays a strong role in whether someone judges him or her to be deceptive. That's not necessarily because these people are honest; it's because they comport themselves in a credible manner. Fernandez thought he had supernatural powers, but it was more likely that he had a smooth and credible style. People who seem credible appear to be honest right from the start, eliciting a gut instinct. They keep a steady gaze, have a round baby-face or charming smile, and they have learned how to work it to seem reassuring or innocent. Participants in the study more often believed liars with high credibility ratings than truth-tellers who were perceived as low in credibility. When Bond and DePaul evaluated numerous other studies about deception, they realized that no one had an innate advantage. There were no "naturals."[15]

"More than anything else," says psychologist Anna Salter, "it is disharmony that signals deception. When people are telling the truth, their hands, facial expression, voice pitch and words will be in harmony." When they're not, even if they're good at lying, something will be off about their timing—"a gesture that is out of synch with what they are saying."[16] However, when someone is posing as an authority figure, these small signals are easy to miss.

Some predators educate themselves on what law enforcement looks for. Timothy Krajcir, a sexually motivated serial rapist who also murdered nine women in three states, actually took courses in criminal justice to dupe both his victims and the cops. He was careful in his surveillance activities and looked for advantages. While he selected victims at random—within certain manageable parameters—he generally checked out the residence to make sure he could get inside without much trouble and that the targeted victim was unprotected. In one situation, Krajcir watched a home until the woman living there left, and then broke in. He cut the phone lines and lay on her bed, waiting for her to return. However, she came home with company, so Krajcir exited without notice. He apparently knew or assumed she had reported the break-in, because he came back a week later, posing with a fake badge as a police officer who was there to "further investigate." She let him in. He took the opportunity to bind, rape, and strangle her.[17]

PLAYING TO THEIR STRENGTH

Sometimes predators are just fortunate, resembling the clean-cut stereotype of health, goodness, and innocence, which they can easily exploit. Because they're attractive or look sweet, people naturally believe them. Paul Bernardo, an aggressive serial rapist in Toronto, and Karla Homolka, his wife and partner in crime, were dubbed "Ken and Barbie" for their blonde good looks and sweet appearance. They seemed to friends and family to be the perfect couple, and even their 1991 wedding was straight from a fairy tale. But their crimes were among the darkest in Canadian history.

Karla was confident, educated, and involved with her loving family. When she was seventeen, she took up with twenty-three-year-old Paul Bernardo, a sexual sadist. Rather than being frightened of him, she encouraged him to do whatever he wanted with her. By Karla's account, when Bernardo demanded to have sex with her fifteen-year-old sister, Tammy, she made all the preparations for the Christmas of 1990. Together they got Tammy drunk, and then raped her. However, she died in the process, so they called for an ambulance and quickly invented a cover story of her "accidental" death. Within a month, Karla was pretending to be Tammy, so Paul could reenact the interrupted seduction.

After they were married a few months later, Paul raped and killed fourteen-year-old Leslie Mahaffy, who was found dismembered, her parts placed into seven blocks of concrete before they were submerged in a lake. Then another schoolgirl, Kristen French, disappeared. She was seen being forced into a car in the middle of the day while walking home from school. Two people were in the car. Then weeks later she was found murdered, her long brown hair hacked off. It turned out that Karla had lured her toward the car because, as she later put it, Paul liked young girls and that way she could keep him happy. Before killing her, they kept Kristin captive for a few days for their pleasure.

As the police closed in, Karla saw the chance to save herself, so she lied about Paul forcing her to cooperate with the rape/murders. There were incriminating videotapes of both murdered girls forced to have sex, and Bernardo was charged with forty-two criminal counts. For her cooperation and a plea of guilty to two counts of manslaughter, Karla was sentenced to only two twelve-year terms, to be served concurrently. She was released in 2005.

Although little research has been done on the remorseless female who uses a man to act out her own violence, that Karla could kill her sister and then continue to participate in more rapes and murders with her sister's co-killer indicates a deviant personality. On videotape, she told Paul that she wanted to get many more young virgins for him. He had not scripted her to say this; it was spontaneous. Karla clearly had her own ideas about how to sadistically torment innocent victims (she has claimed in interviews that she was entirely under Bernardo's influence).[18]

Whether or not there are "naturals" who can spot a groomer, a con artist, or another type of sexual predator, there are plenty of other potential victims who can be easily duped. One skill to learn and teach children is to resist stereotypes; another is to stay alert, watch everything, and respond appropriately when a situation feels wrong. Predators have advantages, but if they suspect a challenge, they may well move on.

When all is said and done, potential victims of predators can only do so much to deflect assault or defend themselves. Social institutions such as law enforcement, the judicial system, and forensic psychiatry and psychology must assist to predict, treat, and contain these offenders. We look next at the efforts so far.

14

Society's Response to the Sexual Predator

HISTORICAL OVERVIEW

Within the past fifteen years, the criminal justice system has enacted a number of significant sexual predator laws to safeguard against violent sexual crimes. For years, law enforcement officials and legislators alike have recognized that the sexual predator is a danger to society, based both on the nature of his criminal acts and the likelihood that he will reoffend, regardless of rehabilitative or legislative efforts. But the concept of a sexual predator is not recent. In the United States, in fact, there have been three distinct periods of intense sexual predator legislation.

The first of these began in the early 1930s, lasting about two decades.[1] Sexual predator legislation followed a series of brutal murders of children that appeared to be sexually motivated, such as those of Albert Fish. J. Edgar Hoover, the head of the FBI at the time, took a harsh stance against sex crimes, making this issue a top priority. He recognized that these types of predatory crimes were more damaging than your standard street crime because of the long-term harm done to children.[2]

One major development of this time period—the first of its kind in this country—was the introduction of sexual psychopathy laws. These laws treated the sexual predator as an individual who has a disease, similar to that of an alcoholic or drug addict. Thus, by this definition, a sexual psychopath was neither criminally nor legally insane. In fact, the common belief was that the offender knew exactly what he was doing. Nevertheless, because of his predilection, and for the best interests of society, he required special considerations.[3]

Criminologists and psychiatrists who studied the sexual psychopath decided that he suffered from emotional instability or behavioral impulsiveness, and a failure to fully appreciate the consequences of his acts. In a sense, the professions involved with the assessment of crime believed the sexual psychopath had little to no self-control; it was not that the offender was unwilling to change, but that he was unable to recognize that his actions were damaging to his victims. He should thus be treated for his condition, not just thrown into prison—exactly as Dr. Fredric Wertham stated about Albert Fish.[4]

Since sexual fetishes, paraphilias, and the desire to commit predatory sexual crimes were considered mental disorders, sexual psychopathy laws were designed to offer treatment in a hospital setting, which allowed for the offender's release, when cured. For the first time, there was professional agreement about how to deal with the sexual predator. Members of both the law enforcement community and the field of criminal psychiatry supported the creation of sexual psychopathy laws, albeit for different reasons. Law enforcement officials were content to get the offenders off the streets and away from the general public. Psychiatrists were pleased with the fact that individuals would not simply be dumped into a prison setting without regard for their mental stability, but that they would be given appropriate psychiatric treatment in a state hospital. The belief was that these individuals could be cured, and putting them under psychiatric care was considered the best course of action.[5]

During this period, psychiatrists played a key role in defining sex crimes and advocating for the way the laws were developed and worded. In a sense, rehabilitation took precedence over punishment. Although it was understood that these offenders had committed crimes punishable by the courts, psychiatrists believed treatment was in everyone's best interest, including society. District Attorneys, policy groups, law enforcement officials, and law and order interest groups pushed for the enactment of psychopathy laws, believing it would result in safer communities.

However, several states eventually repealed their psychopathy laws. Although they seemed like a good idea at the time, over the years it remained unclear whether the treatment had any appreciable effect. Fewer people were convinced that the ideas that had influenced the laws were valid.[6] The fact is that most offenders did not change their behavior after receiving "treatment." Further, there was a real question as to whether sexual psychopathy could even be successfully diagnosed, making the application of the laws entirely subjective.[7] Finally, the idea that sexual predators were receiving rehabilitation did not sit well with the public. If treatment did not have the desired effect for society, they wanted these sex offenders punished.

As it became increasingly clear that the treatment was a failure, public opinion began to shift in support of longer prison terms instead of treatment in a hospital.[8]

The second time period dealing with sexual predators, both socially and legislatively, was during the 1970s, when women's interest groups took the leadership role in legislative activity. To this point in history, women had been considered second-class citizens, subservient to men, with few rights and little respect for their ability to solve social problems. In marriage, women were often seen as chattel, or the property of their husbands. In fact, marital and spousal rape was not even possible; a woman was required to have sex with her husband whenever he was interested. However, during the early part of the 1970s, women gained a stronger collective voice, and legislation soon followed, protecting them as equal citizens.[9]

With this new social status came organizations that examined the need to evaluate the problem of sexual predators. Women's groups raised awareness and ignited social action. With a forum of greater openness, victims of sexual assault came forward to describe their experiences of being raped or molested, as well as to disclose childhood sexual abuse. The pressure was on to become more proactive, so legislatures in all fifty states made significant changes.[10] A widespread issue once ignored had now become a serious focus of law enforcement and legislators alike. Their concentration shifted from stranger attacks to intimate relations and family settings, as it became apparent that the danger was not the creepy man jumping from the bushes to attack, but the husband, father, or relative that a woman might have known for years. Such crimes were difficult to detect unless a victim chose to reveal them, and were difficult for the victim to survive without psychological damage. The response to this emerging issue spread across many disciplines.

One response was to develop treatment-based sentencing alternatives, which encouraged victims to cooperate with the law enforcement system without destroying the relationships they had with the offenders. Although it was still difficult for women to report a sexual assault at the hands of a relative or friend, the goal was to treat the offender so that this type of behavior did not happen again. The ultimate goal of the rehabilitative effort was to reduce sex offender recidivism rates, yet the treatment plans largely failed.[11]

The third period of interest started in 1990 and has continued to the present day. Although spanning almost twenty years, it is evident that the goal has shifted from rehabilitating to offender to protecting the citizenry.[12] In 1990, the Community Protection Act was passed in Washington, DC. Unlike the second wave of sexual predator legislation and reforms, the Community Protection Act did not address the most common forms of sexual assault, including intrafamilial abuse and date rape, because it seemed that prior legislation had adequately done so. Instead, this focus was now on heinous sex crimes involving injury or death. Thus, it was once again about the sexual predator, the psychopath. However, the sexual predator legislation from the 1950s had failed, so a new plan of attack was necessary. The criminal sentences remained in place, but in society's interest there would be an added feature.

In the case of an offender who might be prone to reoffend, there was a way to keep him locked up. The Community Protection Act authorized prosecutors to initiate a civil rather than criminal procedure. For those sexual offenders who had at least one prior conviction for sexual violence and who suffered from a mental abnormality or personality disorder that made them likely to reoffend, prosecutors could seek an indefinite period of treatment and confinement. In essence, the offender would serve a sentence for committing a criminal act, but he might then be brought up on civil charges, with the state acting as the injured party.[13] To gain support, legislators argued that the difficulty lay not in punishing the criminal but in supervising sex offenders, post-sentence, who had served their time. Civil commitment allowed the state to detain the offender for a second sentence under the guise of protection of society, and to offer some level of rehabilitation that the offender may not have received in prison. Ultimately, the goal was safety for society via alternatives to conventional confinement. In 1994, the Supreme Court ruled on this concept, creating a landmark case for the civil commitment of sexual predators.

WHAT TO DO

In 1994, Kansas enacted the Sexually Violent Predator Act (SVPA), which established procedures for civil commitment of the mentally abnormal or those with personality disorders who are likely to engage in predatory sex acts. The Act established civil commitment for sexually violent predators who have completed their prison sentences, but who were still seen as a danger to society. The goal was to keep the most violent of sexual predators locked away from the community.[14]

The enactment was the result of a case heard by the U. S. Supreme Court in 1994. The state of Kansas had committed Leroy Hendricks, an inmate with a history of molesting children. He was scheduled to be released from prison shortly after the SVPA became a law.[15] Although risk assessment was not a sophisticated skill, in Hendricks' case there seemed to be little question, with his record, that he was the type of offender for which the SVPA had been created. Hendricks had agreed that he suffered from pedophilia, that he had an unnatural drive to assault and molest children, and that prison had not cured him of his desire to molest and rape. Moreover, he'd freely admitted that he could not control his sexual urges when he was under stress, and believed that he was likely to reoffend if and when an opportunity arose.

Based on his statements in court, as well as the stipulations of the SVPA, Kansas state officials decided to continue Hendricks' incarceration, arguing that his pedophilia qualified as a "mental abnormality" as defined by the Act, and ordered him to be civilly committed. He was considered incurable, so that releasing him from prison was a guarantee that he would reoffend and thus he posed a danger to the community. The state argued that they had a duty to protect the citizens, and recommitting Hendricks was the safest way to do that.

In the context of this case, it was argued that sexually violent predators have anti-social personality features that are not amenable to existing treatment programs. Unlike drug offenders, such sex offenders will reoffend when given the opportunity. The question is not *whether* they will, but *how soon*. The creators of the Act argued that sex offender recidivism rates were higher than those for other criminal activities, and that the SVPA would be a useful tool in controlling this type of predatory crime. However, this notion proved to be controversial. Not everyone saw the implicit value of the Act as it was intended, and it appeared that the offender's rights were being violated. Since the 1970s, civil liberties attorneys anxious to protect the rights of all citizens had kept an eye on involuntary commitments.

On appeal, in which Hendricks claimed that a certification of mental illness alone was too arbitrary to support an order of civil commitment, the Kansas Supreme Court invalidated the Act, stating that the definition of "mental abnormality" did not satisfy substantive due process requirements of involuntary civil commitment based on the "mental illness" requirement. In essence, the Act was a violation of the defendant's due process rights, because it deemed "mental abnormality" to be the measuring stick by which we judged the sex offender, rather than the more stringent requirement of "mental illness." The court's argument was that, under the Act, an individual deemed to be mentally ill can be civilly committed, but an individual deemed to have only a mental abnormality does not qualify. Committing Hendricks constituted double jeopardy.[16]

However, in a five-to-four majority vote, the U.S. Supreme Court reversed this decision, holding that the Act met substantive due process standards because it required considerable evidence of past sexual violence and a present mental inclination to repeat it. This court did not view psychiatric institutions as de facto prisons. The Act also required the release of those offenders who show mental stability, so it did not violate double jeopardy standards. The legislature was free to define its own notion of a medical condition. More specifically, the legislature was not required to use the specific term "mental illness."[17]

One question that did arise, particularly among defense attorneys and public defenders, was the notion that the SVPA was nothing more than the government's desire to charge a criminal with the same crime more than once. Although conservatives argued that the SVPA was an attempt to keep safe society's children, civil rights activists argued that the offender had served a complete prison sentence, and that putting him back in prison for a second term was tantamount to double jeopardy. However, the U.S. Supreme Court found that the Act did not violate the double jeopardy clause of the Constitution, arguing that the SVPA was an allowable use of the state's civil rights.

Yet this landmark decision does not come without obstacles. Problems arise when definitions of the State do not match those of the medical community, particularly when defining terms such as "insanity" or "abnormal." Psychiatric facilities were not keen to become the dumping ground of sexually violent offenders, especially when there was no clear treatment that could cure them. This issue arose again in another Kansas case.

On January 22, 2002, in *Kansas v. Crane*, the Court issued an additional requirement. Michael Crane was about to end his four-year stint in prison for sexual assault. Since he had a long history of arrests, some of which involved sexual assault, and since he was not exposed to therapy specific to his problems while in prison, he was eligible for consideration for commitment. He was diagnosed with exhibitionism and antisocial personality disorder, so during a commitment procedure under the SVPA, a jury agreed that he should be further confined.

Crane appealed to the Kansas Supreme Court, which reversed the decision, because the state did not introduce evidence that Crane was unable to control his behavior. Then the U.S. Supreme Court reversed the Kansas high court and used the case to clarify its guidelines for *Kansas v. Hendricks.*[18] In essence, the state did not have to show a complete lack of control over sexual behavior, but the state did have to show evidence of an abnormality that made it difficult for the offender to maintain self-control. This could include volitional, emotional, or cognitive impairment, but in no case did the inability to exercise self-control have to be considered absolute.[19]

The American Psychiatric Association publicly disagreed with this decision, stating that psychiatric hospitals are for the truly mentally ill. They were also not keen to have people outside the psychiatric community, such as judges and lay juries, making commitment decisions. Attorneys and mental health experts have long pointed out that even people who work daily with sex offenders cannot tell who may repeat their crimes. Yet rehabilitation practitioners argued that sex offenders are like any other offender: with proper treatment, their desires can be curbed.[20] Practitioners offering cognitive-behavioral therapy argue that recidivism is not destined, and that keeping a watchful eye on an offender in a community setting should be the first avenue pursued.

Further, there is some issue of the government utilizing prior convictions as evidence for reincarceration. Their argument is that an individual's offense pattern should be considered, as it will show what the individual is prone to do in the future. On the other hand, defense attorneys argue that using an offender's prior conviction is prejudicial, and a practice that we should not encourage. They argue that an individual should be adjudicated based only on the crime for which he is currently on trial.

Regardless, the civil commitment of a sexually violent predator has been instituted in many states throughout the country, with the goal of protecting children at the forefront. Although questions arise as to the constitutionality and validity of such governmental actions, particularly when considering an individual's civil rights, this type of legislation receives overwhelming community support.

As of 2008, twenty states and the federal government have passed sexual predator laws, but they vary in terms of wording and requirements. In Missouri, for example, the Repeat Sex Offender Statute creates a life sentence for any individual found guilty of being a sexual predator.[21] In California, the Mandatory Castration Bill was enacted in 1996, allowing judges to choose castration as a sentence for individuals found guilty of committing predatory acts. Society believes that castration is the perfect punishment for the sexual predator, because it takes away the ability of the offender to rape in the future. In fact, the public, generally, favors punishment that represents retribution or revenge for a serious criminal act. However, there is a real question as to whether mandatory castration is an effective solution to the problem. In addition, in the case of innocent men erroneously found guilty, this type of punishment is irreversible.[22]

Although our Constitution does not explicitly state it, the courts have implied that we, as members of society, have a right to procreation. In this sense, castrating an individual is depriving an individual of that right. Even though this is not a concern to the majority of the public, some would argue that this is a right that cannot, under any circumstances, be revoked, and that a less-permanent punishment should be available. With this in mind, Depo-Provera, an inhibitor of sex drive, could be utilized as an alternative punishment, allowing for the chemical castration of the offender. (Recall that Connecticut serial killer Michael Ross said that Depo-Provera treatments had considerably reduced his blinding sex drive.) In either case, the ultimate problem is the assumption that rape, sexual assault, and every other sexually predatory act are, in essence, sexually-driven. Researchers have argued consistently that sex is not the reason for these heinous acts,[23] and that castration, chemical or otherwise, will not reduce the number of sexual predators in our society.

Some offenders just want to be free, so they agree to treatment programs, offering researchers a population for learning what does and does not work. *Milwaukee Magazine* featured the story of Randy Kellner, a man once sexually abused on a weekly basis by his stepfather. Afterward, he'd be locked into a closet, where he'd fantasize about violence against his abuser. By the age of fourteen, Kellner had become a child abuser himself, and he in turn locked some of his victims into trunks. He was caught as an adolescent and received therapy, but he continued to abuse children. He'd been placed into programs where he was constantly confronted, and that didn't work; he simply withdrew into a fantasy life that included abusing other boys. In other words, when disempowered, he sought his secret source of power internally.

In 1989, Kellner was arrested for molesting a thirteen-year-old. He received an eight-year prison sentence. As he came up for release, the state of Wisconsin petitioned to have Kellner civilly committed as a sexually violent person. In May 1994, Governor Tommy Thomson signed Chapter 980 into law for Sexually Violent Persons Commitment. The Wisconsin Supreme Court ruled that this procedure was constitutional. The state had only to prove the presence of a mental disorder and the "substantial probability" of reoffending.

During his civil commitment, Kellner went through a treatment plan that was abandoned after two years when it failed. His case remains open, with no clarity about how well he might ever do on the outside. For Kellner, similar to many offenders in his position, other options have been weighed: chemical castration, freedom with electronic monitoring for life, phone monitoring and a Department of Corrections escort for any trips he made, along with random visitations by officials. He might have to take polygraphs and remain in therapy, and he would not be allowed to own a computer. One more sex crime would get him a life sentence. In terms of community notification, the police might send out a press release or hold a community meeting; Kellner might also be taken door-to-door so residents will recognize him, and information about him would be placed on a public Web site. He remains in treatment, but his future is in limbo.[24]

OFFENDER REGISTRATION AND COMMUNITY RIGHTS

One way that society has taken to protecting their children is to be fully informed about where the offenders reside. Sex offender registration and notification legislation aims toward this goal. The idea behind this type of legislation is that if parents are aware that a sexual predator lives among them, they can take steps to warn and protect their children. Although this notion of notifying the public that a sex offender has moved into the neighborhood is a proactive step in reducing sex offenses, registration and notification laws are not new. In fact, the original initiative was created in the 1930s. Ostensibly the laws were intended to keep citizens informed that a sex offender had moved in to the area; however, it seems more likely that they were created to drive out the "undesirables," giving residents the opportunity to "cleanse" their space and preserve property values.[25]

The first state law requiring sex offender registration was passed in California in 1944, a natural progression from the sexual psychopathy laws of the late 1930s. The hope was that recidivism rates could be reduced if offenders could be monitored, at least where they lived. Almost half a century later, in 1990, Washington became the first state to require community notification.[26]

In 1994, community notification became known as Megan's Law, named for a little girl who was killed in New Jersey. Megan Kanka, a seven-year-old, was raped and murdered by a two-time child molester who, unbeknownst to her parents, lived in her neighborhood.[27] New Jersey passed a law in 1994 requiring sex offenders to register with local police, and other states quickly followed. Although the state of Washington had the first such regulations in 1990, it was not until after Megan Kanka's brutal assault that national attention was focused on the issue of sexual predators living among families. In 1996, President Clinton signed a nationwide Megan's Law that allowed each state to establish its own criteria for disclosure, but compelled all of them to make information on registered sex offenders available to the public.

While Megan's Law has been the subject of many legal challenges, these laws have withstood lawsuits and political pressure from activists who believe they encroach on constitutional rights. The courts have essentially argued that a sex offender does not have a constitutional right to privacy, and that the value of protection to society outweighs an offender's civil liberties; notification of an individual's residence is nothing more than letting people know that a dangerous predator lives in their neighborhood, a service the courts feel they can dutifully allow. President Clinton argued that "we have taken decisive steps to help families protect their children, especially from sex offenders, people who, according to study after study, are likely to commit their crime again and again. . . ."[28]

There are three types of notification laws available to states. The first allows for the *broad and complete dissemination* of all relevant information, including the individual's place of residence and level of offense. In these states, law enforcement officials notify the public of those who pose a risk of re-offending. This notification is done in any number of ways, including posting the information on the Internet, the most likely of methods. However, the distribution of CD-ROM packages, reports on the local news, and articles in local newspapers are other ways of disseminating this information.

The second type allows for dissemination *only for the purpose of protecting* an individual or a vulnerable organization from a specific offender. In this case, law enforcement officials determine who is at risk, and who needs this type of information. Organizations that qualify under this type of notification are those that are responsible for the welfare of children on a daily basis. These can include elementary schools, child care facilities, and any other organization that cares for children.

Finally, the third type of notification allows for access through the local police department, but only after proof of necessity. In this instance, maintenance of all sex offender registration records is done by the local police department within the jurisdiction. In order for the information to be released to an individual, there must be a valid purpose for the dissemination. In states such as Colorado and North Dakota, a requester is allowed to view the registration records for a specific jurisdiction only after demonstrating a need to know such information. Individual babysitters or nanny services would qualify under this level of notification; they may not be registered as a day care facility, but their responsibility for a number of children on a daily basis would qualify them to have access to such information.[29]

Besides state mandates and legislation, the federal government has also attempted to control recidivism by passing its own registration laws. The Jacob Wetterling Act was enacted in 1994, and was the first federal law requiring all states to adopt a sex offender registration system. This federal Act was named after Jacob Wetterling, an eleven-year-old boy whom a masked offender abducted at gunpoint. In addition to requiring all states to adopt a registration system, the Act requires offenders to verify their addresses annually for ten years, and sexually violent predators to verify their addresses quarterly for life.

Two years later, in 1996, the federal government passed the Pam Lychner Sexual Offender Tracking and Identification Act. This Act directs the FBI to establish a national database of sex offenders to assist law enforcement in tracking offenders when they move in or out of state.

Finally, the Adam Walsh Act, named for a boy kidnapped and murdered in Florida in 1981, organizes sexual predators into three tiers; Tier 3 offenders are considered the most dangerous, and are required to update their whereabouts every three months, with lifetime registration requirements; Tier 2 offenders are required to update their whereabouts every six months and must remain registered for twenty-five years; and Tier 1 offenders must update their whereabouts every year, and are required to be registered for fifteen years. In addition, the Act created a national sex offender registry that requires that each state apply identical criteria for posting offender data on the Internet.[30]

SOCIAL POLICY

There are several policy implications from all this legislation. First, in analyzing the idea of civil commitment, a jury decides on an offender's recommitment, not a judge. This procedure seems, on its face, to be prejudicial. The fact is that no individual, if informed that a sexual predator who could recidivate was going to be released into the community, would elect to free the offender. Allowing him out of prison when recommitment is an option is simply unimaginable.

The second concern, and one that more people would question, is the issue of double jeopardy, which means a person is charged twice for the same crime, or, in this case, a second imprisonment without due process. Yet in the case of a civil commitment, a second crime has not been committed. The sexual predator is being reincarcerated because the likelihood of reoffending is great, not because a second offense was committed. Legislators argue that the second sentence is for rehabilitation, but we can imagine that simple fear could have some influence. Perhaps a better alternative is to begin treatment the first day of incarceration. If prison is not the best place, then changing the setting to make it conducive to treatment should be an alternative.

Third, the presumed constitutional right to privacy is at odds with the concept of community notification. Some people believe that community notification extends the court-imposed sentence, placing the offender in the crosshairs of angry citizens. Laws will not help to rehabilitate, which should be the primary goal for anyone allowed back into the community. In fact, community notification can create a false sense of security for parents. In a sense, community notification may be the wrong way to go about protecting the citizenry.

Community notification appears to punish offenders twice, forcing them into a different kind of prison sentence in a neighborhood full of vigilant people. It's not easy to live under constant surveillance and ostracism. Society's desire for retribution has not changed much in the past seventy-five years.

The problem of sexual predators, whether rapists, molesters, stalkers, or murderers, is both serious and complicated: although we don't yet have definitive answers about curing them, many professionals are diligently working on the problem. We can only hope that future efforts will provide relief and safety for communities and effective support for offenders.

Notes

CHAPTER 1

1. "Serial Pedophile Jailed for Life," *BBC News*, August 30, 2007.

2. Stephen T. Holmes and Ronald M. Holmes, *Sex Crimes: Patterns and Behaviors*, 3rd ed. (Los Angeles: Sage, 2009), 63–94.

3. Eric Hickey, "Female Sex Offenders," www.predators.tv. Retrieved May 10, 2009.

4. Anul Aggrawal, *Forensic and Medico-legal Aspects of Sexual Crimes and Unusual Sexual Practices* (Sarasota, FL: CRC Press, 2009), 369–382.

5. J. Reid Meloy, *Violent Attachments* (Northvale, NJ: Jason Aronson, 1992).

6. Emmanuella Grinberg, "Braunstein's Defense Highlights Lack of Rape Evidence in Halloween Attack," CourtTV.com. May 7, 2007; "Braunstein Sentenced to 18 Years to Life," CourtTV.com, June 19, 2007.

7. Ann Rule, *The Lust Killer* (New York: New American Library, 1982).

8. Fredric Wertham, *The Show of Violence* (New York: Doubleday & Co., 1949), 84–85.

9. Accounts in the *New York Times*, June 5, 1928 – January 17, 1936; Harold Schechter, *Deranged: The Shocking True Story of America's Most Fiendish Killer* (New York: Pocket, 1990).

CHAPTER 2

1. "Connecticut Serial Killer Put to Death," CNN.com, May 13, 2005; Martha Elliott, "Michael Ross: Why a Killer Offers to Die," *The Connecticut Law Tribune*, April 29, 1996; Christopher Berry-Dee, *Talking with Serial Killers* (London: John Blake, 2003), 117–158.

2. Sigmund Freud, "On Narcissism: An Introduction," *The Standard Edition of the Complete Psychological Works of Sigmund Freud*, Vol. XIV (1914–1916) (London: Hogarth Press, 1955), 67–102.

3. Alexander Lowen, *Narcissism: Denial of the True Self* (New York: Collier, 1985), 1–24.

4. *Diagnostic and Statistical Manual of Mental Disorders*, IV-TR (Washington, DC: American Psychiatric Association, 1994).

5. W. J. Livesley, K. L. Jang, D. N. Jackson, and P. A. Vernon. "Genetic and Environmental Contributions to Dimensions of Personality Disorder," *American Journal of Psychiatry*, 150, 1826–1831.

6. Robert R. Hazelwood and Stephen G. Michaud, *Dark Dreams: Sexual Violence, Homicide, and the Criminal Mind* (New York: St. Martin's Press, 2001).

7. Carol Vogel, "A Field Guide to Narcissism," *Psychology Today*, January/February 2006.

8. Ann Rule, *The Stranger beside Me* (New York: W. W. Norton, 1980); Stephen Michaud and Hugh Aynesworth, *The Only Living Witness: A True Account of Homicidal Insanity* (New York: New American Library, 1983).

9. Robert Hare, *Without Conscience: The Disturbing World of the Psychopaths among Us* (New York: Pocket, 1993), ix.

10. Robert Rieber, *Psychopaths in Everyday Life* (New York: Psyche-Logo Press, 2004), 82–90.

CHAPTER 3

1. Katherine Ramsland, *Beating the Devil's Game: A History of Forensic Science and Criminal Investigation* (New York: Berkley Publishing Group, 2007), 249.

2. Paula Doneman, *Things a Killer Would Know: The True Story of Leonard Fraser* (Australia: Allen and Unwin, 2006).

3. Gregory Crow with Kevin Osborn and Ralph Earle, *Lonely All the Time: Recognizing, Understanding, and Overcoming Sex Addiction, for Addicts and Co-Dependants* (New York: Simon & Schuster, 1998).

4. Judith Lewis Herman, "Sex Offenders: A Feminist Perspective," in *Handbook of Sexual Assault*, William Lamont Marshall, D.R. Laws, and Howard E. Barberee, eds. (New York: Plenum Press, 1990), 177–193.

5. Helen Singer Kaplan, *The Sexual Desire Disorders: Dysfunctional Regulation of Sexual Motivation* (New York: Brunner/Mazel, Inc., 1995).

6. Stacey L. Shipley and Bruce A. Arrigo, "Serial Killers and Serial Rapists: Preliminary Comparison of Violence Typologies," in *Serial Murder and the Psychology of Violent Crimes*, Richard N. Kocsis, ed. (Totowa, NJ: Humana Press, 2008), 119–139.

7. Bruce A. Arrigo, *Criminal Behavior: A Systems Approach* (Upper Saddle River, NJ: Prentice Hall, 2006).

8. George B. Palermo, *The Faces of Violence*, 2nd ed. (Springfield, IL: Charles C Thomas, 2004).

9. Robert Simon, *Bad Men Do What Good Men Dream: A Forensic Psychiatrist Illuminates the Darker Side of Human Behavior* (Washington, DC: American Psychiatric Press, 1996), 308–309.

10. Stephen Giannangelo, *The Psychopathology of Murder: A Theory of Violence* (Westport, CT: Praeger, 1996), 39.

11. Steven Johnson, *Mind Wide Open: Your Brain and the Neuroscience of Everyday Life* (New York: Scribner, 2004).

12. Katherine Ramsland, *The Human Predator: A Historical Chronicle of Serial Murder and Forensic Investigation* (New York: Berkley, 2005), 282–283.

13. *R v Dupas*, Supreme Court of Victoria, VSC 281, August 16, 2004.

14. Ibid., 3.

15. Ibid., 5.

16. M.J. MacCullough, P. R. Snowden, P. J. Wood, and H. E. Mills, "Sadistic Fantasy, Sadistic Behavior and Offending," *British Journal of Psychiatry* 143 (July 1983): 20–29.

17. Ann Rule, *The Lust Killer* (New York: New American Library, 1983).

18. Vernon Geberth, *Sex-Related Homicides and Death Investigation* (Boca Raton, FL: CRC Press, 2005), 434–457.

19. Louis B. Schlesinger and Eugene Revitch, "Sexual Dynamics in Homicide and Assault," in *Sexual Dynamics of Anti-Social Behavior*, 2nd ed., Louis B. Schlesinger and Eugene Revitch, eds. (Springfield, IL: Charles C Thomas, 1997): 203–223.

20. Robert R. Hazelwood and Janet I. Warren, "The Serial Rapist," in *Practical Aspects of Rape Investigation: A Multidisciplinary Approach*, 3rd ed., Robert R. Hazelwood and Ann Wolbert Burgess, eds. (Boca Raton, FL: CRC Press): 435–462.

21. Robert R. Hazelwood and Janet I. Warren, "The Relevance of Fantasy in Serial Sexual Crime Investigations," in *Practical Aspects of Rape Investigation: A Multidisciplinary Approach*, 3rd ed., Robert R. Hazelwood and Ann Wolbert Burgess, eds. (Boca Raton, FL: CRC Press): 83–95.

22. Vernon J. Geberth and Ronald N. Turco, "Antisocial Personality Disorder, Sexual Sadism, Malignant Narcissism, and Serial Murder," *Journal of Forensic Sciences* 42 (1997): 49–60.

23. Martin P. Kafka, "Sexual Offending and Sexual Appetite: The Clinical and Theoretical Relevance of Hypersexual Desire," *International Journal of Offender Therapy and Comparative Criminology* 47 (2003): 439–451.

24. Eric Hickey, *Sex Crimes and Paraphilia* (Upper Saddle River, NJ: Prentice Hall, 2005).

CHAPTER 4

1. "Sex Offender Who Posed as Child Pleads Guilty," *USA Today*, September 10, 2008, http://www.usatoday.com/news/nation/2008-09-10-sexoffender-school_N.htm (accessed April 1, 2009).

2. Sharon Araji and David Finkelhor, "Abusers: A Review of the Research," in *A Sourcebook on Child Sexual Abuse*, David Finkelhor, ed., with Sharon Araji, Larry Baron, Angela Browne, Stephanie Doyle Peters, and Gail Elisabeth Wyatt (Beverly Hills, CA: Sage, 1986): 89–118.

3. J. M. W. Bradford, "The Antiandrogen and Hormonal Treatment of Sex Offenders," in *Handbook of Sexual Assault*, William Lamont Marshall, D. R. Laws, and Howard E. Barberee, eds. (New York: Plenum Press, 1990), 297–310.

4. John Larson, "The Worst Predator: The Horrifying, True Story of the Man Police Believe Is the Worst Sexual Predator of Our Time—and How He Kept Getting Away with It," *Dateline NBC*, http://www.msnbc.msn.com/id/14306094/ (accessed April 3, 2009).

5. Ibid.

6. Jordan Robertson, "Schwartzmiller Sentenced to 150 years for Child Molestation," *San Francisco Chronicle*, January 29, 2007, http://www.sfgate.com/cgi-bin/article.cgi?f=/n/a/2007/01/29/state/n095125S58.DTL (accessed May 25, 2009).

7. Jim Christie, "Police Say Man Kept 36,000-Entry Journal of Molesting Children," *The Washington Post*, June 18, 2005.

8. Diana Walsh, "Serial Molester Schwartzmiller Gets 152 Years to Life," *San Francisco Chronicle*, January 29, 2007, http://www.sfgate.com/cgi-bin/article.cgi?f=/c/a/2007/01/29/BAGD0NR00H6.DTL (accessed May 26, 2009).

9. Peter Davidson, *Death by Cannibal: Criminals with an Appetite for Murder* (New York: Berkeley Publishing Group, 2006).

10. Carey Goldberg, "System Stands Accused in a Montana Man's Case," *The New York Times*, January 23, 2001.

11. Ann Wolcott Burgess, A. Nicholas Groth, Linda Lytle Holstrom, and Suzanne M. Sgroi, *Sexual Assault of Children and Adolescents* (Lexington, MA: D.C. Heath, 1978).

12. Stephen T. Holmes and Ronald M. Holmes, *Sex Crimes* (Newbury Park, CA: Sage Publications, 1991).

13. Reuben A. Lang and Roy R. Frenzel, "How Sex Offenders Lure Children," *Annals of Sex Research* 1 (1988): 303–317.

14. Alan Gustafson, "Parole Denied in 1980s Abuse Case," *Statesman Journal*, March 5, 2009, http://ww.statemanjournal.com (accessed April 2, 2009).

15. Araji and Finkelhor, "Abusers: A Review of the Research."

16. Eric Leberg, *Understanding Child Molesters: Taking Charge* (Thousand Oaks, CA: Sage Publications, 1997).

17. Dennis Howitt, *Paedophiles and Sexual Offences against Children* (New York: Wiley, 1995).

18. Judy N. Lam, "Child Sexual Abuse," in *Violence in Intimate Relationships: Examining Sociological and Psychological Issues*, Nicky Jackson and Gisele Oates, eds. (Woburn, MA: Butterworth-Heinemann, 1998), 25–56.

19. P. Gilmartin, *Rape, Incest, and Child Sexual Abuse: Consequences and Recovery* (New York: Garland Publishing, 1994).

20. Associated Press, "Fritzl Gets Life in Austria Incest Case," *MSNBC*, March 19, 2009, http://www.msnbc.msn.com/id/29772776/ (accessed May 25, 2009).

21. Linda Lowen, "The Wife Who Knew Nothing—the Josef Fritzl Incest and Imprisonment Case," March 16, 2009, http://womensissues.about.com/b/2009/03/16/the-wife-who-knew-nothing-the-josef-friztl-incest-and-imprisonment-case.htm (accessed April 6, 2009).

22. Blair Justice and Rita Justice, *Broken Taboo: Sex in the Family* (New York: Human Sciences Press, 1979).

23. Ibid.

24. Bryce Marshal and Paul Williams, *Zero at the Bone* (New York: Pocket, 1991).

25. Monte Francis, *By Their Father's Hand* (New York: Harper, 2007).

26. Terry S. Trepper and Dawn Nieder, "Family Characteristics of Intact Sexually Abusing Families: An Exploratory Study," *Journal of Child Sexual Abuse* 5 (1996): 1–18.

CHAPTER 5

1. Bruce Grierson, "The Hound of the Data Points," *Popular Science*, March 21, 2003.

2. A. Nicholas Groth, *Men Who Rape: The Psychology of the Offender* (New York: Plenum, 1979).

3. Julia R. Schwendinger and Herman Schwendinger, *Rape and Inequality* (Thousand Oaks, CA: Sage Publications, 1983).

4. Barry R. Burkhart and Mary Ellen Fromuth, "The Psychology and Social Psychology of Sexual Coercion," in *Sexual Coercion: Its Nature, Causes and Prevention*, Elizabeth Grauerholz and Mary Koralewski, eds. (Lexington, MA: Lexington Books, D.C. Heath and Co., 1991).

5. Ibid.

6. Randy Thornhill and Craig T. Palmer, *Rape: A Natural History of Biological Bases of Sexual Coercion* (Cambridge, MA: The MIT Press, 2000).

7. Dennis J. Stevens, *Inside the Mind of a Serial Rapist* (San Francisco, CA: Austin & Winfield Publishers, 1999).

8. Ibid., 94.

9. Lee Ellis, *Theories of Rape: Inquiries into the Causes of Sexual Aggression* (Levittown, PA: Hemisphere Publishing Corporation, 1989).

10. Sigmund Freud, *The Ego and the Id* (New York: W.W. Norton & Company, 1923).

11. Groth, *Men Who Rape*.

12. Eugene Kanin, "Male Sex Aggression and Three Psychiatric Hypotheses," *Journal of Sex Research* 1(1965): 227–229.

13. "Police: Level 3 Sex Offender Molests Boy at Library," *The Boston Channel.com*, February 1, 2008, http://www.thebostonchannel.com/news/15185914/detail.html (accessed May 26, 2009).

14. Milton Valencia, "New Bedford Library Rapist Sentenced to Life in Prison," *Boston Globe*, April 2, 2009, http://www.boston.com/news/local/breaking_news/2009/04/new_bedford_lib.html (accessed May 26, 2009).

15. "Authorities Slam Release of Accused Despite Rough Childhood," *New Bedford Standard Times*, February 2, 2008, http://www.instituteforlegalreform.org/component/ilr_news/30/article/I2688233905.html (accessed May 26, 2009).

16. Associated Press, "Freed Child Rapist Allegedly Attacks Boy in Mass.," *KDKA.com*, February 1, 2008, http://kdka.com/national/corey.saunders.rape.2.643563.html (accessed May 1, 2009).

17. Cara McCoy, "Girl, 11, Testifies in Trial of Accused Rapist," *Las Vegas Sun*, February 23, 2009, http://www.lasvegassun.com/news/2009/feb/23/girl-testifies-trial-accused-rapist (accessed May 1, 2009).

18. H. Vanderbilt, "Incest: A Chilling Report," *Lear's Magazine*, February, 1992, 49–77.

19. Suzanne M. Sgroi, "Stages of Recovery for Adult Survivors of Child Sexual Abuse," in *Vulnerable Populations: Sexual Abuse Treatment for Children, Adult Survivors, Offenders, and Persons with Mental Retardation, Volume 2*, Suzanne M. Sgroi, ed. (Lexington, MA: Lexington Books, 1989), 111–130.

20. Sandy Lane and Pablo Zamora, "A Method for Treating the Adolescent Offender," in *Violent Juvenile Offenders*, Robert A. Mathias, Paul Demuro, and Richard S. Allinson, eds. (San Francisco, CA: National Council on Crime and Delinquency, 1984).

21. Sandy Lane, "The Sexual Abuse Cycle," in *Juvenile Sexual Offending: Causes, Consequences, and Correction*, Gail Ryan and Sandy Lane, eds. (San Francisco, CA: Jossey-Bass, 1997), 77–121.

22. Ibid., 98.

23. Eugene Kanin, "Male Aggression in Dating-Courtship Relationships," *American Journal of Sociology* 63 (1957): 197–204.

24. Albert Bandura, *Social Foundations of Thought and Action: A Social Cognitive Theory* (Englewood Cliffs, NJ: Prentice Hall, 1986).

25. Edwin Sutherland, *Principles of Criminology* (New York: J. B. Lippincott, 1934).

26. Stevi Jackson, "The Social Context of Rape: Sexual Scripts and Motivation," in *Rape and Society: Readings on the Problem of Sexual Assault,* Patricia Searles and Ronald J. Berger, eds. (Boulder, CO: Westview, 1998), 16–26.

27. William L. Marshall and Howard E. Barberee, "An Integrated Theory of the Etiology of Sexual Offending," in *Handbook of Sexual Assault: Issues, Theories and Treatment of the Offender*, William L. Marshall, D.L. Laws, and Howard E. Barberee, eds. (New York: Plenum Press, 1990), 257–275.

28. Peggy Reeves Sanday, *Fraternity Gang Rape: Sex, Brotherhood, and Privilege on Campus* (New York: NYU Press, 1990).

29. Walter S. DeKeseredy, *Four Variations of Family Violence: A Report Prepared for the Family Violence Prevention Division, Health Canada* (Ottawa, Canada: National Clearinghouse on Family Violence, 1993).

30. Sanday, *Fraternity Gang Rape*, 124–125.
31. Ibid., 138.
32. Carol Bohmer and Andrea Parrot, *Sexual Assault on Campus: The Problem and the Solution* (New York: Lexington Books, 1993).

CHAPTER 6

1. Lori Monsewicz, "Busted: Scuba Diving Pervert Wanted to Drown Young Girls," CDNN, Cyber Diver News Network, July 26, 2007; Andrea Zaferes and Walt Hendrick, "Homicidal Drownings—What First Responders Do," *Fire Rescue News*, Sept. 12, 2007.
2. Stephen Holmes and Ronald Holmes, *Sex Crimes: Patterns and Behaviors*, 3rd ed. (Los Angeles: Sage, 2009), 209–212.
3. Debra Niehoff, *The Biology of Violence* (New York: The Free Press, 1999), 31–53.
4. Michael Newton, *The Rope* (New York: Pocket, 1998).
5. David Buss, *The Murderer Next Door* (New York: Penguin, 2005), 7–9.
6. R. A. Prentky, A. Burgess, F. Rolous, et al., "The Presumptive Role of Fantasy in Serial Sexual Homicide," *American Journal of Psychiatry*, 146, 1989, 887–891.
7. David K. Frasier, *Murder Cases of the Twentieth Century* (Jefferson, NC: McFarland, 1996), 254–256.
8. Robert Ressler, *Whoever Fights Monsters* (New York: St. Martin's Press, 1992), 114–127.
9. Mark Pettit, *A Need to Kill* (New York: Ivy, 1990).
10. Ressler, *Whoever Fights Monsters*, 125.
11. Ibid., 98.
12. Joubert v. Hoskins. 94–3687/94–3849, District Court of Nebraska, January 25, 1996.
13. Louis Schlesinger, "The Potential Sex Murderer: Ominous Signs, Risk Assessment," *Journal of Threat Assessment*, 1(1), 2001: 50.
14. Mark Safarik, John Jarvis, and Kathleen Nussbaum, "Sexual Homicide of Elderly Females: Linking Offender Characteristics to Victim Crime Scene Attributes," *Journal of Interpersonal Violence*, 17(5), May 2002: 500–525.
15. Carol Anne Davis, *Women Who Kill* (London: Allison & Busby, 2001), 22–27, 192; Katherine Ramsland, *Inside the Minds of Serial Killers* (Westport, CT: Praeger, 2006), 159; "Women Killed to Assure Love, One Testifies," *Detroit Free Press*, September 14, 1989.
16. Julia Hislop, *Female Sex Offenders* (Ravensdale, WA: Issues Press, 2001), 219.
17. Brian Masters, *She Must Have Known: The Trial of Rosemary West* (London: Transworld Publishers, 1996); Howard Sounes, *Fred and Rose: The Full Story of Fred and Rose West and the Gloucester House of Horrors* (London: Warner, 1995); Carol Anne Davis, *Women Who Kill* 125–148.

CHAPTER 7

1. "Dutroux Found Guilty in Sex Crimes Case," *BBC News*, June 17, 2004; Craig Smith, "Belgian Gets Life for Raping and Murdering Girls," *New York Times*, June 23, 2004.

2. Numbers derived from author's research.

3. Jaye Slade Fletcher, *Deadly Thrills* (New York: Onyx, 1995).

4. Eric Hickey, *Serial Killers and Their Victims*, 3rd ed. (Belmont, CA: Wadsworth, 2001), 193.

5. Jack Olsen, *The Man with the Candy: The Story of the Houston Mass Murders* (New York: Simon & Schuster, 2001).

6. Hickey, *Serial Killers and Their Victims*, 204–208.

7. Ibid., 198.

8. Vernon Geberth, *Practical Homicide Investigation*, 4th ed. (Sarasota, FL: CRC Press, 2007), 478.

9. Lisa Shaffer and Julie Penn, "A Comprehensive Classification System," in *Sex Crimes and Paraphilia*, Eric Hickey, ed. (Upper Saddle River, NJ: Pearson, 2006), 77.

10. Jim Fielder, *Slow Death* (New York: Pinnacle, 2003); John Glatt, *Cries in the Desert* (New York: St. Martin's Press, 2002).

11. Interview with the authors.

12. R. Hazelwood, "Sexual Sadists: Their Wives and Girlfriends," in *Practical Aspects of Rape Investigation*, 3rd ed., Robert R. Hazelwood and Ann Burgess, eds. (Boca Raton, FL: CRC Press, 2001), 481–483.

13. Thomas Moore, *Dark Eros: The Imagination of Sadism* (Dallas, TX: Spring 1990), 24.

14. Louise Farr, *The Sunset Murders* (New York: Pocket, 1992).

15. Bruce Gibney, *The Beauty Queen Killer* (New York: Pinnacle, 1984).

16. Dee L. R. Graham and Edna Rawlings, "Bonding with Abusive Dating Partners: Dynamics of Stockholm Syndrome." *Dating Violence, Young Women in Danger*, Barrie Levy, ed. (Berkeley, CA: Seal Press, 1998), 119–135.

CHAPTER 8

1. Mark Bourie, *By Reason of Insanity: The David Michael Krueger Story* (Toronto: Hounslow, 1997).

2. Tatiana Pina, "Lynch Seeks to Try Teen Charged with Child Rape as Adult," *The Providence Journal*, July 4, 2008, http://www.projo.com/ri/woonsocket/content/WOONSOCKET_BABY4_07-04-08_E9AOFKM_v40.3bee594.html (accessed April 22, 2009).

3. Sharon Strauss, "Idaho Supreme Court: Reizenstein Will Be Tried as Adult," *Idaho Press-Tribune*, April 8, 2009, http://www.idahopress.com/?2009-04-08-Supreme-Court-Reizenstein-will-be-tried-as-adult (accessed April 22, 2009).

4. Lawrence A. Greenfeld, *Sex Offenses and Offenders: An Analysis of Data on Rape and Sexual Assault* (BJS Publication No. NCJ-163392). Washington, DC: U.S. Department of Justice, 1997.

5. Sarah W. Craun and Poco D. Kernsmith, "Juvenile Offenders and Sex Offender Registries: Examining the Data behind the Debate," *Federal Probation* 70 (3), December 2006. http://www.uscourts.gov/fedprob/December_2006/juvenile.html (accessed April 22, 2009).

6. Frank R. Ascione, Roger B. Graves, D. Kim Openshaw, and Susan L. Erickson, "Demographic and Parental Characteristics of Youthful Sexual Offenders," *International Journal of Offender Therapy & Comparative Criminology* 40 (December 1996): 300–317.

7. Protect-the-Kids.org., "Angel Story 3," http://www.angelfire.com/nj4/savethechildren/COD3.htm (accessed April 20, 2009).

8. The Reporters Committee for Freedom of the Press, "Newspaper's Quest for Juvenile Records Changes State Access Law," *The News Media & the Law*, August 1, 2001, http://www.rcfp.org/newsitems/index.php?i=5812&fmt=print (accessed April 20, 2009).

9. Gail Ryan, "Sexually Abusive Youth: Defining the Population," in *Juvenile Sexual Offending*, Gail Ryan and Sandy Lane, eds. (New York: Jossey-Bass, 1997), 3–9.

10. Ibid.

11. Ibid.

12. Gail Ryan, "Concurrent Psychiatric Disorders" (paper presented at the Annual Conference of the National Adolescent Perpetrator Network, Lake Tahoe, NV, 1993).

13. Gail Ryan, Thomas J. Miyoshi, Jeffrey L. Metzner, Richard D. Krugman, George E. Fryer, "Trends in a National Sample of Sexually Abusive Youths," *Journal of the American Academy of Child and Adolescent Psychiatry* 35 (January 1996): 17–25.

14. Craun and Kernsmith, "Juvenile Offenders and Sex Offender Registries."

15. Malcolm Weatherup, "Boy's Rape Attacks on Disabled Girl," December 14, 2002, http://sci.rutgers.edu/forum/showthread.php?t=9466 (accessed April 22, 2009).

16. Rebecca Leung, "Why Did Eric Kill?," December 10, 2004, http://www.cbsnews.com/stories/2004/12/10/48hours/main660314.shtml?cmp=EM8707 (accessed April 20, 2009).

17. Ibid.

18. Gail Ryan, "The Families of Sexually Abusive Youth," in *Juvenile Sexual Offending*, Gail Ryan and Sandy Lane, eds. (New York: Jossey-Bass, 1997), 136–154.

19. Ibid.

20. Ryan, "Concurrent Psychiatric Disorders".

21. Ibid.

22. B.F. Skinner, *Verbal Behavior* (Copley Publishing Group, 1954).

23. Michael R. Gottfredson and Travis Hirschi, *A General Theory of Crime* (Stanford: Stanford University Press, 1990).

CHAPTER 9

1. Louis Schlesinger, "Homicidal Celebrity Stalkers: Dangerous Obsessions with Nonpolitical Figures," in *Stalking, Threatening, and Attacking Public Figures*, J. Reid Meloy, Lorraine Sheridan, and Jens Hoffmann, eds. (New York: Oxford University Press, 2008), 86.

2. N. Kennedy, M. Donough, B. Kelly, and G. E. Berrio, "Erotomania Revisisted: Clinical Course and Treatment," *Comparative Psychiatry*, January-February 2002; 43 (1), 1–6.

3. Robert Lloyd-Goldstein, "De Clerambault On-line: A Survey of Erotomania and Stalking from the Old World to the World Wide Web," in *The Psychology of Stalking*, J. Reid Meloy, ed. (San Diego: Academic Press, 1988), 197.

4. G. E. Berrios and N. Kennedy, "Erotomania: A Conceptual History," *History of Psychiatry*, 13 (54), December 2002; 381–400.

5. Lloyd-Goldstein, "De Clerambault On-line," 198–200.

6. James Wright, Allen Burgess, Ann Burgess, Anna Lazzio, Gregg McCrary, and John Douglas, "A Typology of Interpersonal Stalking,"*The Journal of Interpersonal Violence*, 11 (4), December 1996.

7. Schlesinger, "Homicidal Celebrity Stalkers," 88.

8. *Mass Murderers* (Alexandria, VA: Time-Life Books, 1992), 71–72.

9. Helen Fisher, *Why We Love: The Nature and Chemistry of Romantic Love* (New York: Henry Holt, 2004).

10. Melita Schaum and Karen Parrish, *Stalked: Breaking the Silence on the Crime of Stalking in America* (New York: Pocket, 1995).

11. J. Reid Meloy, *Violent Attachments* (Northvale, NJ: Jason Aronson, 1992), 145–192.

12. Michael A. Zona, Kaushal K. Sharma, and John Lane, "A Comparative Study of Erotomaniac and Obsessional Subjects in a Forensic Sample," *Journal of Forensic Sciences,* 38(4), 1996, 894.

13. Doreen Orion, *I Know You Really Love Me: A Psychiatrist's Account of Stalking and Obsessive Love* (New York: Dell, 1997).

14. Lloyd-Goldstein, "De Clerambault On-line," 200.

15. Charles Patrick Ewing, *Minds on Trial* (New York: Oxford University Press, 2006), 57–68.

16. Ibid., 91–102.

17. J. Reid Meloy and S. Gothard, "Demographic and Clinical Comparison of Obsessional Followers and Offenders with Mental Disorders," *American Journal of Psychiatry*, 152, 1995, 258–263; R. P. D. Menzies, J. P. Federoff, and C. M. Green, "Prediction of Dangerous Behavior in Male Erotomania," *British Journal of Psychiatry*, 166, 1995, 529–536.

CHAPTER 10

1. Adam Lynn, "Former Teacher Guilty of Rapes," *News Tribune*, April 21, 2009.

2. "Tamara Hofmann's Love Triangle Led to the Death of her 18-Year-Old Math Student," *Chicago Tribune*, April 14, 2009.

3. Stever Gehrke and Jason Bergreen, "Two Bountiful Junior High Teachers Accused of Sex with Same Student," *Salt Lake Tribune*, March 9, 2009.

4. "Female Teachers Accused of Sex with Girls," Associated Press, November 2, 2005.

5. Jim Schultz, "Woman Accused of Having Sex with Boy in Anderson Wal-Mart Parking Lot," *The Record Searchlight*, May 14, 2009.

6. A. J. Cooper, "Female Sexual Offenders," *Serial Offenders: Current Thoughts, Recent Findings*, Louis Schlesinger, ed. (Sarasota, FL: CRC Press, 2000), 263–288.

7. Peer Briken, Andreas Hill, and Wolfgang Berner, "Abnormal Attraction," *Scientific American Mind*, February/March 2007, 58–63.

8. Ken Englade, *Deadly Lessons* (New York: St. Martin's Press, 1991).

9. Gregg Olsen, *If Loving You Is Wrong* (New York: St. Martin's Press, 1999); J. Robinson, *The Mary Kay Letourneau Affair* (Overland Park, KS: Leathers Publishing, 2001); "Letourneau and Fualaau, One Year later," MSNBC.msn.com, June 2, 2006.

10. Janet Warren and Julia Hislop, "Female Sex Offenders: A Typological and Etiological Overview," *Practical Aspects of Rape Investigation*. 3rd ed., R. Hazelwood and A. Burgess, eds. (Sarasota, FL: CRC Press, 2001), 423–431.

11. Owen Lafave, *Gorgeous Disaster: The Tragic Story of Debra Lafave* (Beverly Hills, CA: Phoenix Books, 2006); "Debra Lafave: Crossing the Line," *Dateline*, September 13, 2006, "Sextra Credit: Florida Dismisses Lafave's Charges," Worldnetdaily.com, March 21, 2006.

12. "Boy's 'Raging Hormones' Reduce Woman's Sentence," Associated Press, December 10, 2008.

13. Paulo Lima, "Teacher Molests Student, No Jail Time." *The Record of Hackensack*, May 23, 2002; Supreme Court of New Jersey, Advisory Committee on Judicial Conduct, Docket No. ACJC 2002-171; Cathy Young, "Double Standard," *Reasononline*, June 2, 2002.

14. Jake Easton, "Judge: 7 Years for Pamela Rogers," *Radok News*, January 12, 2007.

15. "'Heartbroken' Teacher Pleads Guilty to Sex with Student," ABC Newsonline.com, January 30, 2006.

16. "Teacher who Seduced Boy Sentenced to 10 Years," Associated Press, March 17, 2007.

17. Eric Hickey, "Female Sex Offenders," www.predators.tv, 2007.

18. Charol Shakeshaft, "Educator Sexual Misconduct: A Synthesis of Existing Literature," U. S. Department of Education, June 2004.

19. Frederick Matthews, *The Invisible Boy: Revisioning the Victimization of Male Children and Teens*. National Clearinghouse on Family Violence, Health Promotion and Programs Branch, Health Canada, 1996.

20. Warren and Hislop, "Female Sex Offenders," 426.

21. Fiona Blackwood, "Vercoe Victims," transcript, www.abc.net.au, July 10, 2005.

22. "Affair between Student and Married Teacher Leads to Teen's Murder in Tennessee," Associated Press, March 18, 2007; "Tennessee Man Eric McLean Avoids Murder Rap in Slaying of His School-teacher Wife's Teenage Lover," Associated Press, September 11, 2008.

CHAPTER 11

1. Rachel Kate Bandy, "Gilbert Gauthe," in *Great Lives from History: Notorious Lives*, Carl L. Bankston, III, ed. (Pasadena, CA: Salem Press, 2007).

2. Ibid.

3. Joseph H. Saunders, "Gilbert Gauthe: Portrait of a Pedophile Priest," Saunders & Walker, P.A., http://www.saunderslawyers.com/practice-areas/physical-and-sexual-abuse/pedophile-priest.html (accessed May 2, 2009).

4. Michael Paulson, *Boston Globe*, June 12, 2002.

5. Thomas P. Doyle, "Clergy Sexual Abuse: The First Decade," (1993), http://www.votf-li.org/doyle_decade.pdf (accessed April 2, 2009).

6. Alan Sayer, "Gilbert Gauthe Arrested for Not Registering as a Sex Offender," Associated Press, April 24, 2008.

7. Philip Jenkins, *Pedophiles and Priests: Anatomy of a Contemporary Crisis* (New York: Oxford University Press, 1996).

8. John Jay College of Criminal Justice, *The Nature and Scope of Sexual Abuse of Minors by Catholic Priests and Deacons in the United States, 1950–2002* (Washington, DC: United States Conference of Catholic Bishops, 2004).

9. Ibid.

10. Denise Noe, "Pedophile Priest: The Crimes of Father Geoghan," *Crime Magazine: An Encyclopedia of Crime*, January 25, 2006, http://www.crimemagazine.com/03/geoghan,1201.htm (accessed May 5, 2009).

11. "The Archdiocese of Boston Sex Scandal," http://www.mtholyoke.edu/˜carr20c/classweb/fathergeoghanintro%20htm.html (accessed May 5, 2009).

12. "Abuse in the Catholic Church," *Boston Globe*, 2003, http://www.boston.com/globe/spotlight/abuse/geoghan/ (accessed May 5, 2009).

13. Linda Matachan, "Town Secret," *Boston Globe*, August 29, 1993.

14. "Victims Testify of Porter Assaults," *Boston Globe*, April 24, 2004.

15. Kevin Cullen, "Experts Say Law Rejected Advice," *Boston Globe*, June 7, 2002.

16. Jason Berry, *Lead Us Not into Temptation* (Chicago, IL: University of Illinois Press, 2000).

17. Ibid.

18. Jenkins, *Pedophiles and Priests.*

19. Ibid.

20. United States Conference of Catholic Bishops. *Report on the Implementation of the Charter for the Protection of Children and Young People.* Washington, DC: United States Conference of Catholic Bishops, 2005.

21. Anne B. Burke and Robert S. Bennett, *A Report on the Crisis in the Catholic Church in the United States*. Washington, DC: United States Conference of Catholic Bishops, 2004.

22. A.W. Richard Sipe, *Sex, Priests, and Power: Anatomy of a Crisis* (New York: Brunner/Mazel, 1995).

23. Jenkins, *Pedophiles and Priests.*

CHAPTER 12

1. Bill Draper, "Robinson Admits Five Killings in Missouri," Associated Press, October 6, 2003; John Douglas and Stephen Singular, *Anyone You Want Me to Be: A True Story of Sex and Death on the Internet* (New York: Scribner, 2003).

2. Julia Juttner, "Garman Chatroom Addict on Trial for Two Murders," *Der Spiegel*, January 14, 2009.

3. Douglas Montero and James Fanelli, "Craigslist Killer: More Is Coming Out," *New York Post*, April 25, 2009.

4. Robert Lloyd-Goldstein, "De Clérambeault On-line: A Survey of Erotomania and Stalking from the Old World to the World Wide Web," in *The Psychology of Stalking*, J. Reid Meloy, ed. (San Diego: Academic Press, 1998), 209–210.

5. Carla van Dam, *The Socially Skilled Child Molester* (New York: Haworth Press, 2006), 41–45.

6. Bruce Bower, "Growing Up Online," *Science News*, June 17, 2006.

7. Detective Joe Pochron, Southeastern Pennsylvania Computer Crimes Task Force; personal interview with authors.

8. Monique Mattei Ferraro and Eoghan Casey, *Investigating Child Exploitation and Pornography: The Internet, Law, and Forensic Science*. (San Diego, CA: Academic Press, 2004), 51–74.

9. Joel Kurth and Amy Lee. "MySpace: More Girls Flirt with Danger," *Detroit News*, June 13, 2006.

10. Edward Baig, "Keeping Internet Predators at Bay," *USA Today*, January 29, 2003.

11. Mary Jayne MaKay, "Secret Lives," CBSnews.com, June 25, 2003.

12. Todd Richmond, "More Internet Predators Are Challenging Agents," *Chicago Tribune*, March 21, 2009.

13. Detective Richard Peffall, Pennsylvania's Montgomery County Major Crimes Unit; personal interview with the authors.

14. Ferraro and Casey, *Investigating Child Exploitation and Pornography*, 5–18.

15. Janis Wolak, David Finklehor, Kimberly Mitchell, and Michelle Ybarra, "Online 'Predators' and Their Victims: Myths, Realities, and Implications for Prevention and Treatment," *American Psychologist*, 2008, 63(2).

16. "Attorney General Corbett Announces Arrest of 'Traveling' Internet Predator Who Flew from Texas to Pittsburgh," Associated Press, April 30, 2009.

17. Tara Parker-Pope, "Teens Exposing Themselves in Cyberspace," *New York Times*, January 7, 2009.

18. Ed Kemmick, "'Sexting' Draws Greater Scrutiny in Area," *Billings Gazette*, February 13, 2009.

CHAPTER 13

1. Anna Flowers, *Bound to Die: The Shocking True Story of Bobby Joe Long, America's Most Savage Serial Killer* (New York: Pinnacle, 1995).
2. Bernie Ward, *Bobby Joe: In the Mind of a Monster* (Boca Raton, FL: Cool Hand Communications, 1995).
3. Joe Navarro, *What Every Body Is Saying* (New York: Collins Living, 2008).
4. Pars A. Granhag and Leif A. Strömwell, "The Detection of Deception," in *Applied Criminal Psychology*, Richard Kocsis, ed. (Springfield, IL: Charles C Thomas, 2009), 103.
5. Mark McClish, *I Know You Are Lying* (Police Employment.com, 2008).
6. A.Vrij, *Detecting Lies and Deceit: Pitfall and Opportunities*, 2nd ed. (Chichester, UK: John Wiley & Sons, 2008).
7. M. K. Johnson and C. L. Raye, "Reality Monitoring," *Psychological Review*, 1981, 88, 67–85.
8. James W. Pennebaker, Roger J. Booth, and Martha E. Francis, "Linguistic Inquiry and Word Count," LIWC.net. Retrieved May 10, 2009.
9. D. Grubin and L. Madsen, "Lie Detection and the Polygraph: A Historical Review," *Journal of Forensic Psychiatry and Psychology*, 2005, 16, 357–369.
10. Lawrence Farwell, "Farwell Fingerprinting Testing." Forensic Report prepared by Farwell for Sheriff Robert Dawson, August 5, 1999.
11. Robin McKie, "It's the Thought That Counts for the Guilty," *The Observer*, April 25, 2004.
12. "German Scientists Reading Minds Using Brain-scan Machines." Associated Press, March 6, 2007.
13. Kalman Seigel, "Three Lonely Hearts Murders Trap Pair; Body Dug Up Here," *New York Times*, March 2, 1949.
14. Paul Ekman and Maureen O'Sullivan, "Who Can Catch a Liar?" *American Psychologist*, 1991, 46, 913–920.
15. Bruce Bower, "Life Defectives," *Science News*, July 4, 2008.
16. Anna Salter, *Predators: Pedophiles, Rapists & Other Sex Offenders* (New York: Basic Books, 2003), 222.
17. Steven Walker, *Predator* (New York: Kensington, 2010).
18. Nick Pron, *Lethal Marriage* (New York: Ballantine, 1995); Stephen Williams, *Invisible Darkness: The Strange Case of Paul Bernardo and Karla Homolka.* (New York: Bantam, 1996).

CHAPTER 14

1. Estelle B. Freedman, "Uncontrolled Desires: The Response to the Sexual Psychopath, 1920–1960," *Journal of American History* 74 (1987): 83–106.

2. J. Edgar Hoover, "How Safe Is Your Daughter?" *American Magazine* 144 (1947): 32–33, 102–104.

3. Manfred S. Guttmacher and Henry Weihofen, *Psychiatry and the Law* (New York: Norton, 1952).

4. Roxanne Lieb, Vernon Quinsey, and Lucy Berliner, "Sexual Predators and Social Policy," *Crime and Justice: A Review of Research,* vol. 23, Michael Tonry, ed. (Chicago: University of Chicago Press, 1998): 43–114.

5. Frederick J. Hacker and Marcel Frym, "The Sexual Psychopath Act in Practice: A Critical Discussion," *California Law Review* 43 (1955): 766–780.

6. Paul W. Tappan, "Sentences for Sex Criminals," *Journal of Criminal Law, Criminology and Police Science* 42 (1951): 332–337.

7. James D. Reardon, "Sexual Predators: Mental Illness or Abnormality? A Psychiatrist's Perspective," *University of Puget Sound Law Review* 15 (1992): 849–453.

8. Robert M. Wettstein, "A Psychiatric Perspective on Washington's Sexual Violent Predators Statute," *University of Puget Sound Law Review* 15 (1992): 597–634.

9. Lieb, Quinsey, and Berliner, "Sexual Predators and Social Policy."

10. Cassia Spohn and Julie Horney, *Rape Law Reform: A Grassroots Revolution and Its Impact* (New York: Plenum, 1992).

11. Ibid.

12. Lieb, Quinsey, and Berliner, "Sexual Predators and Social Policy."

13. Governor's Task Force on Community Protection, *Task Force on Community Protection: Final Report* (Olympia, WA: Washington State Department of Social and Health Services, 1990).

14. Wayne A. Logan, "The Ex Post Facto Clause and the Jurisprudence of Punishment," *American Criminal Law Review* 35 (1998): 1275–1277.

15. *Kansas v. Hendricks,* 117 S. Ct. 2072 (1997).

16. Ibid.

17. Ibid.

18. *Kansas v. Crane.* 534 U.S. 407 (2002).

19. Ken Hausman, "High Court Tries to Clarify Sex Offender Ruling," *Psychiatric News,* March 1, 2002.

20. D. Richard Laws, "Relapse Prevention or Harm Reduction?" *Sexual Abuse: A Journal of Research and Treatment* 8 (1996): 243–247.

21. *Missouri Revised Statutes Title* 38, ch. 558, §558.018, House Bill 974, Laws of 1996.

22. B. Drummond Ayres, Jr., "California Child Molesters Face Chemical Castration," *New York Times,* August 27, 1996.

23. Craig T. Palmer, "Twelve Reasons Why Rape Is Not Sexually Motivated: A Skeptical Examination," *Journal of Sex Research* 25 (1988): 512–530.

24. Pegi Taylor, "I am a Child Molester," *Milwaukee Magazine,* February 2002.

25. University of Pennsylvania Law Review, "Criminal Registration Ordinances: Police Control Over Potential Recidivists," *Pennsylvania Law Review* 103 (1954): 60–112.

26. Lieb, Quinsey, and Berliner, "Sexual Predators and Social Policy."
27. William Glaberson, "At Center of Megan's Law Case, a Man the System Couldn't Reach, *New York Times*, May 6, 1996.
28. *Radio Address of the President* (Chicago: Office of the U.S. Press Secretary, 1996).
29. Lieb, Quinsey, and Berliner, "Sexual Predators and Social Policy."
30. *Adam Walsh Child Protection and Safety Act*, Pub.L. (July 27, 1996): 109–248.

Selected Resources

Aggrawal, Anul. *Forensic and Medico-legal Aspects of Sexual Crimes and Unusual Sexual Practices.* Boca Raton, FL: CRC Press, 2009.

American Psychiatric Association. *Diagnostic and Statistical Manual of Mental Disorders* IV. Washington, DC: 1994.

Araji, S., and D. Finkelhor. "Abusers: A Review of the Research." in D. Finkelhor, with S. Araji, L. Baron, A. Browne, S.D. Peters, and G.E. Wyatt, *A Sourcebook on Child Sexual Abuse.* Beverly Hills, CA: Sage, 1986.

Berry, Jason. *Lead Us Not into Temptation.* Chicago, IL: University of Illinois Press, 2000.

Bourie, Mark. *By Reason of Insanity: The David Michael Krueger Story.* Toronto: Hounslow, 1997.

Buss, David. *The Murderer Next Door.* New York: Penguin, 2005.

Cauffiel, L. *Forever and Five Days.* New York: Zebra Books, 1992.

Cooper, A.J. "Female Serial Offenders," in Louis B. Schlesinger, ed., *Serial Offenders: Current Thought, Recent Findings.* Boca Raton, FL: CRC Press, 2000.

Davis, Carol Ann. *Women Who Kill.* London: Allison & Busby, 2001.

Doneman, P. *Things a Killer Would Know: The True Story of Leonard Fraser.* Australia: Allen and Unwin, 2006.

Douglas, John, and Stephen Singular. *Anyone You Want Me to Be: A True Story of Sex and Death on the Internet.* New York: Scribner, 2003.

Earle, R., G.M. Crow, and K. Osborn. *Lonely All the Time: Recognizing, Understanding, and Overcoming Sex Addiction, for Addicts and Co-dependants.* New York: Simon & Schuster, 1989.

Ellis, Lee. *Theories of Rape: Inquiries into the Causes of Sexual Aggression.* Levittown, PA: Hemisphere Publishing Corporation, 1989.

Farr, Louise. *The Sunset Murders.* New York: Pocket, 1992.

Ferraro, Monique M., and Eoghan Casey. *Investigating Child Exploitation and Pornography: The Internet, the Law, and Forensic Science.* Burlington, MA: Elsevier, 2005.

Fielder, Jim. *Slow Death.* New York: Pinnacle, 2003.

Fletcher, Jaye S. *Deadly Thrills.* New York: Onyx, 1995.

Flowers, Anna. *Bound to Die: The Shocking True Story of Bobby Joe Long, America's Most Savage Serial Killer.* New York: Pinnacle, 1995.

Geberth, Vernon J. *Practical Homicide Investigation,* 4th ed. Boca Raton, FL: CRC Press, 2007.

———. *Sex-Related Homicides and Death Investigation.* Boca Raton, FL: CRC Press, 2005.

Giannangelo, Stephen J. *The Psychopathology of Serial Murder: A Theory of Violence.* Westport, CT: Praeger, 1996.

Gibney, Bruce. *The Beauty Queen Killer.* New York: Pinnacle, 1984.

Gilmartin, P. *Rape, Incest, and Child Sexual Abuse: Consequences and Recovery.* New York: Garland Publishing, 1994.

Glatt, John. *Cries in the Desert.* New York: St. Martin's Press, 2002.

Greenfeld, L.A. "Sex Offenses and Offenders: An Analysis of Data on Rape and Sexual Assault." BJS Publication No. NCJ-163392. Washington, DC: U.S. Department of Justice, 1997.

Groth, Nicholas. *Men Who Rape: The Psychology of the Offender.* New York: Plenum, 1979.

Hare, Robert. *Without Conscience: The Disturbing World of the Psychopaths among Us.* New York: Guilford Press, 1999.

Hazelwood, Robert R., and A.W. Burgess, eds. *Practical Aspects of Rape Investigation: A Multidisciplinary Approach,* 3rd ed. Boca Raton, FL: CRC Press, 2004.

Hazelwood, Robert R., and Stephen Michaud. *Dark Dreams: Sexual Violence, Homicide, and the Criminal Mind.* New York: St. Martin's Press, 2001.

Hickey, Eric. *Serial Murderers and Their Victims,* 3rd ed. Belmont, CA: Wadsworth, 2002.

———. *Sex Crimes and Paraphilia.* Upper Saddle River, NJ: Prentice Hall, 2005.

Hislop, Julia. *Female Sex Offenders.* Ravensdale, WA: Issues Press, 2001.

Holmes, Stephen T., and Ronald M. Holmes. *Sex Crimes: Patterns and Behaviors,* 3rd ed. Los Angeles: Sage, 2009.

Howitt, D. *Paedophiles and Sexual Offences against Children.* New York: Wiley, 1995.

Jenkins, Philip. *Pedophiles and Priests: Anatomy of a Contemporary Crisis.* New York: Oxford University Press, 1996.

Johnson, Steven. *Mind Wide Open: Your Brain and the Neuroscience of Everyday Life.* New York: Scribner, 2004.

Justice, B., and R. Justice. *Broken Taboo: Sex in the Family.* New York: Human Sciences Press, 1979.

Kaplan, H.S. *The Sexual Desire Disorders: Dysfunctional Regulation of Sexual Motivation.* New York: Brunner/Mazel, Inc., 1995.

Keppel, Robert D., and William J. Birnes. *Serial Violence*, Boca Raton, FL: CRC Press, 2009.

Lafave, Owen. *Gorgeous Disaster: The Tragic Story of Debra Lafave.* Beverly Hills, CA: Phoenix Books, 2006.

Lane, S., and P. Zamora. "A Method for Treating the Adolescent Offender," *Violent Juvenile Offenders*, R. Mathias, P. Demuro, and R. Allinson, eds. San Francisco, CA: National Council on Crime and Delinquency, 1984.

Lang, R.A., and R.R. Frenzel. "How Sex Offenders Lure Children," *Annals of Sex Research* 1, 1988, 303–317.

Laws, D. Richard. "Relapse Prevention or Harm Reduction?" *Sexual Abuse: A Journal of Research and Treatment* 8, 1996, 243–247.

Leberg, E. *Understanding Child Molesters: Taking Charge.* Thousand Oaks, CA: Sage, 1997.

Lieb, Roxanne, Vernon Quinsey, and Lucy Berliner. "Sexual Predators and Social Policy," *Crime and Justice: A Review of Research,* vol. 23, Michael Tonry, ed. Chicago: University of Chicago Press, 1998, 43–114.

Lloyd-Goldstein, R. "De Clérambault On-line: A Survey of Erotomania and Stalking from the Old World to the World Wide Web," in *The Psychology of Stalking*, J. Reid Meloy, ed. San Diego: Academic Press, 1988.

Lowen, Alexander. *Narcissism: Denial of the True Self.* New York: Collier, 1985.

Marshal, Bryce, and Paul Williams. *Zero at the Bone.* New York: Pocket, 1991.

Marshall, William L., D. Richard Laws, and Howard E. Barberee, eds. *Handbook of Sexual Assault: Issues, Theories, and Treatment of the Offender.* New York: Plenum Press, 1990.

Masters, Brian. *She Must Have Known: The Trial of Rosemary West.* London: Transworld Publishers, 1996.

Matthews, Frederick. *The Invisible Boy: Revisioning the Victimization of Male Children and Teens.* National Clearinghouse on Family Violence, Health Promotion and Programs Branch, Health Canada, 1996.

Meloy, J. Reid. *Violent Attachments.* Northvale, NJ: Jason Aronson, 1992.

Michaud, Stephen, and Hugh Aynesworth. *The Only Living Witness: A True Account of Homicidal Insanity.* New York: New American Library, 1983.

Navarro, Joe. *What Every Body Is Saying.* New York: Collins Living, 2008.

Newton, Michael. *The Rope.* New York: Pocket, 1998.

Niehoff, Debra. *The Biology of Violence.* New York: Free Press, 1999.

Olsen, Gregg. *If Loving You Is Wrong.* New York: St. Martin's Press, 1999.

Olsen, Jack. *The Man with the Candy: The Story of the Houston Mass Murders.* New York: Simon & Schuster, 2001.

Orion, Doreen. *I Know You Really Love Me: A Psychiatrist's Account of Stalking and Obsessive Love.* New York: Dell, 1997.

Palmer, Craig T. "Twelve Reasons Why Rape Is Not Sexually Motivated: A Skeptical Examination." *Journal of Sex Research* 25, 1988, 512–530.

Pettit, Mark. *A Need to Kill.* New York: Ivy, 1990.

Prentky, R.A., A. Burgess, F. Rolous, et al. "The Presumptive Role of Fantasy in Serial Sexual Homicide." *American Journal of Psychiatry* 146, 1989, 887–891.

Pron, Nick. *Lethal Marriage.* New York: Ballantine, 1995.

Purcell, Catherine E., and Bruce A. Arrigo. *The Psychology of Lust Murder.* Burlington, MA: Elsevier, 2006.

Ramsland, Katherine. *Inside the Minds of Serial Killers: Why They Kill.* Westport, CT: Praeger, 2006.

———. *The Human Predator: A Historical Chronicle of Serial Murder and Forensic Investigation.* New York: Berkley, 2005.

Reardon, James D. "Sexual Predators: Mental Illness or Abnormality? A Psychiatrist's Perspective." *University of Puget Sound Law Review* 15, 1992, 849–853.

Ressler, Robert K., and Tom Schachtman. *Whoever Fights Monsters.* New York: St. Martin's Press, 1992.

Rieber, Robert. *Psychopaths in Everyday Life.* New York: Psyche-Logo Press, 2004.

Rule, Ann. *The Lust Killer.* New York: New American Library, 1983; revised 1988.

———. *The Stranger beside Me.* New York: W.W. Norton, 1980

Ryan, Gail and Sandy Lane, eds. *Juvenile Sexual Offending: Causes, Consequences, and Correction.* San Francisco, CA: Jossey-Bass, 1997.

Safarik, Mark, John Jarvis, and Kathleen Nussbaum. "Sexual Homicide of Elderly Women," in *Profilers*, John H. Campbell and Don DeNevi, eds. Amherst, NY: Prometheus, 2004.

Salter, Anna. *Predators: Pedophiles, Rapists & Other Sex Offenders.* New York: Basic Books, 2003.

Sanday, Peggy Reeves. *Fraternity Gang Rape: Sex, Brotherhood, and Privilege on Campus.* New York: New York University Press, 1990.

Schaum, Melita, and Karen Parrish. *Stalked: Breaking the Silence on the Crime of Stalking in America.* New York: Pocket, 1995.

Schechter, Harold. *Deranged: The Shocking True Story of America's Most Fiendish Killer.* New York: Pocket, 1990.

Schlesinger, Louis. *Sexual Murder: Catathymic and Compulsive Homicides.* Boca Raton, FL: CRC Press, 2004.

———. "Homicidal Celebrity Stalkers: Dangerous Obsessions with Nonpolitical Figures," in *Stalking, Threatening, and Attacking Public Figures*, J. Reid Meloy, Lorraine Sheridan, and Jens Hoffmann, eds. New York: Oxford University Press, 2008.

Schlesinger, Louis B., and E. Revitch, eds. *Sexual Dynamics of Anti-Social Behavior*, 3rd ed. Springfield, IL: Charles C Thomas, 1997.

Schwendinger, Julia R., and Herman Schwendinger. *Rape and Inequality.* Thousand Oaks, CA: Sage, 1983.

Shipley, S.L., and B.A. Arrigo. "Serial Killers and Serial Rapists: Preliminary Comparison of Violence Typologies," in *Serial Murder and the Psychology of Violent Crimes*, R.N. Kocsis, ed. Totowa, NJ: Humana Press, 2008.

Simon, Robert. *Bad Men Do What Good Men Dream: A Forensic Psychiatrist Illuminates the Darker Side of Human Behavior.* Washington, DC: American Psychiatric Press, 1996.

Sipe, A.W. Richard. *Sex, Priests, and Power: Anatomy of a Crisis.* New York: Brunner/Mazel, 1995.

Sounes, Howard. *Fred and Rose: The Full Story of Fred and Rose West and the Gloucester House of Horrors.* London: Warner, 1995.

Spohn, Cassia, and Julie Horney. *Rape Law Reform: A Grassroots Revolution and Its Impact.* New York: Plenum Press, 1992.

Stevens, Dennis J. *Inside the Mind of a Serial Rapist.* San Francisco: Austin & Winfield Publishers, 1999.

Terry, Karen. *Sexual Offenses and Offenders.* Belmont, CA: Wadsworth, 2006.

Thornhill, Randy, and Craig T. Palmer. *Rape: A Natural History of Biological Bases of Sexual Coercion.* Cambridge, MA: The MIT Press, 2000.

Trepper. T.S., and D. Nieder. "Family Characteristics of Intact Sexually Abusing Families: An Exploratory Study." *Journal of Child Sexual Abuse* 5 (4), 1996, 1–18.

Vrij, A. *Detecting Lies and Deceit: Pitfall and Opportunities*, 2nd ed. Chichester, UK: John Wiley & Sons, 2008.

Vronsky, Peter. *Serial Killers: The Method and Madness of Monsters.* New York: Berkley, 2004.

Walker, Steven. *Predator.* New York: Kensington, 2010.

Warren, Janet, and Julia Hislop. "Female Sex Offenders: A Typological and Etiological Overview," in *Practical Aspects of Rape Investigation*, 3rd ed., R. Hazelwood and A. Burgess, eds. Boca Raton, FL: CRC Press, 2001, 423–431.

Wertham, Fredric. *The Show of Violence.* New York: Doubleday & Co., 1949.

Wolak, Janis, David Finkelhor, Kimberly Mitchell, and Michelle Ybarra. "Online 'Predators' and Their Victims: Myths, Realities, and Implications for Prevention and Treatment." *American Psychologist*, 63, 2008, 111–128.

Zona, Michael A., Kaushal K. Sharma, and John Lane. "A Comparative Study of Erotomaniac and Obsessional Subjects in a Forensic Sample." *Journal of Forensic Sciences* 38, no. 4, 1996, 894–903.

Index

Acrophilia, 4
Adam Walsh Act, 164
Addiction, 23–34, 101
Agonophilia, 62
Agoraphilia, 4
American Psycho, 78
Andrews, Tommie Lee, 23
Anti-stalking laws, 101
Apotemnophilia, 5
Aquaerotism, 5, 61–62
Arachnophilia, 4
Araji, Sharon, 36
Attention deficit hyperactivity disorder (ADHD), 95
Autoeroticism, 4

Bandura, Albert, 56
Barberee, Howard, 57
Bardo, John, 102–103
Bar-Jonah, Nathaniel. *See* Brown, David Paul
Barkdall, David, 58
Barron, Anthony, 1–2
Beck, Martha, 151–152
Bench-Salorio, Sarah, 111
Bernando, Paul, 153–154
Biology of Violence, The, 62
Blevins, Patrick, 143
Bohmer, Carol, 59
Bond, Charles, Jr., 152
Brain Fingerprinting, 149–150
Brainwashing. *See* Stockholm syndrome.
Braunstein, Peter, 6–7
Brooks, David, 77
Brooks, Pierce, 63
Brown, David Paul, 38–39
Brudos, Jerome, 8, 32–33
Bundy, Carol, 81–82
Bundy, Theodore Robert, 18–20
Buss, David M., 63

Candaulism, 4
Cannibalism, 5, 9
Catholic Church, 125, 126, 128, 129, 130–132
Casey, Eoghan, 141
Child molestation. *See* Pedophilia
Child Molestation and Research Prevention Institute, 119

Child pornography. *See* Pornography
Child Predator Unit, 142
Civil commitment for sex offenders, 157–160
Clark, Doug, 81–82
Collectors, 136
Collector, The, 84
Comeaux, Ernest Randy, 47–48
Community Protection Act, 157–158
Compliant accomplice, 80–81
Cooper, A.J., 110
Coprolagnia (Coprophilia), 4, 9
Corll, Dean, 77
Craigslist, 134–135
Crime Classification Manual, 100
Criteria-Based Content Analysis (CBCA), 149
Cyber-predator, 133–144; chatters, 136; collectors, 136; manufacturers, 137; travelers, 136,140–141
Cycle of violence, 55, 94

Deception detection, 145–154; behavioral signals, 147–148,152; Brain Fingerprinting, 149–150; Criteria-based Content Analysis, 149; Linguistic Inquiry and Word Count, 149; naturals, 152, 154; Polygraph, 149; Reality Monitoring, 149; standard assessments, 148; Statement Validity Analysis, 148
de Clerambault's syndrome, 99
DeBardeleben, James Mitchell, 17
DeKeseredy, Walter, 57
DePaulo, Bella, 152
Depo-Provera, 161
DeSalvo, Albert, 50
Diagnostic and Statistical Manual of Mental Disorders (DSM-IV-TR), 3, 16–17
Diehl-Moore, Pamela, 115–116
Dietz, Park, 80
Dissociative disorder, 95
Doland, Jeff, 61–62
Dopamine, 28, 101
"Dr. Evil," 139
Dufort, William, 41–42
Dupas, Peter Norris, 29–32, 58
Dutroux, Marc, 75–76

Ekman, Paul, 152
Ellis, Lee, 52
Erotic enthrallment, 27. *See also* Addiction
Erotolalia, 4
Erotomania, 97–107, 135; definition of, 99; secondary, 99; statistics, 100. *See also* Stalkers
Erotophonophilia, 62
Escalation. *See* Addiction, Cycle of violence
Exhibitionism, 4

FaceBook, 136
Facial Action Coding System, 152
Fantasy, function of, 2–3, 4, 64, 85, 146
Farley, Richard, 101
Farwell, Lawrence, 149–150
Female offenders: lust killers, 70–73; part of team 75–86, 153–154; teachers predators, 109–122
Fernandez, Raymond, 151–152
Ferraro, Monique, 141
Fetishism, 4, 8
Finkelhor, David, 36
Fire water complex, 5
Fish, Albert, 8 10, 36, 155, 156
Fisher, Helene, 101
Foster, Jodie, 105
Fowles, John, 85
Fraser, Leonard, 24–27
Frenzel, Roy, 40
Freud, Sigmund, 15, 52
Fritzl, Josef, 42
Frotteurism, 4
Fualaau, Vili, 111–112, 121

Gaeta, Bruce, 116
Gauthe, Gilbert, 123–125
Geberth, Vernon, 34
Gecht, Robin, 76
General Theory of Crime, 95
Geoghan, Father John, 126–128
Geographical profiling, 47–48
Gerontophilia, 5
Giannangelo, Stephen, 28
Glatman, Harvey, 63
Gottfredson, Michael, 95
Graham, Gwendolyn, 70
"Green Man." *See* DeSalvo, Albert
"Green River Killer," 20
Groth, Nicholas, 53

Haarmann, Fritz, 9
Hare, Robert, 21
Hazelwood, Robert R., 17, 80–81
Hebephilia, 4
Hendy, Cindy, 79
Henley, Elmer Wayne, 77
Hickey, Eric, 3, 34, 70, 77, 119
Hinckley, Jr. John, 105
Hirschi, Travis, 95
Hislop, Julia, 70, 113, 120
Hofmann, Tamara, 109
Holmes, Ronald, 62
Holmes, Stephen, 62
Holt, Rachel, 118
Homolka, Karla, 153–154
Hoover, J. Edgar, 155
Horney, Karen, 15–16

Incest, 42–45
Infantilism, 5
Infibulation, 5, 9
Insanity defense, 105
Internet Solutions for Kids, 141
Investigating Child Exploitation and Pornography, 141

Jackson, Stevi, 56–57
Jacob Wetterling Act, 164
Jarvis, John, 69
Jenkins, Philip, 130
Joubert, John, 64–68
Juvenile sex offender, 87–96;
demographics of, 89–90;
developmental factors, 91–94;
mixed offense offender, 90;
pedophile, 90;
sexual assault offender, 90

Kansas v. Crane, 160
Kansas v. Hendricks, 159–160
Kaplan, Helen Singer, 27
Kellner, Randy, 162
Kernberg, Otto, 16
Klismaphilia, 5
Kohut, Heinz, 16
Krajcir, Timothy, 152–153
Krueger, David Michael. *See* Woodcock, Peter

Lafave, Debra, 113–115
Lane, Sandy, 55
Lang, Reuben, 40
Letourneau, Mary Kay, 111–112, 121
Lilley, Amy Gail, 110
Linguistic Inquiry and Word Count (LIWC), 149
Lloyd-Goldstein, Robert, 135
Long, Bobby Joe, 145–146
Love sickness. *See* Erotomania, Stalking.
Lust murder, 68–69; among females, 70–72
Lynn, Robert, 115–6

Malingering, 148
Mandatory Castration Bill, 161
Markoff, Phillip, 135
Marshall, William, 57
Masochism, 4
Masturbation, 51
Mathews, Frederick, 119
McLean, Eric, 120–121

McLean, Erin, 120–121
"Measuring Man." *See* DeSalvo, Albert
Megan's Law, 163
Meloy, J. Reid, 103, 107
Miklosovic, Elizabeth, 110
Millon Clinical Multiaxial Inventory (MCMI), 17
Minnesota Multiphasic Personality Inventory (MMPI-II), 148
Moore, Julie, 122
Mowery, Robin, 115
Mud eroticism, 4
Mutilomania, 5
Mysophilia, 4
MySpace, 117, 136, 137, 138, 142–143

Narcissism, 11–22; as personality disorder, 16–17; immunity, 17–18; malignant, 15; related to psychopathy, 18–22
Narcissistic Personality Inventory (NPI), 17
Narratophilia, 4
National Center for Missing and Exploited Children (NCMEC), 139
Nau, Ralph, 100–101
Necrophilia, 4
Newton-John, Olivia, 100
Niehoff, Debra, 62–63
Nolan, Bridget Mary, 117–118
Nussbaum, Kathleen, 69

Obsessive Compulsive Disorder (OCD), 7, 95
Operation Blue Ridge Thunder, 139
Orion, Doreen, 103–104
O'Sullivan, Maureen, 152

Palmer, Craig, 51
Pam Lyncher Sexual Offender Tracking and Identification Act, 164
Paraphilia, 3–5, 26, 137, 156
Parrot, Andrea, 59
Partialism, 4
Pedophiles and Priests, 130
Pedophilia, 4, 9, 35–46; adolescent regressive, 43; angry retaliator, 43; fixated child offender, 40; in families, 42–45; in females, in juveniles, 90; 112–113; in males, 9, 39–41, 139, 140–144; in priests, 123–132; mysoped, 39; naïve pedophile, 40; regressed child offender, 40; sexually preoccupied, 43; *See also* Incest
Peffall, Richard, 140–141
Penn, Julie, 79
Pictophilia, 4
Piquerism, 9
Pochron, Joe, 137
Poddar, Prosendijit, 105, 106
Pornography, 21, 36
Porter, Father James, 128–9
Post-Traumatic Stress Disorder (PTSD), 95
Price, Casey Edward, 35–36
Price, John, 88–89
Priests who offend, 123–132. *See also* Pedophilia
Psychopaths in Everyday Life, 21
Psychopathy, 21–22, 146
Psychopathy Checklist (PCL), 21
Psychosexual Disorders. *See* Paraphilias
Psychosis, 94
Pygmalionism (Statuphilia), 4
Pyrolagnia (Pyrophilia), 5

Rape, 23–34, 47–60; biological theory, 51; characteristics of, 23, 34, 49; motivation for, 33–34, 48–49; psychological theory, 51; ritual in, 32; sadistic, 32, 48; serial, 33–34; sociological theory, 55–60
Ray, David Parker, 15, 78–80
Reality Monitoring (RM), 149
Reizenstein, Trevor, 89
Repeat Sex Offender Statute, 161
Ressler, Robert K., 65–67
Rice, Jennifer, 109
Rieber, Robert, 22

Risk assessment, 156, 158, 159–161
Ritualism, 32
Robinson, John Edward, 133–134
Rodreick, Neil Havens, 35–36
Rogers, Pamela, 117
Ross, Michael, 11–14, 15
Rossmo, Kim, 47–48
Rotramel, Robert, 90–91

Sadism, 5, 78–79, 173. *See also* Lust Killers
Safarik, Mark, 69
Saliromania, 5
Salter, Anna, 152
Sanday, Peggy Reeves, 57, 58
Satyriasis, 5
Saunders, Corey Deen, 53–54, 57
Scatophilia, 4
Schaffer, Rebecca, 102–103
Schlesinger, Louis, 68
Schwartzmiller, Dean Arthur, 36–37
Scoptophilia, 5
Serial killers (lust killers), 61–74; as teams, 75–86
Serial Murderers and Their Victims, 70
Sexting, 144
Sexual addiction. *See* Addiction
Sexual Predator Legislation, 155–156
Sexual Psychopathy Laws, 155–156
Sexually Violent Predator Act (SVPA), 158–160
Shaffer, Lisa, 79
Shakeshaft, Carol, 119
Simmons, Ronald Gene, 44
Simon, Robert, 28
Sipe, A.W. Richard, 131
Skinner, B.F., 95
Smart, Pamela Ann, 111
Smith, Eric, 92–93
Spillman, Jack Owen II, 33–34
Stalkers, 97–107; domestic, 100; love obsessional, 103; non-domestic, 103; simple obsessional, 103
Statement Validity Analysis, 148
Steinhagen, Ruth Ann, 97–99
Stevens, Dennis, 51
Stiles, Chester Arthur, 54, 57
Stockholm syndrome, 76, 84
Structured Interview of Reported Symptoms (SIRS), 148
"Sunset Strip Murders." *See* Bundy, Carol and Clark, Doug
Sutherland, Edwin, 56

Tarasoff, Tatiana, 106
Team offenders, 75–85; forced teaming, 82–83
Testosterone, 36
Thornhill, Randy, 51
Torture. *See* Sadism
Transvestitism, 5
Travelers, 136
Triolism, 5
Trophies, 23
Urolagnia (Urophilia), 4

Vampirism, 5
Vercoe, Sarah Jayne, 120
Violent Criminal Apprehension Program (ViCAP), 20
Vomerophilia, 5
Vrij, Aldert, 149

Waitkus, Eddie, 97–99
Warren, Janet, 80, 113, 120
Weber, Jeanne, 70
Wertham, Fredric, 8–9, 156
Wesson, Marcus, 45
West, Fred, 71–73, 77
West, Rosemary, 71–73, 77
Wilder, Christopher, 83–85
Without Conscience, 21
Wood, Catherine, 70
Woodcock, Peter, 87–88
Wuornos, Aileen, 70

Yancy, Dennis Roy, 79
Young, Cathy, 115–116
Youtube, 144

Zamora, Pablo, 55
Zona, Michael, 103

About the Authors

KATHERINE RAMSLAND has a master's degree in forensic psychology from the John Jay College of Criminal Justice, a master's degree in clinical psychology from Duquesne University, and a doctorate in philosophy from Rutgers. She has published thirty-seven books, including *The CSI Effect, Inside the Minds of Serial Killers, Inside the Minds of Healthcare Serial Killers, Inside the Minds of Mass Murderers, The Human Predator: A Historical Chronology of Serial Murder and Forensic Investigation, The Criminal Mind: A Writers' Guide to Forensic Psychology,* and *The Forensic Science of CSI.* She has been translated into ten languages and has published over 900 articles on serial killers, criminology, forensic science, and criminal investigation. She currently writes a regular feature on historical forensics for *The Forensic Examiner* and is an associate professor of forensic psychology at DeSales University in Pennsylvania, where she is department chair. She is a frequent commentator, appearing on *Larry King Live, Montel Williams, 20/20,* NPR, and numerous true crime documentaries.

PATRICK N. MCGRAIN has a master's degree in criminal justice from the State University of New York College at Buffalo and a doctorate in criminal justice from Temple University. He currently serves as assistant professor and Director of the Master of Arts in Criminal Justice program at DeSales University. He has published articles in the field of drug treatment, focusing on the effects of prison-based programming and the predictors of therapeutic engagement in a correctional setting. His current research interests include the treatment of sex offenders and the motivation of sexual predators.

www.ingramcontent.com/pod-product-compliance
Lightning Source LLC
LaVergne TN
LVHW010012040626
840463LV00003B/53